ARCTIC RENDEZVOUS

A MAN'S QUEST FOR MEANING

BY GRAHAM L. McGILL

A.R.E. Press • Virginia Beach • Virginia

A.R.E. Press
Sixty-Eighth & Atlantic Avenue
P. O. Box 656
Virginia Beach, VA 23451-0656

Edgar Cayce Readings © 1971
by the Edgar Cayce Foundation
Reprinted by Permission

Library of Congress Cataloging-in-Publication Data
McGill, Graham L., 1933-
    Arctic rendezvous : a man's quest for meaning / Graham L.
McGill.
        p.   cm.
    ISBN 0-87604-305-8
    1. McGill, Graham L., 1933- . 2. Reincarnation—Case stud-
ies. 3. Psychics—United States—Biography.   I. Title.
BF1027.M17A3 1993
133.9'013-dc20
    [B]   93-10866

Cover by Don Dyen Illustrator

DEDICATION

For Billy,
Who, having dreamed of
Seven golden candlesticks,
And having completed his appointed task,
Departed whence he had come.

"Go fish and hunt, day by day—farther and wider—and rest thee by many brooks and hearthsides without misgiving. Rise free from care before the dawn and seek adventures. Let the noon find thee by other lakes and the night overtake thee everywhere at home . . . Let not to get a living be thy trade, but thy sport."

Henry David Thoreau
Walden, Chapter 10
"Baker Farm"

ACKNOWLEDGMENTS

I am deeply grateful to:

Sherrill, my wife, who became our sole breadwinner when I quit a newspaper job to write, who set aside her own desires so I could pursue mine, who, despite the subject matter—my first marriage—and her full-time job as an editor, read every chapter, often many times. She was my No. 1 Crud Detector, my first defense against turbidity and stupidity. We learned during the birthing process—she to be assertive and I to appreciate and trust her judgment. Also she cooked, picked up, ran errands, soothed my brow, massaged my shoulders, and reminded me by word and deed that all life does not transpire in the head.

Joseph W. Dunn, Jr., editor-in-chief, A.R.E. Press, for the vision to see potential where others could not, for faith, friendship, enthusiasm, and a patient touch; for a thousand-and-one suggestions about what to point up, tone down, develop, and delete.

William R. (Bill) Baker, English teacher, who, despite a heavy class schedule, ripped through every chapter with his lovable red pen, stiffening flaccid verbs, brightening murky adjectives, tightening sloppy phrases, tidying unclear syntax, and adding sparkle where my story had been dull and gray.

William C. (Bill) Getz, director of staff development for the New York State Education Department, old friend; stickler for details; canoeing, fishing, and hiking buddy; for encouragement, understanding, and a special emphasis on clarity and accuracy, and for drawing my map.

Dr. Robert H. Wentorf, Jr., inventor and engineer, a living example that science does not contradict spiritual truth, swimming buddy and post-workout lunch guest, for many better words, correct spellings, and much-needed pats on the back; he gave freely of his limited time and almost unlimited linguistic prowess.

David Pitkin, friend of twenty years and founder of Saratoga Search for God Study Group No. 1, for insights into "big dreams," punchy phrases, and many instances of better judgment.

Laura Beth, my daughter, whose praise of *A Raft of Wood* persuaded me to keep writing.

G. Scott, my son, ultralight pilot and mechanical wizard, who, despite a barrage of distractions, seemed to read avidly.

Bruce Burns, brother-in-law and Alaska-lover, who, despite interruptions for critique, didn't seem able to put it down.

Aleta Ker-Burns, sister-in-law, resident of Seattle and mother of two imps, for asserting her especially feminine views.

Also Judy Baker, Gail Pitkin, Ann Hauprich, Lawrence Alan Duaine, Chuck McLoughlin, Louis Deinzer, Ralph Thompson, Tim Coakley, Carl Buell, Harold Buell, Olya Legg, Paul Dwyer, Richard Yauchler, and Barry Riemer.

PROLOGUE

The seed for this book was planted one night in 1987 during a backpack trip near King's Canyon National Park in the Sierras, when my son and daughter, relaxing around our high-altitude campfire, asked, "Dad, what happened between you and Mom? Why did you split up?"

They had grown up without their father, didn't know who I was, and now had established separate lives, thousands of miles from me. My son was a skilled private pilot and refrigeration engineer in Chicago; my daughter had settled into a San Diego suburb as a wife and mother of two; and I, a newspaper editor, had spent the last fifteen years as father to my wife Sherrill's three children in upstate New York. This was our first experience together as a family, a brief respite in the ache of our lifelong isolation—since Scott was six and Laura Beth two.

That night their questions seemed a chance to set matters straight, correct any misconceptions, explain my own view of the circumstances surrounding their mother's and my divorce. And yet I sat stunned. Nothing I could think of at that moment seemed able to breach the great gulf of understanding I felt, a gulf not only of age and experience, but of years of loneliness, sleepless nights, and desperate soul searching. So I remained struck dumb in the firelight, skewered by the youth and innocence of my now-grown children.

Yet youth and innocence eventually disintegrate under the press of years, and it is my hope that this book may prove helpful in the longer backpack trip that is the life journey of all of us.

BOOK I

MILES

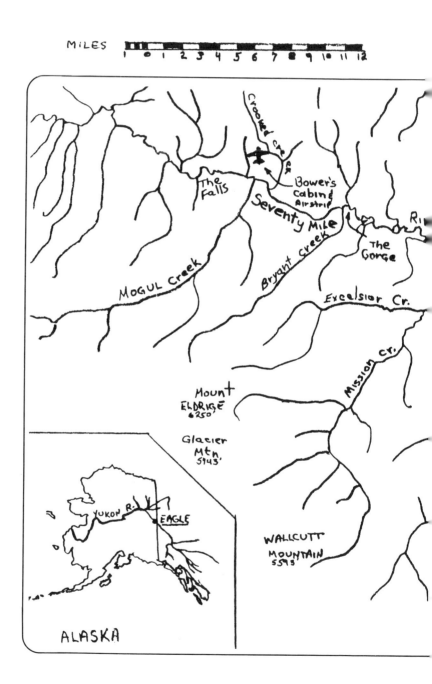

= AIR STRIP   141°00'

65°00'

YUKON RIVER

Pickerel Slough

Calico Bluff

CANADA
U.S.A.

er

Ford Lake

Shade Cr

Last chance Cn

Hayfield & Sod House

Eagles Bluff

Eagle Creek

EAGLE

American

Taylor Highway

Wolf Cr.

EAGLE Village

5

WICKIUP Creek

Boundry Creek

QUARTZ CR.

YUKON RIVER

YUKON TERRITORY
ALASKA

YUKON RIVER

Getz

TETLIN JUNCTION & TOK

A RAFT OF WOOD

Facing my first winter in Alaska, 1959, I listened carefully to Anton Merly, my neighbor. He believed I'd need eight or ten cords of wood to get through until spring. He suggested I trek upriver to Boundary Creek and cut a stand of dead spruce—seasoned on the stump and right next to the Yukon River. He advised me to build a raft and float it back to town.

Tall and bald, Anton had come to Alaska from a homestead in North Dakota in 1949. Adept with his hands and wise in the ways of survival, he knew his way around the back country. Soon after we arrived in Eagle, he and his wife Esther had befriended me and my family, had taken us under their wing.

I packed enough dry salmon and moose jerky to last two weeks, kissed my wife Kate and infant son Scott, called my dog Zeke, shouldered my backpack, swung my canoe up and headed out. It was a short portage from our rented cabin across the dirt road, which was Main Street, Town of Eagle, to the Yukon, which, except in sloughs and backwaters, is too swift for paddling upstream. I didn't own an outboard, so I towed the canoe with a rope, a procedure known as "lining."

First, I rigged a bridle, a short line from bow to stern

slightly longer than the canoe. From this I knotted my tow rope, which let the canoe "fly" into the current like a kite, kept it away from the shore. To the other end of the tow rope I hitched a singletree, a short stick whose ends were tied to a belt around my waist, a plow-horse device which allowed me to swing my hips.

The silty Yukon made a "Sh-h-h-h-h-h" on my canoe's yellow canvas bottom, a noise like an endless, cushiony belt of wet sandpaper.

Lining upstream didn't seem like work to me on this bright autumn day. True, it lacked the lazy abandon of a downstream drift, yet it was accompanied by the same exultant music—the vociferous ravens, the mewing gulls, the keening sandpipers, the twittering swallows—and it was accompanied by the syncopated clopping of my swinging, frisky feet.

Headed upstream, Eagle is the last U.S. settlement on the Yukon River before you enter Canada, hence the name of my destination, Boundary Creek. Summer here is two months long—June and July—but with almost twenty-four-hour daylight, temperatures sometimes reach the 90s. Yet this was August. The aspens were already tinged with yellow, and I could sniff the tang of winter in the air.

The nearly empty canoe skittered over the surface so that, when I spotted the dead swatch of spruce, I still felt invigorated and optimistic, and the day was still young. I knew I'd be here awhile. So why not build a shelter?

Following directions in Vilhjalmur Stefansson's *Arctic Manual,* I wove an inverted basket of saplings—"a wickiup," he called it—and covered it with two ponchos and a tarp. But I'd built it a little too big. No amount of fudging would close the hole in the roof. Finally I shingled it with my jacket, which, I hoped, at least for the time being, I could do without. Aside from that though, standing back and admiring my handiwork, I decided it was sturdy and serviceable, an assessment I had cause to affirm that night when it began to rain.

No brief, spattering shower of summer, this was the cold, steady drizzle of autumn, and it lasted all night. In the morning, I lifted the door flap and peered out. Across the river, slightly upstream, a rampart of slate jutted into the current. Yesterday it had been backdropped by sun-drenched, grassy hills; today it was veiled by whispy fingers of scud reaching down from the thick overcast. A pair of ravens swept past, dark, mute. I shivered.

I didn't feel like getting up. I had dry wood for cooking, plenty of grub, a down sleeping bag, a few books, a flash-light for reading, extra duffel for a pillow and a warm dog for company. Further, I had no bells to answer or clocks to punch. Yet I had not come here to loll around. I slipped into my boots, donned a wool sweater, hefted my ax and buck-saw, and climbed the hill to my woodlot.

This stand of trees had been killed by a lightning-ignited blaze which had burned itself out at its perimeter. Sprigs of fireweed grew between the trunks, but without their flashy red blossoms this late in the season. I peeled off my sweater, set it and my saw against a root, and stepped up to a tree. Appraising it with my ax, I spread my legs and dug in my heels. The incline was too steep for surefootedness, but I swung my blade. The dry bole rang like a Chinese gong— BONG! The edge bounced, keen steel barely making a dent. My next harder swing did the same. I dug in my heels and swung with all my might. BONG! Again, BONG!

Having excised only a few splinters, I was already winded. This was going to be a struggle. Maybe the bucksaw would be easier, I thought. Sure enough, its slithering column of jagged teeth bit into the dessicated fibers, where a live tree would've bound it in gummy resin. I had the hulk down in about thirty minutes.

Glancing across the river, I spied a small black bear

downstream from the slate cliffs. Now and then he'd vanish into the brush.

When I knocked off for lunch, I had three trees on the beach. They'd stay there unless the river rose.

On and off all day it rained, and that night turned colder. I built a driftwood bonfire a short way from our wickiup, and Zeke and I enjoyed its warmth for hours.

When we turned in, the wickiup was cold and damp. Zeke began to shiver. I missed my jacket, but it was doing us both good on the roof. I slept fitfully.

In the morning the bear was still there. A pelt would cover that hole in the roof, I thought. Then I could put my jacket where it belonged—on my back. I waited until the bear ambled into the brush, took my '06, leaned into the canoe ropes, and lined upstream so our crossing would carry us to the bear. Then I clucked Zeke aboard and shoved off.

I really didn't want Zeke along on this bear hunt, but she had me over a barrel. If I told her to stay, she'd make a show of obedience, then leap into the river and swim after the canoe. If I tied her to a log or rock, she'd stay for a while, then whine or bark, finally chew the rope and swim after me. Usually eager to please, she was too smart to tolerate being confined alone in the bush. After all, wolves and grizzlies abounded. So I compromised by bringing her along and leashing her to the canoe thwart. This at least might keep her from spooking the bear when we landed on the other side.

"Zeke" was a strange name for a female, but I figured she didn't care. I'd picked up the moniker from Kate, who, then my girlfriend, had picked it up from a cowboy, who'd tagged her girlfriend with it. I'd grown fond of its one syllable, which, when hollered, carried across the miles like a wolf's howl.

Zeke looked nothing like an Alaskan dog. She weighed a mere sixty pounds, compared to over a hundred for a husky.

Her ruff was brown and black with a chest patch of white; huskies were mostly gray or white. Her mom was a shelty, her dad a German shepherd; native huskies were descended from wolves.

And there were cultural differences. Life to Zeke was basically a game. Starting with a rubber ball rolled across the living room floor, she'd learned to play fetch while she was still a pup. From that we graduated to tennis balls in the yard, sticks tossed into fields, woods, lakes, and rivers, and finally live ducks and grouse. Before she was a year old, she'd learned to ride on the back of my Harley and carry her own pack on hikes in the Sierras.

Compared to the huskies at Eagle Indian Village in 1959, Zeke was spoiled rotten. Native dogs were draft animals—chained outdoors, fed once a day, never allowed to run except in harness, never invited indoors, never played with or made part of the family. From the Native point of view, this wasn't cruel. Traditionally, huskies were the sole means of transport in a harsh land, a requisite to survival. A native would no sooner turn loose his sled dog than a farmer would turn loose his horse.

Zeke, on the other hand, seldom wore her collar, stayed close of her own volition, usually came when called, was rarely on a leash, and could often be found leaning against my leg. But I had never actually trained her to hunt, a fact which jumped out at me as we beached about a hundred yards from where I'd last seen the bear.

He appeared on the shore again as I was pulling the canoe up, in plain sight but evidently too naive to perceive us as danger. I knelt and aimed my '06. The long canoe stalk across open water had unsettled my nerves. I could not hold my rifle steady, so I snapped off a shot as the sight wavered near the bear's chest.

He lunged into the thicket. I worked the bolt. I didn't relish stalking a wounded bear, but had I actually wounded him? Perhaps I'd merely scared him. I was headed toward the bear's last position when something crashed in the brush nearby. I whirled. The bear was wounded all right and had run in my direction. He seemed on his last legs. I finished him with one more shot.

When he lay still, I began the dressing out. Stefansson claimed Eskimos used to eat the stomach contents of animals they killed—"Eskimo salad," he called it. This bear's stomach was full of blueberries. I sniffed. It smelled like blueberry relish. But jaws were not as selective as a hand: the mixture contained twigs, leaves, and green berries. I couldn't bring myself to sample it.

After the bear was gutted, I loaded the meat into the canoe, lined upstream again, and recrossed to our wickiup. Bears are noted for "b'ar grease," but this one was young and lean, yielding several nice steaks. I cut saplings and built a meat rack on a level spot a short way from camp. The air was too moist for drying, but hanging would at least discourage blowflies. The pelt was just big enough to replace my jacket.

That night I laid a circle of rocks around my bonfire and carried them into our wickiup when we retired. Between their warmth and my jacket's, Zeke and I slept snugly.

In the morning I awoke with a smile. I now had what Thoreau listed as "the three necessaries of life"—food, shelter, and clothing—two of which I'd gleaned entirely from the land. This was what I'd dreamed of while I was an air force pilot. This was my ideal life style, the way I imagined I'd escape the incessant treadmill of civilization. For the first time in my life I felt close to self-sufficient, part of and one with the land. All I had to do now was make it sound sensible to Kate.

The next day, despite continued rain, I felled ten more trees. Canada jays, also called camp robbers, found my bear meat, and a raven joined them. My cache soon began to look pecked and scraggly. I hollered and threw stones, but to little avail.

The next day more rain, more tree felling, more rock throwing. The raven, fresh from the meat rack, swooped low over our wickiup, taunting. I killed it on the wing with my .22.

Sawing away on the hill above camp that afternoon, I hardly noticed a second raven flapping and cawing upriver. And I paid little attention a few hours later when it beat back down on my side, still cawing. A few hours later, up again. Then down again, cawing more frantically. Finally it dawned on me. That raven was the mate of the one I'd killed. They were probably the same pair I'd seen the first morning. The cawing was a question with no answer—"Where are you? Where are you?" Each time the bird passed, late into that evening and all the next day, its cries pierced my heart.

Holding the lifeless body aloft, I called: "Oh, raven, see! I have killed your mate in a thoughtless moment. I am very sorry. But I cannot undo what I have done."

My words echoed back to me from across the wide canyon, but the live raven did not appear to notice. Finally I arranged the dead bird atop the wickiup, hoping that the live one would spot it. For myself I viewed it as a mark of shame, for I had killed it on a whim and in anger, with no thought of using the meat.

The next day Amund Hagen, an old Norwegian returning to Eagle from the Fortymile River in a motorboat, stopped by to chat. Amund had become famous many years ago for betting some trappers he could beat their dog teams in a race over the 160-mile trail from Tok to Eagle (later the Taylor Highway). Amund would travel on one ski, the way he used to in the old country, both feet on the ski when coasting downhill, pushing with his free leg and two poles when climbing. Everyone except Amund had bet on the dog teams, but Amund had won.

Now he was working for Alan Innes-Taylor, my former employer, setting up tent sites along the Yukon for tourists. I gave him most of my bear meat in a duffel bag to take home to Kate.

Laboring on the hillside another week, I cut all except the tiny trees. When I had rolled and skidded about sixty logs onto the beach, I followed Anton's instructions for building a raft:

"First build a three-sided trap. Lay the inside log against the shore, the middle log straight out from the shore and the outside log pointing upstream—an open-ended rectangle with the open end upstream. Rope the outside log to a high point on the shore, canting it out a little so the current holds it out, but not so much that it gets away! Float the loose logs under the rope and into the trap. See?"

With an auger I drilled holes in the ends of three logs and wired them loosely together, configuring them as Anton described. I floated the loose logs inside, one by one. When the trap was full, I closed it with a fourth log and wired it in place at the corners. Then I laid a second tier of logs across the first and a third tier across the second, cinching it with wire so it wouldn't roll apart.

Anton had told me to build a sweep—a fulcrum at one end of the raft to be used with one long oar.

"How does it work?" I asked.

"I'm not sure," Anton admitted. "But that's the way the old-timers did it."

In Alaska, invoking the old-timers is like invoking God.

"O.K.," I had nodded.

And now, not trusting my own judgment, I drilled three holes in the deck logs, drove in short poles and lashed them together about three feet up, making a tripod oar lock or, in this case, a sweep lock. Next I lashed my stoutest paddle to a long pole as the sweep. Then I tossed another pole aboard for good measure, packed all my gear, set my canoe in the middle, whistled for Zeke, and shoved us into the current. We were away!

My first feeling at trusting my entire winter's wood supply to the vagaries of the Yukon was sheer fright. Leaping to the sweep, I hauled it this way, then that, rotating my craft nicely. But how to project it cross-current? I felt I must be making some obvious mistake and, blaming my inexperience, began wielding the tiller furiously. But the raft merely rotated. I even tried sculling, which I'd only seen done, never properly learned it. It was no use. Before long I realized I had no navigational control. We were completely at the mercy of the river. If we drifted too near the middle, we'd careen past Eagle and, well, there would go all my winter wood. Too close to the shore and we'd take out Charlie Steve's fish wheel about seven miles, at most forty-five minutes, away. But my raft would not stop. I had to do something. I had to do something immediately.

Feeling the first stages of panic, I wrenched the sweep from the water, sliced the lashings, grabbed my paddle, bounded to one side, and began flogging the water. I doubted this would have any effect; the raft weighed many tons; surely my paltry force could only do what the sweep had done—spin us uselessly. And sure enough the raft again commenced a slow, leisurely revolution. I vaulted to the other side and paddled against the torque, thereby making a crucial discovery: the paddle force applied against the pivoting momentum produced a lateral vector that gave me a modicum of control. Not much, but some, as long as, squirrel-like, I hopped back and forth and paddled like mad. Though panting hard, I could now breathe easier. I had found a way to steer, barely.

Were we too close to the shore or too far away? Impossible to tell. But we were really moving—eight to ten knots, I judged. There was no way to stop. Yet I made myself sit back. A gull winged by, a moose cracked a branch in the woods, a hawk circled lazily overhead. I'd feel better after we passed that fish wheel.

Fish wheels were crucial to the Natives in Eagle. All summer long they yielded salmon, first the oil-rich kings, starting in July, then the silver or dog salmon, which kept running into September. The Natives dried the meat, ate it themselves, and fed it to their huskies.

A wheel consisted of a central axle and four blades, two opposing horizontal paddles and two opposing chicken-wire-covered scoops. Buoyed by double rows of empty fifty-five-gallon drums, it was anchored to the beach with steel cables and kept offshore with planks. As the current turned the wheel, the salmon were trapped in the scoops, hoisted out of the water, rolled back toward the axle, into side-angled chutes, thence into boxes at the sides of the wheel.

At the height of the season and in an ideal location, a fish wheel could catch hundreds of pounds of salmon every day, from twenty to thirty pounds each, and in prime condition, despite their not imbibing a morsel while swimming upstream for 2,000 miles from the Bering Sea.

For me, who loved fishing above all human endeavors, to wipe out the support mechanism of the village's fisherman emeritus with my out-of-control log raft would be humiliating, to say the least, and perhaps even fatal to my continued good standing on the Eagle social register.

I eyeballed the shore and tried to imagine the fish wheel. I thought we were about right, but what would the currents do between here and there? No way to tell. And no way to move this hulking mass quickly. Six feet too close with a half mile to spare and I'd surely crash into the wheel.

I tried to control my breathing. The shoreline looked familiar. The village was around the next bend. Getting closer now. The raft seemed to drift toward mid-river as the shore curved gently away. There was a cabin, and another—the upstream limits of the village. At last, in the distance, I saw the fish wheel.

Native boys called from the bank, "Look! There's MaGeel." "Hi, MaGeel!" "What you doin', dibicha (rascal)?"

I moseyed to the front with my pole, just in case. Would we miss? Or wipe out? I held my breath. The gap narrowed. A hundred yards. Fifty. Twenty. Ten. We missed! A few yards to spare. Breathing again, I grinned. And there was Charlie, fisherman emeritus, waving happily.

"Hi, Charlie," I saluted, a gesture full of bravado. Was he aware that I'd chewed my fingernails almost down to my elbows? From his perspective I doubted it. I had arrived and departed too quietly, too suddenly.

Then we'd gone beyond the village and were alone again. Just me, Zeke, my canoe, my logs and tons and tons of irresistible momentum. Now I only had to worry about how to keep the raft from sliding too far into the current.

The river widened beyond the village. Not wanting to trust my logs to the swift stretch above town, I poled into the shallows. "Yo oh, heave ho," I grunted. The raft grounded on the flats. Raising my arms in triumph, I hitched my wood to a boulder with a long hank of parachute cord, hoisted my pack and rifles, and strode down the car road toward home.

A few days later Anton towed my raft to a landing at the edge of town with his motorboat. Barney Hansen threw a choker cable around it and dragged it to my backyard with his D-8 cat. I cut the trees into fifteen-foot lengths, stacked them in a snow-and-rain-shedding teepee, built a sawbuck, and started sawing stove lengths.

As the nights grew colder and snow accumulated, our woodpile began to grow and grow.

GENIES IN THE BOTTLE

Kate had spurned the bear meat I'd sent home with Amund Hagen, had set it down in the cold cellar, a space under the kitchen, where it had spoiled. "It wasn't easy to shoot that bear," I complained. "They don't grow on trees, you know. We can't just sashay down to the corner grocery and buy more of it."

"In case you've forgotten, I was here alone while you were out playing Eskimo, tending Scott and taking care of the house. I didn't have a lot of spare time."

"I haven't forgotten." She hadn't even mentioned being pregnant.

"I don't like bear meat. It's gamey and too greasy."

"Like mutton or pork," I snapped.

"And why did you put the head on top of the bag? It had no lips or eyelids. Made me want to puke."

"Didn't bite you, did it?" Head, ribs, hindquarter—I couldn't see much difference, hadn't given it a second thought. To me it was all meat. *She could've at least tried to act grateful,* I fumed.

Dumping the whole mess in the woods, I tramped to the wood pile to vent my spleen. After about twenty cuts, I realized I shouldn't have been surprised.

Kate and I had met while she was a coed at the University of Arizona and I an aviation cadet at Marana Air Base. She'd been a "blind" date, I recalled, smiling at the word, because I'd been the one who proved blind in the deeper sense, that is, lacking a controlling consciousness, having little regard for rational discrimination, unable to discern or judge. She'd swept into my life that warm Arizona night in a red-and-white floral print "squaw dress," she called it, which swished when we danced and showcased the bareness of her arms and neck. Blue-eyed, solid-jawed, with a saucy nose, long blond hair and an oo-la-la physique, she made me feel like an inarticulate dolt, able only to smile and gulp.

That spring and summer, stretched out on the diving board at the cadet pool, she made the most exotic travel posters look pale and drab. Though proud to be seen with her in public, I spent most of my spare time figuring how to get us off by ourselves. But when I succeeded, she nearly always wanted to discuss religion—at times when I was feeling anything but religious.

Church life was important to Kate. Our trouble began when she announced that hers was "the *only true* religion," which struck me as outrageous. Then she insisted that I had to believe it to be "saved," at which I blew my stack.

"Don't you know that billions upon billions of Indians, Chinese, Japanese; Hindus, Muslims, Jews; Bushmen, Eskimos, aborigines; countless tribes, whole cultures, myriad generations of unheard-of peoples have lived and died without ever hearing of your religion? And what about the Israelites, 'God's chosen people' of the Old Testament, plus millions of other alleged Christians who quarrel among themselves, while rejecting the tenets set forth by your church? Do you really believe none of them have ever been worthy of being 'saved' by 'the *only true* church'?"

If so, I insisted, it was she, not I, who needed saving, "FROM BEING A BIGOT!"

My vehemence astounded me and astounded Kate, too, since she'd expected me to acquiesce. "Why should you care?" she challenged. "You NEVER go to church."

She was right there. Church had been optional in our family, and I'd opted out. I believed in the bounty of Mother Nature, my strong arm and my keen eye. Religious folk, in my opinion, were basically blockheads. So I had no ready answer to Kate's churchless charges, at least none that sounded reasonable to me.

Gradually we found that, though we could begin a religious discussion amicably, we couldn't keep it that way, and before long we'd find ourselves goading, lashing out, sulking, and parting. But our last argument would fester, haunt, and challenge us to try again. Though armed with the best intentions, we always wound up wrangling. Religion became our "genie in the bottle"—a trickster who, once loose, became difficult to recork.

All through my first year in the air force—five months of primary at Marana near Tucson and seven months of basic at Williams near Phoenix—Kate and I flailed away at each other. Finally I transferred to gunnery school at Laughlin in Del Rio, Texas, 1,500 miles from Kate, and at last our verbal jousting foundered. When my roommate was killed in a plane crash, I suffered a personal crisis, taking many walks alone at night, pondering life's ultimate purposes and everyone's ultimate fate.

Ashes to ashes, and dust to dust—what the dickens did it all mean?

Besides that, I was beginning to suspect that the brave slogans of the Mighty U.S. Air Arm were a coverup for a national unmentionable fear, and that the arms race with the Soviets, though allegedly initiated and precipitated by the majority, could lead to nothing but world destruction. It disgusted me to be part of it.

And so, with enough tumult in my life just trying to keep

my jet pilot's tail in one piece and desiring a less tumultu-
ous significant relationship, I didn't send Kate my new
address when transferring to Florida, thus insulating me
from her irresistible charms, I thought. But six months later
I received a letter. Kate had found out my address by writing
to my mother, my own mother, who, years later, would wonder airily about this lapse in her usually good judgment.

At last my training as a USAF pilot was over; I was as-
signed to McClellan Air Force Base in Sacramento. Kate,
with a bachelor's in social work, moved to Sacramento, too.
And we found that the intervening year had softened us
both. We got along better. We shared a love for hiking, camping, swimming, canoeing, reading. We enjoyed each other's
company immensely—as long as we managed to keep our
"genie in the bottle."

Still sawing away at my woodpile, I began to reflect upon
events that led to Alaska.

In 1955-'59, after I'd separated from the air force and was
attending the University of California at Berkeley, while Kate
and I were still newlyweds, I'd tried to interest her in
Vilhjalmur Stefansson, anthropologist and arctic explorer.
He'd persuaded me that food preferences are purely preju-
dice, have nothing to do with race, climate or geography,
are variable from culture to culture, depend strictly on habit
and, like all habits, are changeable. From his conclusions
I'd made what I thought a brilliant leap in logic—that real
freedom is achieved only through insight into one's own
thought processes.

One night reading in bed, I asked Kate, "Did you know
humans can live on nothing but fish?"

"Huh?" she said, engrossed in her own book.

"Humans can live on nothing but fish. Did they ever
teach you that at college?"

"No. And I don't believe it. It flies in the face of all modern
dietary practice."

"Not so. Stone Age Eskimos lived on nothing but fish for months at a time. Stef and his pals learned to do it, too."

"Like the all-meat diet you were talking about yesterday, only now it's all-fish."

"Right!"

"How can you be sure of this?"

"Stef tells the whole story right here in this book, *The Friendly Arctic*. It's very convincing."

"In other words, you've only read about this. You've never tried it. You don't know anyone personally who has."

"True, but . . . "

"I can cite a hundred books that insist on the need for balanced diets."

"Kate, Stefansson is a respected scientist. He has not made this up. I *know* he's right about it!"

"You 'know'? Seems to me you'd need more evidence to say you 'know.'"

She was wrong. I didn't need more evidence. I *knew*, and I *knew* that I knew. But I couldn't explain how. "Think about it," I queried. "Where would an Eskimo find a carbohydrate?"

In bed the next night:

"You seem to be going bananas over Stefansson," she remarked.

"'Bananas' doesn't seem the right word. Too tropical."

"You're thinking you'd like to go north, aren't you? Live up there?"

"Well . . . "

"You'd like to take me and this baby," she placed my hand on her belly, "and go live on nothing but fish."

The way she put it, without my air force background, made it seem heartless, too intentional. But she had a way of piercing through to my core thoughts. I couldn't help smiling.

"Give me one good reason why I might want to do that," she pressed.

I gulped. "I don't know . . . off the top of my head. As an adventure maybe? A new experience?"

She glared.

I cleared my throat. "To have something to tell your grandchildren?"

She gritted her teeth.

"To . . . er . . . see what the Arctic looks like?"

She shook her fist and growled.

"How 'bout 'cause you love me?" I grinned.

"All those reasons stink," she snapped. "Alaska is too COLD."

I knew I'd have to try another approach.

The next opportunity came at breakfast, but Kate seized the initiative. "It's too dark in Alaska. The sun sets in the fall, doesn't come up until spring. And Eskimos have no electricity."

"Well, it depends on . . . "

"There are too many mosquitoes!"

"Only in June and July."

"June and July! That wipes out the whole summer. And we haven't even talked about dirt."

"Whaddya mean, 'dirt'?"

"I mean *dirt*. Camping out is dirty. For a week or two, you can stand it. But forever? You'd get filthy—your skin, your hair, your clothes, everything! And there'd be no way to get clean!"

"We might get used to it."

"Used to it! You think our baby will be able to get used to it?"

"Sure! It's *clean* dirt!" Had I really said that?

"What did the Eskimos do for diapers?"

"Moss and rabbit fur, Stef says."

"Yuk!"

"Well, they're handy and disposable. And the price is right."

"If we went to Alaska, I'd never see my parents or sisters again."

"You never saw them that much while you were at college."

"I saw them every summer."

"Well, all young couples have to start somewhere. You never can tell what life might bring." I tossed down my last swig of coffee, stuffed toast in my mouth, grabbed my books, my jacket, called Zeke and headed out. No one could say I didn't know when to retreat.

"I like supermarkets, laundromats, and movie theaters," Kate yelled after me. "I like hot weather, long summers, nice clothes, and warm showers. I hate frozen wastelands!"

I vaulted down the stairs.

"Do you hear me?" she screeched as I swept through the door. I had, yes, but knew I had to let her cool off.

I broached the subject again a few nights later while she was fixing dinner. "How'd your day go?"

"O.K. Went shopping."

"How's the baby?"

"Still kickin'." She meant literally. "How'd your day go?"

"Found another Stefansson book."

"Thought you'd have read them all by now."

"This was the last one in the stacks."

"More about Eskimos?"

"What else?" I dragged it out and started thumbing pages. "*Hunters of the Great North*. May I read you something?"

"Sure."

I began with Stef's description of an old Eskimo fisherman, a pillar of his small community. He fished long hours and caught much, but gave freely to all who lived nearby, including those outside his immediate family. He was the perfect image of the kind, old father, never became dictatorial or cantankerous. "'He had no formal or legal power,'" Stef wrote, "'but he commanded the respect and good will of everyone.'"

"Nice," Kate observed. "Does Stef mention the cold?"

"Yes . . . let me find it . . . here . . . 'When I praised the southern climate in San Francisco, the old fisherman asked me whether it was not always summer there. On my replying yes, he said that undoubtedly white men might like that sort of climate, but an Eskimo couldn't understand how any country could be pleasant when it was always summer. In winter, he said, a hot house is good, for you can always go outside and cool off; but where can you flee from the heat of summer?' "

"You see," I put in, remembering my belief that real freedom is achieved only through insight into one's own thought processes, "it all depends on what you get used to."

"Does Stefansson speak of the darkness?"

"In other books, yes. But I can tell you, it didn't inconvenience the Eskimos much. They burned seal-oil lamps in white snowhouses. Their walls were ultrareflective. Outdoors everything was white. The moon, the stars, the northern lights gave them all the light they needed. 'Darkness' is a misnomer. Also, this so-called complete darkness only lasted a few months."

As Kate put the food on the table, I detected a softer look.

"Dark and light are like any of life's opposites," I continued. "Rough and smooth, fast and slow, hard and soft, joy and sorrow. Any sensory condition is only perceivable because it exists in juxtaposition to its opposite. Yin and yang, you know?"

From that day forward she never objected strongly to my wanting to quit school and go to Alaska. I never found out exactly why, what actually happened inside her head, and I avoided asking directly for fear it would crumble under the weight of explanation. But she liked to travel, see new places. Perhaps her initial resistance had dissipated because of that. Perhaps she was just exercising a woman's prerogative—the right to change her mind. Or perhaps, I

mused, still sawing, still ranting over the spoiled bear meat,
I'd just uncorked another "genie in the bottle."

GROCERIES

Near the end of September our winter order of groceries arrived from Seattle, which meant a two-day car trip over the Taylor Highway, Eagle's only vehicle link to the Outside, a 160-mile dirt road to Tetlin Junction and the Alaska Highway. Zeke and I piled into my gray '54 Chevy, gassed up at the Northern Commercial Company and headed out.

Straddling my lap, Zeke stuck her head out my window, let me steer under her belly and gave me her spine as a furry chin rest. Squinching down, dropping my eyes to the level of her back, I imagined how we'd look to a man in a city street—a car driven by a dog!

Autumn had painted the landscape in brilliant swatches of magenta, yellow, ocher, and scarlet, all backdropped by a sparkling blue sky and dazzling snippets of opalescent clouds—almost too gaudy to be real.

We were in no hurry. Indeed, there was no way we could hurry over this dirt. So I settled back and watched the scenery go by. As the tires rumbled and jiggled between the here and the there, so my thoughts flitted and jiggled between the then and the now, settling me into that half meditative, half dreamy state that merges past, present, and future into one immediate stream of consciousness.

At twenty miles we passed the site of my first moose hunt a couple of months ago. Charlie and Isaac Junebee, two Native youths with jet black hair and flashing smiles, had supplied the license, I'd supplied the transportation, and we agreed to split our take fifty-fifty. We'd been bumping slowly over the road, a pair of eyeballs at every window, when a bull moose appeared to the left at about 400 yards. As we stopped, he took off. The boys bolted out the passenger side while I, the cheechako or newcomer, eased out on the moose's side and stared. A yearling, he'd attained his full height but was still lanky, had small antlers, long ears, a bulbous snout, and a shiny black and mahogany coat. I thought he was too far for a shot, but Charlie grabbed my '06 and levered a shell into the chamber.

"Hadn't you better give me that?" I snapped.

The moose was gathering momentum.

"Shoot!" Charlie insisted.

"He's a quarter of a mile away!"

"Shoot!" Isaac echoed.

"He may be the last one we'll see all day," Charlie goaded.

The moose was in the open, trotting across a creek and heading for cover. I checked the chamber, sat, thumbed off the safety, wrapped the sling around my arm, placed my elbows on my knees, peered through the scope and, recalling my trajectory charts, aimed about a yard over his back and a yard in front, and squeezed.

BOOM!

I thought I'd missed, but we found him an hour later, shot through the heart. By that evening the whole town had heard about it. And the Junebees and the McGills enjoyed moose meat for a month. Thanks to my '06.

At thirty miles Zeke and I came across several dozen ruffed grouse, sitting in the highway like targets in a shooting gallery, inviting me to drive close and pick them off. We encountered them often during the trip. Sometimes I'd get as many as three before the flock spooked, but then they'd only fly into the trees and wait, their only known enemies having four legs; they didn't understand bullets.

"The best chicken you'll ever eat," the Natives said, evoking no argument from me or Kate.

After a while we passed the stretch where, on my first trip to Eagle in the spring, I'd followed two caribou, a mother and calf, galloping down the road in front of my car. Caribou usually run to escape wolves, and my car contained a pseudo-wolf—Zeke.

At first it was a thrill to have caribou loping along a hundred feet from our bumper, but when I approached too close, they'd speed up to 40 mph and hog the middle of the road, keeping me from passing; I could only proceed at caribou pace, which slowed to 10 mph as the miles slipped by. Zeke had never seen caribou, let alone a prolonged view, and began clawing at the windshield and shrieking—in short, going berserk.

Finally fed up with her madness, I braked and said, "O.K., Zeke, you want caribou? Go get 'em!"

She bolted through the door and dashed off. But her enthusiasm soon waned and she settled into a trot, then a walk. When I invited her back in, she complied but immediately began shrieking again.

I let her out and back in three times, while the caribou pounded on ahead, seemingly unfatigued. After the third round, even Zeke seemed awed. The caribou raced on and on for perhaps ten miles, finally leaped into the snowbank and gaped at us as we gawked past. I understood how wolves might be hard pressed to catch a meal which could run as fast and as far as that.

Even Kate would like caribou, I thought.

As we neared Tetlin Junction and descended into the Tanana (Ta' na naw) valley, I nearly ran over a porcupine. His head had become stuck in a tin can, which doomed him to starvation. I stopped, taking care not to let Zeke out, found a stick and, staying clear of that spiny tail, smacked the can. That failing, I found another stick, placed them both against the can, and held it while the porcupine pulled. Head free at last, he grinned me a thanks, I thought, as he waddled out of sight.

I picked up our food order at the Tok (Toke) general store, a few miles up the road from Tetlin, sacked out beside the car that night and started back in the morning.

The road seemed an unbroken chain of ups and downs and lefts and rights to whose engineers "straight-and-level" must have been an abstract concept—imagined and dreamed about but never plotted or experienced. On the map this Taylor Highway was a pale and wiggly hairline, as if the cartographer, contemplating it, had had an attack of apoplexy. I constantly down-shifted and up-shifted as we ground up, whined down or tilted around. Dust plumed behind our tires. Many signs warned of SOFT SHOULDERS, a phrase which never failed to remind me of Kate.

After my arrival in Alaska, I'd ended up in Eagle because of a chance meeting with Alan Innes-Taylor at a restaurant in Fairbanks. He'd spotted my yellow canoe and asked me to work for him as a Yukon River guide. He'd called Eagle "the most beautiful town in Alaska," and his offer seemed like a good omen. So I accepted and sent for Kate, who arrived soon afterward at Fairbanks airport with Scott, six months, in tow.

I recalled Kate's excitement as we traveled this same road four months ago, a glint of adventure in her clear blue eyes, an uptilt to her firm jaw, an eagerness tinged with trepidation for the vast, unpeopled unknown—everything, including Scott, so spanking new. Kate loved camping so much; I was convinced I could get her to love this campers' haven of the north, too.

After we arrived in Eagle, I helped Innes-Taylor build a

tent site at Boundary Creek, helped clean and paint a tourist headquarters in Eagle, and made one trip with tourists on a rubber raft from Dawson. But whenever I mentioned money, he'd put me off, change the subject, and spout promises. Finally, I spouted back, was fired, and took a job fighting a local forest fire.

I'd saved $3,000 as an air force pilot, Dad had almost doubled it in the stock market, and I wanted to make it last as long as possible.

Gradually I got to know Eagle's permanent residents: Anton and Esther Merly, who ran the post office; the three Biedermans—father Horace, mother Sarah, and adult son Junior—proprietors of the Northern Commercial Company general store; Amund Hagen, Dick Bower, George Montgomery, and "Grasshopper" Joe Brissette, retired miners; and "Silent" Bill, who talked nonstop, and his wife Hazel, a pair of pensioned tourists.

There were also about a dozen summer residents and perhaps thirty-five at the Indian village—the Juneboos, the Malcolms, the Pauls, the Davids, and the Steves.

This handful of people shared the Yukon River valley east and west for a couple hundred miles, an area the size of Massachusetts. A mile from town in any direction and you'd be totally isolated.

Eagle is the only community in Alaska where whites and Natives live apart, the Indian village being three miles upstream. The division is more accidental than prejudicial, the white town having developed during the gold rush, when the town became the exit port for placer miners from the Klondike.

About halfway down the last grade before home, I pulled off at a wide spot and gazed.

The town at this distance seemed to nestle against Eagle Bluff, a rocky promontory on the left where eagles once nested. On its summit was a twenty-foot cross, built and

painted by Anton Merly, agleam in the last rays of the setting sun. Every occupied dwelling sent up pencil-straight
shafts of woodsmoke, which merged and stratified at bluff
height. The town's four main buildings—the Northern
Commercial Company, the wellhouse, the library, and the
post office—were all white with green trim. Between the
post office and the Bluff was a wide grass airstrip, one of the
town's two runways. I could distinguish the roof of our
rented house this side of the post office. Beyond the town
was the pewter swath of the Yukon River; beyond that ocher
willow flats and dark green patches of spruce; and in the
distance the Ogilvie Mountains. The scene took my breath
away.

Zeke and I pulled up in front of our house. Kate and Scott
greeted us warmly. As Scott watched, Kate helped unload
our winter rations—flour, corn meal, dry milk, dry baby formula, canned fruit and vegetables, shortening, vegetable
oil, oranges, and apples.

Also in the trunk were several dozen ruffed grouse. Plac-
ing them carefully in the cold cellar, determined not to let
them spoil, I'd pluck, clean, and can them tomorrow.

HOMESTEAD

The next time I left Eagle it wasn't to get wood or meat. I left simply to get out of the house. I'd been prowling back and forth like a caged polar bear, trying to assuage my wanderlust between the kitchen and the crib. Wherever I turned in our rented house, there stood my mate. Cut the wood! Haul the water! Do the dishes! Start a fire! I felt enswathed in an endless loop of familial responsibilities—the great arctic hunter transformed into an assistant housewife. And worse, the pattern had begun to look set, like a sneak preview of the rest of my life. My precious vision of self-reliance seemed to be slipping through my fingers, even as I watched. Rent, groceries, white gas—expenses had whittled my $5,000 to $2,000 in six short months. And we hadn't yet begun to live the life of my dreams. I felt I had to transfer my family into the bush, shove us toward self-sufficiency, or gird myself for the commercial treadmill.

"See you in a couple of weeks," I called from the door, knowing Kate, growing heavy with child, and Scott would be looked after by the Merlys.

My destination was the Hayfield, three miles up the Yukon to the Indian village, another mile beyond that to Eagle Creek on the other side, and four miles up it toward the Ogilvie Mountains. Presumably I was "exploring," but I also wanted to build a sodhouse, wanted my family to live there until I could build a log cabin. If Kate had plumbed my sense of urgency in this matter, she'd think I'd gone bonkers. The same for the Merlys. So I hadn't told any of them. I'd just do it and let the chips fall where they might.

Since my separation from the air force, the Soviets had launched *Sputnik* and entered an all-out missile race with the United States, a policy later termed MAD, for Mutually Assured Destruction. Americans everywhere were building backyard bomb shelters, and many, including me, were sure that the entire world faced imminent nuclear holocaust. But not Kate. Somehow she maintained a serenity, a state which she ascribed to her abiding faith, but which I ascribed to her never having been a jet pilot. I'd done all in my power to persuade her that once The War started, which I was sure it would SOON, Alaska would be a safe haven. Stefansson had convinced me that war was a perversity, that civilization since the Industrial Revolution had warped and twisted us, that certain primitive people—Eskimos, Hopi, Bushmen, for instance—knew more than we moderns about peace, brotherhood, and living in harmony with nature. I was absolutely certain. But Kate proved impervious to my best rhetoric. Either I could not articulate my fears clearly, or she was unimpressed by my self-purported authority in this matter of life and death. Whatever the reasons, we were unable to communicate meaningfully. So we did what we'd always done—pushed it into the background. Therefore, I had taken it upon myself to act in what I thought were the best interests of all of us, but autonomously, independently, keeping my "genie in his bottle."

I lined the canoe up the Yukon, passed the Indian village, crossed to the mouth of Eagle Creek, carried the craft up the bank, hid it under the brush, hefted my pack with its long-handled assortment of building tools, and began hiking.

The old Indian trail meandered through birch and alder groves beside Eagle Creek, and now and then angled across grassy flats. The U.S. Army Corps of Engineers had begun a supply road up the creek during World War II, intending to push it through to the Arctic Ocean. They'd abandoned the project after the first winter, but dozer scars were still visible in the fragile earth.

During the gold rush in 1898, the Hayfield had been used by the Canadian Northwest Mounted Police as a source of fodder for their horses. Their old barn still stood at the back edge of town, a half mile from the Yukon. But the Hayfield was deserted now. I didn't see why I couldn't use it—squatters' rights, they called it.

My sodhouse would be one room, with a dirt floor, stone fireplace in the middle, roof and walls made of poles and covered with sod—like the ones used by early American settlers and some Eskimos in Stef's day.

When we arrived I shrugged off my pack and broke out lunch, while Zeke sniffed the area. After quaffing what was left in my canteen, I refilled it in the creek and splashed water on my face. Returning to the pack, I found my battered copy of the *Arctic Manual* and opened it to the chapter on "Shelters."

First I had to decide where to build. My house should be far enough from the creek to be safe from spring runoff, but not so far as to make water-hauling impossible. It should be near enough to the field for sod, but not too far from firewood. I paced around before making up my mind, then marked four outside spots for corner posts and four inner ones for center posts. Then I began to dig. Soon I was reveling in the sheer joy of exertion, my cares passing from me with the perspiration.

I worked steadily until almost dark, built a fire, and had supper—nuts, raisins, cheese, and jerky washed down with instant coffee. Then I threw on more logs, crawled into my sleeping bag, and snuggled up to Zeke.

The dawn was bright and crisp, temperature maybe 40° F. After breakfast I picked up my shovel and started digging again. Over the next few days I excavated four center holes a yard deep and a yard apart, and found four dry spruce logs for center posts, all about the same length and diameter. I inserted each post into a hole, propped them vertical, filled in around them and tamped them tight. This complete, I lugged a dozen bushels of stones from the creek and piled them between the center posts. This would be the fireplace, hold the heat after the flames had gone out, and keep the sodhouse warm at night. Over the fireplace would hang a Dall's sheepskin, my survivalist diploma. We'd draw it aside to let the smoke out, pull it back to keep the heat in. Translucent, it would act as a skylight.

Then I set to work on the outer walls and roof, a long process of exhuming the four outer postholes, finding, felling, and dragging trees, chopping, sawing, lifting, carrying, eating, and sleeping. Zeke mostly hung around the fringes or tried to entice me into playing fetch by bringing me sticks. She wasn't used to staying in one place or to such single-minded devotion to a stationary project.

At some point I moved camp next to the sodhouse fireplace so I could watch my structure take shape. So far, it looked more like the skeleton of some prehistoric beast than a potential dwelling. I was glad Kate couldn't see it at this stage.

One evening, needing a break, I took my rifle and binoculars, called Zeke and climbed a hill overlooking the valley. At the top I sat down and scanned the countryside. Back home atop Eagle Bluff, I'd never failed to spot moose within ten minutes, but this hill was lower, the viewing area smaller, and the angle flatter. I began glassing the slope where Zeke and I had encountered the brown bears in June.

We had passed by the Hayfield on the other side of the

creek and had headed into the mountains. A few hours later, while taking a lunch break, a mother brown bear and her cub, a lethal combination, ambled by not thirty feet away on the far side of the creek. I ceased breathing, put my hand on my '06, but they didn't even glance in our direction. Perhaps the wind was just right, or the creek masked our sound and scent. Zeke never looked up, a lucky thing, too—one woof and that mother would've charged. At that range against a berserk sow bear, I wouldn't have trusted my aim. Later, on the way home, stumbling blindly into the Hayfield, we encountered spikes so tall that I couldn't see over and so dense I couldn't see through. I felt isolated from everything except the green wall in front of my face and, if I looked up, the blue dome overhead. As we passed through, the stalks slithered and clacked, a not unpleasant song which nevertheless terrified me because I was sure it was telegraphing our position to every monster bear within a mile, even as it hampered my hearing them. The farther we went, the more claustrophobic I felt. Yet I was thrilled to find green grass this far north. A land that supported grizzlies, I knew, would also support humans, and my goosebumps arose not only from fear of becoming a bear morsel, but from the promise of future feasts of my own. And this site was beside a creek full of grayling, mountains full of Dall's sheep, and valleys full of moose and caribou. I paused often to listen, but also to imbibe the sweet odor of succulent meadow. At last, the stems began to thin, and trees and hills became visible again.

The Hayfield was much like what I imagined in the Great Plains before cultivation, a patch of wildflowers and perennial tall grass.

But that had been summer; it was October now. The Hayfield was brown and flat. Still searching for game, I noted that the binocs emphasized the scene's three-dimensionality, accentuated the apparent separation between objects. Disappointed at not seeing movement, I finally sauntered back to camp with Zeke.

Sitting beside the campfire at dusk, we were buzzed by some large bird. I heard it whoosh, ducked instinctively, then scanned the sky. Ravens, hawks, and ducks don't fly in the dark and owls stoop soundlessly. I never did see it, but finally decided it must have been a golden eagle. They're large enough to carry off a lamb. And what else would've been that brazen?

Over the next several days I erected corner posts, tied them together with cross members, installed four rafters between the corners and the center posts, and began laying horizontal poles to form the roof. More poles slanted from the cross members to the ground to form walls. All this took time because I'd already used up the closer trees and had to range farther to find others. During the next week, the house began to take shape.

Under the south wall I dug a trench about belly deep, which, when covered with poles and sod, would be a tunnel entrance, less convenient than a door, but designed to conserve heat. Hardpan and shale lay under the topsoil, and it all had to be picked apart and shoveled out. My palms grew thick with calluses.

One day while I was swinging my pickax, Zeke charged off, barking furiously. A bull moose with a rack wider than my outstretched arms had stalked to within fifty yards. No doubt he believed that the sounds of my digging were made by a rival bull, scraping antlers in his territory. When he saw Zeke, he turned and trotted up the hill. I gawked. Immense and sleek, he had a long bell and huge shoulders. If I'd intended to stay the winter, I'd have killed him without batting an eye.

That night snow began to fall and it turned bitter cold. I stuffed my mummy sleeping bag into my larger down bag. Zeke crawled in beside me. I donned all the clothes I'd brought—T-shirt, long-johns, jeans, down underwear, sweater, jacket, parka, wool stocking cap, three pairs of wool socks, even my heavy mittens with wool liners. I had to get up once to gather more hay for bedding. Zeke burrowed to the bottom and relaxed there, head-down, nose next to my feet. I wondered how she could breathe, and why she didn't suffer claustrophobia. Though warm, we were trussed up like a hay bale. I couldn't sleep. The clock ran as if oiled with molasses, and the stars looked so bright I thought we'd been rocketed into orbit. When it finally began to get light, I called softly, "Zeke." She didn't move. "Zeke!" Finally, like a ferret, she squirmed around and stuck her nose out. Our combined breath escaped in a cloud. But we couldn't stay here. Gritting my teeth, I rassled myself up and braced myself against the elements.

My boots, which I'd slept with to keep from freezing, were frozen anyway. I couldn't get my feet into them. I'd laid out kindling the night before, but couldn't walk to it in my socks. Finally I raced around on tiptoe, gathering hay for scarecrow socks, which kept my feet warm until I could start a fire to thaw my boots.

We grabbed snacks for breakfast, while I shivered and packed to leave. I didn't pack my shovel and pickax. No one would bother them here, and I wouldn't need them in Eagle before spring.

I shrugged into my pack and we headed out, Zeke in the lead. I turned for one last look.

There was half the framework for a sodhouse, logs but no sod, bones but no flesh. To the north was the front lawn, the Hayfield, now under the snow, a summer playground for Scott and his brother or sister. To the east was Eagle Creek, brimming with salmon and grayling, thoroughfare for furbearers—beaver, ermine, mink, fox, fisher, marten, otter, wolverine, and wolf. Nearby roamed all the game I'd ever need—sheep, caribou, moose, and bear; grouse, ptarmigan, hare, squirrels. To the west was a low ridge, a buffer against wind, birch-dotted and aspen-cloaked. In the distance was a snow-covered peak, our personal shrine.

For many minutes I stood staring with a lump in my throat, feeling at one with all the unnamed pioneers who'd found their niche in a land called America—explorers, trappers, voyageurs, pot-hunters, mountaineers, squaw men, homesteaders, sheepherders, ranchers.

I turned and headed home.

"What more could any woman want?" I said to Zeke.

What more could any woman want?

IMPASSE!

About halfway back along the trail to the Yukon, thinking I heard something, I stopped. It sounded like "Shhhh," barely audible. *It's only in my head,* I thought. *Been out by myself too long. Must be gettin' bushy.* I kept walking.

Soon I realized that the sound was not in my head but was varying in volume, growing louder then softer, louder then softer. Again I halted. It seemed to come from everywhere at once—front, back, left, right, even from above.

I'd spent thousands of hours in diverse wilderness places and never heard a sound like that—not like something live. *Too harsh, too mechanical, too weird.* I shrugged and kept walking.

In the next half mile, trying to identify it, I stopped and started a half dozen times. It didn't help. But the sound seemed definitely louder now; I was getting closer; whatever it was, it was ahead.

After another half mile, it had become a droning hiss. I walked faster, sure it must be coming from the Yukon, that vast undulating body which reigned over the landscape and now seemingly the airwaves, too. I grabbed my pack frame to keep it from banging my back, and, befuddlement rising with the rising sibilance, broke into a lope. Finally, I rounded the last bend, topped the last rise, and there it was:

ICE!

The Yukon was choked with it. Crammed full. From this side to the other. Upstream. Downstream. As far as the eye could see. A gigantic frozen serpent, half a mile wide, slithering, crawling, rasping past me in an endless unbroken column.

I shrugged off my pack and side-stepped down the slick bank to look close. This wasn't the same as breakup ice. No bergs, no chunks. No booming or crashing. Just flat wheels, thin panes. Sharp-edged plates of all sizes, the large ones looking frail, but exerting great horizontal force. Barely jutting above the surface, they revolved in the current, with thousands of bits and pieces in between. Nothing awesome about this freeze-up ice. Just a "Shhh." A whisper. But hundreds of miles long.

At my feet the ice plates dragged against the shore, not digging or gouging, just twirling in a lazy pirouette.

A mill of ice. Grinding slowly. But exceeding fine.

I climbed back up the hill to my canvas-covered canoe, which suddenly looked frail and delicate. The cloth would be shredded by those jagged shards. I was stuck. Stranded. No way to get home.

I sat down on my pack, wondering what to do. Go back to my unfinished sodhouse? Hope for another moose? Wait for the river to freeze solid? Or wait for it to run clear again?

Yet, Kate was expecting me tonight, and if I didn't show up, she'd surely worry, might even initiate a search; I didn't want that. If I could just let her know I was O.K. . . .

I decided to walk the three miles toward the Indian village and holler across to someone who could get a message to Kate. Then I'd return to my sodhouse. I leaned my pack against a scrub spruce and started out.

Strange, I thought, *I haven't been consistent. At home, I'd felt imprisoned. Now all I wanted was to get back.*

Nearing a point opposite the village, I saw children playing between the cabins about a half mile away. I waited for them to notice me. At last I cupped my hands, leaned back and bellowed:

"CAN YOU HEAR ME?"

The roar of my own huge voice after two weeks of perfect quiet was a tremendous shock. I shuddered involuntarily, but tried again.

"CAN YOU HEAR ME?"

Some of the kids stopped playing.

"TELL MY WIFE I AM ALL RIGHT."

No answer. Other kids were still milling around. I could hear words, snatches: "Look, there's . . . " "What does . . . " " . . . telling us?" "Do you . . . " Bits and pieces came to me like that, on the errant wind.

But if I could catch partial phrases spoken by normal voices, surely they could comprehend my shouts. So I leaned back and brayed again:

"CAN YOU HEAR ME?

"TELL MY WIFE I AM ALL RIGHT."

Silence. Some were still playing, not even looking up.

"CAN YOU HEAR ME?"

No answer.

Feeling foolish, wondering what to do next, I heard an airplane. Of course! Today was Wednesday—mail day. That was the twin Beech making its approach to Eagle airport, or rather the dirt strip that passed for one between the village and the town. It would land, unload its bags, pick up outgoing mail, and take off again for another village. If the pilot spotted me, he might fly close enough to read a message. He might relay it to Esther by radio, and she might relay it to Kate.

I found a flat place to tramp words in the snow. But what to say? It had to be terse and pithy. Straight to the point.

Finally I had it—NEED NO AID. I shuffled through the white mantle until the letters were distinct. Nine capitals.

Big. Plain. As readable as I could make them. From my low angle, they didn't look like much, but I hoped they'd be clear from the air.

It took about fifteen minutes; I'd worked up a sweat.

I waited.

And waited.

And waited.

At last the mail plane took off, but set course and climbed out without dipping a wing in my direction.

The first hint that my shouts had been misunderstood was the sight of two figures on the other shore, mere dots at this distance, but determined, decisive dots. They were lining a boat upstream, one on the shore, towing, the other in the boat, fending off ice. Oncoming floes intermittently halted them, but they persisted.

"Oh, no! They're not coming across?" I groaned. But that was exactly what they were doing.

"WAIT! STOP! GO BACK! I DON'T WANT YOU! NEED NO AID!"

All my shouts were stifled in my throat. I'd already tried bellowing. There must be some other way to signal. But how? Waving my arms? Jumping up and down? Turning cartwheels? I could think of no gesture equal to the simple idea: I'm O.K.

I leaned back and roared again.

"CAN YOU HEAR ME?"

The dots didn't pause. The sounds of the ice and their own breath were probably louder than my now hoarse voice.

Finally I decided I should just walk away. Maybe they'd get discouraged if I were no longer visible. Maybe they'd see my wife later and tell her they'd seen me but I'd gone away. She'd assume I'd gone back to my homesite and planned to stay until crossing was safe. But before I could move, the dots boarded the boat and cast off.

From where I stood the crossing appeared frenzied. The men didn't rest for an instant. From the bow, the stern, seemingly all sides at once, they thrust and prodded the ice. Now in the pack, now in the clear, they worked furiously as I watched transfixed. The gap between us narrowed. The dots acquired heads and torsos, then faces and limbs. Finally recognizing Bob Stacey and Tim Malcolm, I marched downstream to greet them.

Bob had lived on the river for many years, running a fish wheel in summer and trapping in the winter. His lined and weathered brow showed evidence of many moose hunts and many seasons at fish camps. Tim was young, athletic, and quiet. He grinned at me through a missing front tooth. I'd never asked him how he lost it, but if it had been in a fight, I pitied the other guy.

Sweat-soaked but smiling, they were hauling their boat out as I approached. "I've been standing here, gawking at you," I said, "telling myself no one could do what you just did. But here you are. At least I think you're here. I'm still in shock."

They laughed and Bob said, "It's not so hard." But I'd seen them in action and their faces were drenched. "We thought you needed help."

"Of course, you did," I replied. "I couldn't think of any way to make you understand. All I needed was someone to tell my wife I'm O.K."

Bob's old eyes lowered. "We heard you shouting, 'Can you help me?' "

"It was 'Can you *hear* me?' "

"The kids said you were writing S.O.S. in the snow."

"It was NEED NO AID. It's still there." I pointed. "You can read it yourself."

Tim said, "You mean we made that trip for nothing?"

I felt sheepish.

Bob said, "I have a feeling McGill isn't too angry. Maybe

he'll even come back with us. It'll be easier with three."

"Four," I corrected. "My dog Zeke."

"Will she sit still in the boat?"

"She will," I said. "But I have another problem. I left my pack at the mouth of Eagle Creek. If I leave it there all winter, the bears will rip it apart. It'll take an hour or more to retrieve it. It's not fair to ask you to wait."

My friends stood silently, considering this.

"Listen," I put in, "maybe I could make it across in my canoe."

"No!" Bob said. "The ice will cut the canvas."

"We don't mind waiting," Tim said.

"All right," I said, then set off at a trot.

These sudden developments left me numb. Two weeks ago I'd wanted to leave home and did. Two hours ago I'd wanted to return home and couldn't. And now I'd been unexpectedly coaxed into being ferried home. I ran nearly all the way.

I dragged my canoe onto high ground and under a bush, retrieved my pack, and returned to my Native friends.

Bob and Tim were hauling their boat upstream to increase our distance above Eagle Bluff, the huge promontory that juts into the Yukon just below town. "If we don't make shore before the Bluff, the boat might be crushed," Bob mused.

"Looks like a black bear has been here," I said, pointing to tracks.

"Wolverine," Bob said. "Smaller, shorter, the tracks are closer together."

"Ferocious," I said.

"Powerful," Bob agreed. "Can break into anything."

We scrambled aboard—Tim in the bow with a pole, me in the center with an oar, Zeke next to me, and Bob in the stern with another oar. The boat was too small for its extra freight; we three could almost touch hands. We had only a few inches of freeboard—the distance between the water line and the gunwale; scarred and dented planks were our only protection against razor-sharp ice. To capsize was to freeze to death.

With my feet braced against the sideboards, I slammed away at the ice like the Natives, but my oar kept slipping and pitching me over. Bob and Tim scowled when I nearly tipped us twice. "It might be cool for swimming," Bob suggested.

I felt the hull give against my feet as we wedged our way into the ice field. I thought I heard the old boat groan, then realized it had been me.

We took advantage of small leads, tried to widen new ones. A yard here, a foot there, we crept forward.

I glanced up briefly to catch my breath. The day was old now. The sun had fallen below the Bluff with its landmark—the silver cross. I'd seen it often from many angles, but at that moment, from the middle of the icy Yukon, aglow in the eerie twilight, it looked vibrant, unreal, fraught with significance. I recalled Bob's casual remark as we shoved off, "I hope we make shore before the Bluff." I bent to my oar again.

There was a trick to this ice poling, I discovered—move quick but don't push too hard. My concentration seemed total while my awareness remained diffuse. We three seemed commanded by one voice, a silent cry that pulsed through our feet, urging, imploring, exhorting, "Push, damn it, push!"

But the ice closed in, fixing us at its center. We could only move forward by smashing the crust and propelling the hull into the space. Our poles bobbed and slashed. My neck, shoulders, back, arms, and hands burned as the Bluff loomed overhead.

"Is the whole damn Yukon gonna freeze solid right now?" Bob growled.

As we worked closer to the other shore, I saw people in the dim light, Natives and whites, adults and children, a mob jammed together, shuffling en masse, matching its pace to ours.

"Paddle like hell!" someone shouted. "It's your last chance!"

But it was no use to paddle like hell. We could only chop and inch forward.

As we drifted past the main part of town, I saw Kate, not walking after us like the others, just standing at the edge of the crowd, as if sensing our helplessness and her own. With a medium hard fling she could've reached us with a stone, but she just stood there, staring, alone and looking forlorn. Then the ice began to wobble and gurgle, as we threw ourselves into a final assault.

We struggled to attach ourselves to shoreward moving ice and detach from the rest. We scoured the gloom for cracks that might become gaps, and gaps that might become leads. The temperature was below zero, but the sweat poured from our faces and our breath came in gasps. Tim hopped onto the gunwales and rocked to keep the hull from freezing. We wielded our poles with desperate fury as the Bluff eclipsed the stars.

Only two figures followed us now. Anton Merly was in the lead with a rope. He cocked his arm. We crouched for the catch. He tossed, missed, retrieved, and threw again. The line snaked toward us. The weight thumped close. Bob grabbed it, passed it to me, I passed it to Tim in the bow, who held on and grunted as the line grew taut.

"No!" shouted Bob.

"We'll swamp!" I yelled.

The rope went slack. The men on shore had dropped their end. We stood dumbly in our craft, squinting through our sweat, twenty feet from safety.

The Bluff towered over us. Up there somewhere out of

sight in the moonlight stood the proud landmark of the town—the silver cross; perhaps, I thought, it will acquire another meaning tonight.

Ahead I could see ice plates breaking against the Bluff, rearing up, sliding over each other—the October voice of the Yukon, rumbling, mocking. I felt the towering indifference of inanimate granite, the innate supremacy of solid rock, which persisted through eons while men came and went. Then I heard the creak of overstressed hullboards. How long would we last in that frigid tumult? A minute? Two? I remembered my last view of Kate, stark and still against the snow; Scott, our son, just learning to walk. I reached out, fondled Zeke's head and waited for death.

But the huge floe with our boat at its center drifted around and floated past the Bluff. Then the pressure let up and the ice loosened and parted. We bent to our poles again, pushed toward the shore, and landed in a cove about a quarter mile downstream. Clawing our way up ice-coated boulders, we dragged our boat after us and wedged it tightly among the rocks.

"I thought we were goners when we lost that rope," I said.

"Me, too," Tim said.

"The river let us go this time," Bob said.

All we had to do now was climb the ridge around the Bluff. I lost track of my friends on the way up. Zeke and I angled too far left and found ourselves at the foot of the cross. Before backtracking, I reached out and put my hand on its timbers.

It took me several hours to wend my way over the ridge in the dark. Bob and Tim were already in town when I arrived. The Merlys had radioed for helicopters from Eilsen Air Force Base to begin a full-scale search in the morning, but called it off when we all showed up.

Kate, who I'd thought would be worried stiff, greeted me calmly. "I wasn't worried," she said. "You told me not to. You had Zeke and your rifles. Even if you had to stay on the other side, you had plenty of game."

MY PEN PAL

Having neglected my correspondence during a furious autumn push, I started looking around our house for a place to write. The kitchen, dining room, and living room, though warm, were ruled out as hubs of family activity. Eventually I settled into an upstairs bedroom and improvised a table with Blazo-box sides and a loose door for a top. Shims lent a certain stability, but my desk had insets, wells, ridge lines, a keyhole, a knob, and rough spots in the enamel, which didn't do much for my already squiggly scrawl. Without electricity, I balanced a flashlight on its backside and aimed it at the ceiling, which yielded a soft glow.

Over the last seven years Mom's letters had followed me to air force bases in Texas, Arizona, California, and Florida; the Grand Canyon, where I'd worked as a park ranger; Berkeley, and now Alaska. I admired her artistic penmanship, starting with the address on the envelope, each line evenly spaced, each character beautifully shaped and flowing into the next, the result symmetrical, firm, and perfectly legible, not ostentatious, yet suggesting vigor, a tribute to her prowess with paintbrush and oils. And neither was she fickle as a correspondent, but always dependable, often stimulating, whimsical, and now and then provocative. Topics included

Bill, my dad; Don, my brother; friends, acquaintances, her
students, flowers, and gossip—all delivered in an airy, mischievous tone, never dour or doleful, as from one who
enjoyed the limelight, but who, motherlike, was primarily
interested in entertaining me:

Nov. 2, 1959

Dearest Graham,
    We're ecstatic about your ice-crossing story. We've
shared it with all our friends, including your old
schoolteachers—Carl Spear and Melba Carpenter.
Both insisted it kept them on the edge of their seats.
In all my days as an English teacher I've never read
anything so exciting. Your father and I think you
should send it to one of the outdoor magazines, taking care with your spelling, which still seems to
confound you at odd moments.
    As you know, I spend much of my spare time writ-
ing short stories for magazines. I speak as an author
and not as your mother when I say, SOME EDITOR
WILL BUY IT.
    Enclosed is a typewritten copy of your letter. Your
father did this of his own volition, without prompting
from me. I'm sure he wouldn't have thought of it unless he'd been immensely impressed.
    In a rush now. Must fly off to school. Keep writing.
We adore your letters. We are very proud of you!
Love,
Mom

I respected my parents' literary judgment. They weren't
your average run-of-the-mill readers, in my opinion, Mom
being, in her own words, "the most squinchy-eyed English
teacher at New Rochelle High," yet one who often sought
the advice of Dad, who, though not a professional linguist,

had found a more lucrative calling as a financial analyst on Wall Street. But he loved reading. The entire living room in their house was wall to-wall books. Both had bachelor's and master's degrees, subscribed to a dozen magazines and read constantly. Their approval was better than an A+ in English, which I'd never actually received.

I titled my story "Impasse!" and wrote it out in my most meticulous pen, then sent it to *Sports Afield*, following it with a letter to Mom:

Nov. 10, 1959

Dear Mom,

Tonight, pausing to catch my breath from sawing and beholding an eye-popping aurora borealis, I dashed into the house to alert Kate and Scott.

I was reminded, Mom, of that time long ago at 17 Wood Place [in New Rochelle], when you woke Don and me in the wee hours. We were too groggy to understand the fuss. But you dragged us downstairs, threw our coats over our pajamas, pushed us out the door, pointed toward the sky, and 'oo'd' and 'ah'd' until we paid heed.

"Behold! Aurora borealis!" you exclaimed. "You may never see it again in your whole life." Remember, Mom? I recall it as a faint flickering around the horizon, spectacular only because we had nothing to compare it to.

Here we see northern lights so often we forget to look. Polaris is almost directly overhead. The lights shoot straight down from the zenith, not a smog-dulled ambience, but an unrestrained glare of relentless intensity, a projection to bedazzle and bewitch. And not just white, mind you, but yellows and reds and greens, a full palette of hues, dancing and shimmering in curtains, rays, swirls, arcs, pinwheels, and coronas—the firmament bestreaked with celestial fireworks, with God as the Artist and the whole cupola as His canvas, and not a hint of a moon or a street light to dim its luster.

It was so bright, I could've read a book by it! And this is the so-called *dark* season!

Standing there, gazing upward in a hush, Kate, Scott, and I discovered we could actually hear a hiss or fizzle, very faint, very subtle, very far away, like the crackling in a thunderstorm before the lightning strikes.

I wish you could've been here to share it with us.

Love,

Graham

P.S. I've sent our ice-crossing story to *Sports Afield*, though I think you should know the event has not been trumpeted unanimously. Under the headline, "EAGLE NEWS BRIEFS," Alan Innes-Taylor, correspondent for the *Fairbanks News-Miner*, wrote of my "heroic" rescue by Bob Stacey and Tim Malcolm. He referred to newcomers who don't know the country, neglect to thank their rescuers, and cause everyone needless worry by failing to consult old-timers like himself. Yet Innes-Taylor, though a neighbor, wrote and printed this without consulting me! Humph!

"Impasse!" came back from *Sports Afield*. I sent it to *Outdoor Life*, and began another letter home:

Nov. 22, 1959

Dear Folks,

You remember the summer forest fire I wrote you about. Well, I forgot to tell you an adventure Kate had while I was away.

Looking out the kitchen window, she was startled

to see a huge husky in our yard, pure white with a
proud thick tail, obviously bred for sleds. He terrified
her because she'd left Scott outside in his home-built
playpen. And this dog was staring at Scott. Was he
contemplating a human breakfast? She dashed outside, whisked Scott to safety, then high-tailed it to the
post office.

In Eagle the post office is sort of a back-country
news center. When you need to know something,
you go there first. But no one could tell Kate anything
about the strange dog. Some said they'd seen him
wandering around by the river and at the Indian village. Others surmised he belonged to a trapper or
miner and had become lost. No one would claim
him, and no one was sure.

The dog kept showing up every day—proud,
stately, Kate said, but never wagging his tail, never
dropping his ears or head, staring in the manner of
an alpha male. Never responding to her overtures, he
looked cocky, powerful. Made her feel intimidated,
she said. Perhaps attracted by Zeke's scent, he began
hanging around constantly, showing up early and
staying late, keeping Kate from letting Zeke out or
putting Scott in his playpen. Where did he go at
night? What did he eat? Was he crouched in our yard
in the dark, waiting to pounce as she hustled to the
outhouse? The possibility terrified her.

After two weeks of this, at the end of her rope, she
took my .30-30, levered a shell into the chamber,
leaned across the car hood, aimed at his heart and—
her own heart pounding like mad—squeezed the
trigger.

The dog ran away. Had she missed? She didn't
know, but at least she'd routed him. Later she told "Silent Bill," acting police chief, who agreed the dog

might be wounded and suffering. Finally he paid Kate a visit, searched for and found the dog cowering near the garbage dump, did his duty and dispatched him with his revolver.

A tragic story. An ignominious end to someone's escaped lead dog, perhaps; a potentially splendid animal, whose crime was needing and trusting man. It left me choked with ambiguity—you know how I am about dogs. Where had he come from? Who was his owner? I was sure I could've befriended him, if only I'd been there.

Yet I didn't blame Kate. She had Zeke, Scott, and herself to take care of. I was sure she did what she thought was best.

Love,
Graham

Postcard from Mom:

Nov. 27, 1959

Dearest Graham,

Yesterday was Thanksgiving, the day we had set aside to sample your provender—canned moose, canned salmon, and homemade cranberry relish (with orange rind)—what a banquet! The Spears came over to share it with us, as is our custom, and we spent half our time talking about you.

We are all well and looking forward to your next letter.

Love,
Mom

Dec. 8, 1959

Dear Folks,

Our house has two stoves—a flat-topped cast-iron cook type and a knee-high blue-steel barrel model I acquired in Berkeley; I have to keep both filled and stoked constantly.

Barney Hansen, a miner who owns a home in Eagle, tried to teach me to make "fuzz sticks," useful as fire starters because we have no newspaper or accessible birch bark. He can whittle them from dry spruce at the rate of three a minute, feathering them on all sides, knife flashing like lightning and eyes twinkling with an inner fire. Though I tried mightily to get the hang of it, I was only able to "fuzz" my first stick after weeks of practice. And that took me ten minutes and left me thankful I still had my fingers.

Anton and Esther make our lives easier at every turn, showing us how to build a makeshift dresser from the wooden Blazo boxes used to ship lantern fuel, stacking them four-high, open end to the front, and filling them with empty cardboard cartons for drawers. Many Alaskans use cut-and-flattened Blazo cans to shingle their cabins. With two Blazo cans suspended from a yoke on loan from Anton, I tote water from the wellhouse, a 200-yard round trip.

Esther has invited us over so often that we're wearing a rut in the snow, her kitchen being the principal allurement, with home-baked bread, sourdough pancakes, and many kinds of cookies and cakes. We also spend hours in their living room, playing crokinole (finger pool on a card table), usually falling victim to Anton's unerring digit.

Kate, with three months to term now, is growing larger by the day. I help her with Scott as much as I can. Sometimes I growl at him when he wakes up squalling in the night, but that only makes him squall louder. Sometimes I bundle him up, tuck him into my backpack and walk him around town. Or I strap him into his car seat, lash it onto our dog sled, and let

Zeke pull him until he falls asleep.

My story came back from *Outdoor Life*. I touched it up in a few spots, sent it to *Field & Stream*. Wish us luck!

> Love you all,
> Graham

Dec. 15, 1959

Dear Folks,

We're snowed in now, cut off from the Outside except for the mail plane, a tiny outpost of humanity on the fringe of a vast wilderness, nothing between us and the North Pole except a few clumps of Eskimos. The true "Land of the Midnight Sun" lies 200 miles north, above the Arctic Circle. But on June 21, the longest day of the year, if you drive ten miles up the Taylor Highway, climb the highest peak, and gaze south, you can just see a sliver of the sun at midnight.

In the winter the mountains obscure its disc completely for about five weeks. The night is twenty-four hours long now, broken only by a glow in the south around noon. The Taylor Highway is blocked by drifts, some of which will be thirty feet deep by spring. It's snowing now, incidentally, fine sparkly flakes which just shimmer down, and through which we can see quite well. It may only amount to a fraction of an inch, but it'll all be here until spring. It snows even at 20 below, tiny, gritty crystals, no slippier than sand and very hard to push a sled through. We don't do much except eat, sleep, browse in the library (heavy on Zane Grey), read, write, play with Scott, take (brief) walks, and saw wood.

The freezing of the Yukon has improved the local climate a bit, eased the damp chill. I scooted outside to pee the other night in my moccasins and T-shirt, discovering when I looked that it was 50° below. In those few minutes I hadn't even begun to shiver, my skin having been warmed deep by radiance from the stove. What feels COLD at 50° below is the outhouse seat! We usually sit on a towel.

Normally, when the thermometer's plummeting, it's also dead calm. All the town's stoves send up straight ropes of smoke, breathtaking when the moon is full and wolves are "talking" in the hills.

You'd think we'd be bored with so much inactivity, and we are, some. Yet I remain intrigued by eerie moonlit snowscapes, and the pale and creased faces of our fellow shut-ins.

We've arranged to have Kate flown to Dawson, Canada, in March when the baby is due, only twelve weeks away now. They have socialized medicine there; it should save us a bundle.

Love,
Graham

P.S. It's not true that at 50° below your urine freezes before it hits the ground.

Jan. 5, 1960

Dear Folks,

We've passed the winter solstice now, and that faint glow in the south is presumably lengthening.

Scott looks fat and sassy in his new red snowsuit, Kate loves her Revereware set, and I love the painting, Mom. All these gifts have made us feel like something we're actually not—rich!

Anton ran a wire from his diesel-powered generator to our house. We now have a light bulb in the kitchen, and I can use the Coleman lantern for writing! Much better!

We spent a quiet Christmas afternoon with the

Merlys around their beautiful tree, as tall as the ceiling and as big around as three oil drums. In Alaska, when looking for your tannenbaum, you can afford to be discriminating. Time is of no essence. You can turn your nose up at thousands of scraggly specimens. And they're all free!

We haven't collected many ornaments yet, so our own tree is modest, lucky for us—Scott tried to pull it over twice!

Kate, I'm sure, misses attending Catholic mass. She had to make do with Murray Trelease, an Episcopalian minister who's also a bush pilot.

Murray, a carrier pilot during Korea, drags his Cessna over the strip, power on, as if landing on a deck. My air force instructors would've chewed me to ribbons for that. They taught us to land with the throttle at idle so we'd be able to glide in if the engine quit in the pattern.

Murray and I had an arm-wrestling contest at a recent town dance. He's 6 foot 2, built like an orangutan with arms to match. But in shape from much sawing, I thought I might stand a chance. We faced each other across a narrow table, adjusting our elbows, fussing with our grip, breathing deep, and glaring at each other in mock ferocity. A crowd gathered, to which we played, with which we toyed. But finally, after much stalling, we declared ourselves ready. Someone yelled, "Go!" and we leaned into it and grunted.

Murray won in thirty seconds, which made me instantly aware of a personal quirk: Along with a perverse sense of fairness which causes me to root for the underdog, I also possess a perverse sense of self-worth—I hate being an underdog.

Murray has special problems when he lands his

plane at 40° below. He must drain all the oil from the engine and immediately take it indoors. If he stays out long enough for the engine to cool, he must cover it with a canvas hood and put a gas burner under it. (Not a few planes have burned up this way in the course of Alaska's aviation history.) Then he reheats the oil on a stove and pours it back into the engine. Otherwise, the oil would turn to cement and his engine wouldn't turn over.

Murray conducted a Christmas service for us in the tiny chapel across from the post office, and then another for the Natives at the Indian village. We attended both. Very homey, with carols, candles, even store-bought fruitcake! But despite Kate's influence, I always feel hypocritical in church. It's as though I'm tacitly agreeing to something I don't really believe in. Like you, Mom, I guess I'm agnostic. I see the Divine in the sky, the mountains, the rivers, not the Bible or a church.

Love,
Graham

Feb. 21, 1960

Dear Mom, Dad, and Don,

Guess what! *Field & Stream* bought "Impasse!" and will publish it soon! They sent me $200 for the first American serial rights. Kate and I are celebrating. We hope you do the same. It would never have happened without you!

Hugs and kisses,
Graham

The story was published in May, 1960, and a few weeks later, Innes-Taylor visited. He asserted he was sorry about what he'd written in his newspaper column. I told him I didn't believe it. I confessed to being furious over the back wages he still owed me. Pay me first, I insisted, then we can discuss apologies. He hemmed and hawed. Curtly, bluntly, I ordered, "Get out!"

BILLY

Anton and I were doing chores at the Hansens' place Sunday, Feb. 25, 1960, about a quarter mile from my house, when Esther, wheezing, burst through the door.

"Kate needs you ... NOW!" she gasped.

"She all right?"

"Didn't say ... Wants you home ... IMMEDIATELY!"

I ran all the way and, upon arrival, also burst through the door, wheezing.

"Kate?"

"Here." The bedroom.

"You all right?"

"Yes, but a lot of water leaked out."

Kate needed a Caesarean; in Eagle this was an emergency.

"Any labor pains?"

"No, but I'm afraid they might start."

"We'd better ... get you ... to a hospital ... I'll get Esther."

I ran full speed back to the Hansens' and, still wheezing, burst through that door.

Esther said, "Well?"

"No pains yet ... She's O.K."

"But?"

"Water ... she ... "

"She broke her waters."

"Yes."

"She could go into labor any second. We should call the doctor. I'll get on the radio. Hope I can get through."

"Shall I ... ?"

"You go home. Stay with Kate. Let me know if there's any change."

"You'll be home?"

"Yes. By the radio."

I ran full speed back home again, and burst in, wheezing harder.

Kate said, "What did Esther say?"

"You broke ... your waters ... "

"She's calling the doctor?"

"Yes ... on the radio ... "

"In Dawson?"

"Don't know ... "

"How will the doctor get here?"

" ... Fly ... "

"Will you come with me?"

" ... Sure ... "

I sat on the edge of the bed and held her hand while emergency gears began to mesh. First Esther had to contact someone by radio; that someone had to locate an available pilot and doctor; pilot and doctor had to get to the airport; the pilot had to preflight a plane, gas up, warm up, and take off for Eagle. I began packing Kate's bags.

Esther entered. "Good place for you, Kate, in bed."

"Contact someone?" Kate asked.

"Fairbanks weather station. Couldn't rouse Dawson."

"We were planning on Dawson."

"Not now," Esther said. "You'll have to go to Fairbanks."

Stifling a groan, I said, "I was planning to go, too."

"You'd best wait for the mail plane, Graham. There'll be

one in tomorrow. Wednesday at the latest. It's cheaper than charter. If you go now, you'll just be in the way."

I glanced at Kate.

Esther said, "You two talk it over. I'll be back later." She departed.

I said, "Still feeling O.K.?"

"Yup."

"You want me to go with you now or shall I wait?"

"Mail plane will probably be O.K."

"You be all right alone?"

"I'll have the doctor."

Esther came back in about an hour. "The plane and doctor are on their way. You ready?"

"We're ready," Kate said.

"You taking the mail plane, Graham?"

"Sounds like the best bet."

"O.K. I'll come back when Anton gets his truck ready."

Anton entered in about fifteen minutes. "Eagle Taxi Service!" he called.

Kate climbed out of bed like an egg with legs. Anton and I helped her to the truck. It was dark and bitter cold, the headlights glowed, the engine purred. We maneuvered Kate into the warm cab. Esther took Scott. Anton and I grabbed the luggage and threw it in the back. In down parka, pants, and mukluks, I vaulted into the back with the bags. Anton started up and we headed for the airstrip.

The wind was an icy blast. Anton drove slowly, carefully, but I winced for Kate at every bump.

Anton pulled onto the runway and drove its length, searching out obstructions, then turned, drove back, and parked with the engine running. After a while he got out and glanced at his watch. "About ten minutes," he said, his breath enveloping his head. "Too cold out here." He climbed back in and shut the door.

My down parka was warm, but I turned my face toward

the cab to shield it from the wind. The sky was alight with a million stars.

In about five minutes Anton shut off the motor, got out, snatched off his hat and put his cupped hand to his ear; I pulled off my hood and cupped my hand to my ear—two two-legged birddogs, listening for a motorized partrige.

"I hear it," he said.

I squinted skeptically.

"I'm used to it," he chuckled. "I do this every week. You get to know what it sounds like."

"I've heard plenty of airplanes," I said.

"You'll hear another in about a minute." He grinned.

In about a minute I did.

The twin Beech cleared the surrounding peaks and became a blinking conglomeration of red, green, and white lights. It descended into the traffic pattern and dropped the gear. Landing lights glared. It turned onto base leg, then final, lined up with the runway, descended, approached, skimmed the trees, flared out, touched down, rolled toward us, and braked. The engines stopped. Except for metal, groaning as it cooled, all became still.

Esther climbed out of the truck with Scott, while Anton and I helped Kate. We turned toward the plane as its door slid open. A man lowered the stairs. Another appeared behind him and said, "You must be Mrs. McGill." He reached for her hand. "Still feeling all right?"

"Yes thanks," she said.

"Any pains?"

"Not yet."

"Good." He turned to me. "You're Mr. McGill."

"Right."

"I'm the doctor."

Anton was trading quips with his old friend, the pilot. When Kate was safely aboard, the doctor said, "Let's go!"

"Take care of Scott," Kate called.

"Don't worry. You just have that baby," Esther replied.

The door closed. The left prop turned, the engine sputtered, and caught; then the right prop turned. Engines revved. The plane lunged forward, wheeled, kicked snow, and taxied downfield. At the far end it whipped around. Engines whined. The plane grew larger, lifted off, and roared past at about twenty feet altitude. Growing smaller, it climbed, turned right, again became a blinking conglomeration of red, green, and white lights, and disappeared over the mountains.

"Come on," Anton said. "It's cold!"

We climbed into the pickup, Esther and Scott in the middle and me in the cab. "There, there," Esther said, bouncing Scott on her knee. She had often expressed a longing for children. Now she had one on loan.

We spoke little on the way home. Our minds were in the sky with Kate, winging over the frozen landscape. Whatever happened now was in the hands of the pilot, the doctor, the baby, and fate.

Thinking what it meant to be a woman, I was feeling proud of Kate and at the same time humble that she had decided to be my wife.

A few days later I took the mail plane to Fairbanks, found the hospital, and paid the bill. I greeted Kate, who somehow managed to look lovely—in spite of her delivery ordeal—even without makeup. I stayed overnight in a motel.

Exhibiting her usual faculty for almost instantaneous recovery, Kate was ready to leave the hospital the next day, and the three of us took the mail plane back to Eagle.

We named the baby William R. McGill, after my father.

From the moment of his debut, Billy was a delight. He spent most of his awake time cooing, grinning, or suckling. He radiated joy. Nothing seemed to irk him. Even when he needed a burp or a diaper, his whimpering said, please.

Soon he'd twisted everyone around his little finger—his dot-
ing mother, his now-destitute father, and Esther, his
borrowed Alaskan grandmother.

I blamed his sunny disposition on his north country
pedigree, but Mom wrote that it conformed to a pattern:
firstborns were often more demanding, second ones more
amicable. She claimed this had been true of my brother and
me, attributed it to the now-experienced mother's more relaxed attitude. Kate and I had been firstborns, she noted.

Billy was born on leap year day, Feb. 29, 1960, a day which
occurs only once in every 1,460 ordinary days, a day which
compensates for calendar errors, which, as I think back on
it now, over thirty years later, seems fitting: Billy ultimately
compensated for errors in my conception of myself. At the
time, however, I was too dismayed for perspective. Expenses connected with his arrival had demolished my
bankroll and threatened my goal of living in an Alaskan
sodhouse.

ADDITION AND DIVISION

Of course, my folks were delighted to hear about Billy and immediately sent a package of baby stuff, all practical and helpful, but of less interest to me than the moral support in Mom's letters and the incentive they gave me to write back:

April 10, 1960

Dear Mom and Dad,

Kate amazes me with her powers of recuperation, was up and about a week after her C-section, and even attended the town dance last week, polkaing with me around the hub of slower couples until we were breathless. I could hardly believe it!

Shindigs here are nothing like the ballroom dance lessons you, Mom, foisted upon Don and me, when we were teens—you remember?—all the girls on one side of the church in pinafores and corsages, all the boys on the other in tuxedos and white gloves? Remember how I hated that? Well, Mom, you may find this incredible, but here I'm a hoppin' hoedowner.

To start with, the dance hall is a log building with a fifty-five-gallon oil-drum heat—a backwoods ambience New Rochelle could never match. Then we have

an array of humanity ranging from old bachelor miners who haven't kissed anyone but their sled dogs in
months, but wouldn't think of showing up without
their yearly bath (whether they need it or not), to
cute little Indian girls you can dandle on your knee.
Further, there is no social pressure to attend. Yet no
one ever stays home unless both legs are broke. And
fancy duds are out; it's strictly come-as-you-are, with
Anton Merly, our accordion player, perhaps the most
natty in western shirt with mother-of-pearl buttons,
string bow tie and cowboy boots, offsetting our jolly
old squaws with no teeth.

Anton is a one-man-band on that accordion, pro-
viding music all night, though Horace Biederman
sometimes fills in on the fiddle while Anton takes a
breather. And once in a while, someone puts a record
on a battery-operated phonograph.

Kate has plenty of admirers at these dances, with
her blond hair, blue eyes, and statuesque physique,
but especially at the last event when she attempted
to breast-feed Billy. Inured to this homey scene, I
wasn't paying much attention until I noticed a wall of
levis, hip-to-hip in front of her like a picket fence. I
felt like standing up and shouting: "STEP BACK,
PLEASE—BACK, I SAY! GIVE THE LADY SOME
ROOM! WHAT DO YOU THINK THIS IS—A SIDE-
SHOW!" But that would've only mortified Kate, and
demonstrated lack of confidence. I'd seen her handle
similar situations with finesse. So I just watched. But
finally, to me privately, she confessed her anxiety and
absconded.

While she was gone, I polkaed with Esther and a
few old squaws, bigger around and harder to steer
than Kate. At our dances, nearly everyone does a
twirl with everyone else before the night's over, the

music serving as an excuse to hop, jump, or just bounce, depending on your talent and arthritis. Racial bias has never been a problem in Eagle. Our rare instances of ill will occur mainly between individuals; some folks just don't like each other. But mostly we just gather together, without regard to skin tone or ethnic origin, like one big happy family, a tiny stewpot of humanity in step with an American ideal. I don't think we're necessarily better than other folks; we just have the advantage of being hemmed in by a vast wilderness which reminds us we need each other. Yet we don't hardly take time to notice.

Love,
Graham

The fact was, even in our living room back home, Billy drew a crowd like nectar draws bees. His visitors included many ladies from the Indian village, more curious than beneficient, perhaps. But often it was just Esther, who sometimes seemed a crowd by herself—not that she didn't mean well, not that she didn't help, but her affection for my newborn developed a tenacity which I blamed on unfulfilled maternity. "Kids are a woman's responsibility," she once informed me. Yet Kate seemed to need Esther, and the two often spent the whole day clucking away in one kitchen or the other, bathing and feeding Billy and Scott like a pair of contented hens, and making me feel locked out.

A few weeks after his birth, Kate tried to wean Billy, and her breasts became painfully engorged. Questioning basic assumptions, I stuck my oar in muddy water, or in this case, milk. Why wean Billy at all? How could formula milk be as healthy as her own? Did she think I would admire a firm, youthful breast more than a droopy one? (I assured her this was untrue.) What good was a breast anyway, if not for what Nature intended? And—a sidelight I thought should interest a Catholic—did she know that extended nursing is a natural form of birth control? Stef claimed that Eskimo mothers often nursed their babies until they were four.

But my questions were dismissed out of hand. Nursing was a mater matter, beyond the ken of a man. I was sure Kate often felt like telling me to keep my mouth shut, but in this case it proved inconvenient.

Our nursery kit lacked a breast pump. She had ordered one from Seattle, but it was slow in arriving. Enduring considerable agony, she grumbled about it to Esther after each pumpless mail delivery. "Won't that darn thing ever get here!"

"You could help her, Graham," observed Esther, by which she meant that I might . . . that I could . . . that I possessed the maxillary apparatus to . . . relieve Kate's engorgement. Shocking! But an idea to which I could not pay mere lip service.

O.K. But how to go about it? And where? First, we tried the living room, with me sitting in a chair and Kate, topless, perched on the chair arm; ah, she was gorgeous, but this strained her back and crimped my neck. Next we tried Kate sitting in the chair and me leaning over her shoulder; novel and upside down she was still gorgeous, but I couldn't swallow uphill. Then, we tried Kate leaning forward from the chair and me kneeling on a pillow in front, but that wrenched my spine and hurt my knees. Finally, we repaired to the bedroom, where Kate propped me up with pillows and cradled my bulbous head in her comely arms.

This solved our spacial problems; psychological ones proved more formidable.

Kate kept smiling preposterously, beatifically down on me, which made me want to smile back. But I could not smile and pucker at the same time, and I had to keep swallowing or choke. If I relaxed for an instant, my lips would slip, milk would seep out, and I'd be stricken with an uncontrollable urge to murmur "ga, ga," which would produce instant hysteria. But once started, Kate's milk didn't staunch just because I stopped sucking. It had mom-entum, a mind of its own. If my concentration wavered, it completely drenched me and drenched Kate, too, since her other breast spritzed in sympathy.

True, Kate's breasts were lovely and her milk tasted like warm vanilla ice cream, but I never felt a sensation as a human breast pump. The undignified procedure always left my face sticky, my loins tense, and my mind awash with lactiferated debaucheries. That I continued to do it, despite my stated opposition to the whole process, only showed the loftiness of my devotion and the depths to which I would stoop for my beloved wife.

At last the real breast pump arrived from Seattle, and the unwieldy substitute was relieved.

As the father of two now, established in the community, and having revealed my financial state to the Merlys, I could hardly say no when Anton, Eagle town mayor, asked if I'd paint the library and wellhouse for $200.

A professional carpenter, he showed me how to build a scaffold as beautiful as it was simple. First he nailed three-foot and four-foot two-by-fours together at right angles, with a five-foot hypotenuse. Then he nailed short boards across the apex to stiffen and triangulate. Building two of these triangles, he placed the four-foot legs against the building about ten feet apart, fitted spruce poles into the apex, and hoisted the triangles while wedging the poles into the ground. Then I carried a plank up his ladder and clamped it to the out-thrust three-foot legs. Thus, I had a stable work station in the sky.

One morning after a hard frost, Anton happened by while I was slathering paint onto clapboards thirty feet up. "This ground is frozen!" he noted. "If one of your poles slips, you'll come down in a hurry!"

"They won't slip," I shot back.

"They might," he insisted, and without even asking me to descend, he dug depressions in the icy ground and slid the pole butts into them. Of course, seeing later that he was right, I appreciated it.

He had a way of being both direct and indifferent with his advice, rarely ruffling my feathers.

As April arrived and the days grew longer by an hour each week, I began dreaming of my sodhouse. I often passed townsfolk in the street, faces turned toward the sun's warmth and eyes squinched against its brilliance. Even the mighty Yukon, still locked in its icy mantle, seemed to bulge muscularly in anticipation of deliverance.

I took several snowshoe trips to my sodhouse, crossing the Yukon above the Indian village on ice thick enough to support a bulldozer. The McGill food stocks were running low, so I always took my '06, but none of my excursions produced meat.

Often on these trips I'd hear the village sled dogs howling, their voices yodeling up and down the scale, reverberating back and forth between the hills. About halfway back across the Yukon on one return trip, I realized that one of those sled dogs was out of place, behind me. Turning, I spotted a wolf in a clearing about 500 feet up the opposite slope, maybe a thousand yards away. I broke out the binocs, shrugged off my pack and sat on it to admire him.

He was cocking his head, then howling, cocking his head, then howling, and his music filled the whole valley. The first wild wolf I'd ever seen, he put me in a trance. "Zeke, look!" I said. "See that cousin of yours up yonder? What's he saying?" But she didn't recognize his voice as being out of place, nor did she have a reason to focus on that distant spot.

Soon I picked out a second wolf beside a nearby spruce.

Sometimes one would howl, sometimes the other. Were they mates? I watched a long time from the middle of the Yukon, then took my binocs, '06, and Zeke, left my pack on the ice, and snowshoed toward the hill.

Reaching its base, I could still see the wolves about 300 yards away, each worth a $50 bounty and perhaps another $100 each for the pelt, $300 together, more than I'd made in a month of painting. Having killed my first moose at a greater range than this, I squinted through my '06 scope. But standing I couldn't hold the cross-hairs steady. If I squatted or sat, my view was obstructed. I was afraid I might miss or wound them. Besides, they looked too much like Zeke.

I kicked off my snowshoes, leashed Zeke to my belt and began climbing. The hill was steep and slippery, and we lost sight of our quarry on the way up. When we reached the spot where I'd last seen them, they'd vanished. The snow was littered with splayed tracks, twice as wide and long as Zeke's, as big as my flat hand. I admired them for many minutes.

Zeke sniffed, hackles up. "They're gone, girl," I assured her. "Too smart to wait around for a man with a rifle. They're headed home now, I bet, minding their own business. And that's what we're gonna do, too." We side-stepped back down the hill, recrossed the ice to my pack, and picked up the trail toward the village.

Familiar faces smiled and nodded as we meandered between cabins. Charlie Steve, fisherman emeritus, invited me in for soup. I tied Zeke near the front door, knowing Charlie wouldn't want her inside. He offered her water, which she slurped.

Charlie served a delicious moose-rice-and-carrot concoction with homemade bread and butter on the side.

Afterward he asked about my '06 and I led him to the living room to demonstrate. As I picked it up, my finger brushed the trigger.

B-O-O-O-O-O-M!

The walls bulged outward and the roof up. Charlie grimaced, cupped his hands over his ears, rocked from the waist, and moved his lips. Deafened by the blast, I couldn't hear a word. The acrid smell of powder permeated the room. Mortified, I bent to examine the floor. All I could find was a small hole. I stood and shouted into Charlie's ear, "I'M VERY SORRY."

He yelled into my ear, "I'M STILL SHAKING!"

"MY EARS ARE RINGING? ARE YOURS?"

He nodded. "LUCKY NO ONE WAS HURT."

I shrugged. "MAKES ME FEEL STUPID. I HONESTLY DON'T KNOW HOW IT COULD HAVE HAPPENED. THE SAFETY MUST'VE BEEN OFF."

At that moment a half dozen Native kids traipsed through the back door. "What you guys doin', shootin' mice?"

We all laughed, especially the perpetrator.

I thanked Charlie for the meal, apologized again, swung into my pack, took up my '06 again (carefully), untied Zeke, and departed.

Anton accompanied me and Zeke on our next trip to the sodhouse. With a vast fund of interesting stories, he was always fun to have along. Dark sideburns framed his long face, his bald head, twinkling blue eyes, and a mischievous smile. He looked like an overgrown elf.

Privately, I felt proud of my sodhouse, but coming upon it with Anton, seeing it through his eyes, I felt chagrined. His house had asphalt shingles, painted siding, fiberglass insulation, hot-and-cold running water, a full basement with a wood furnace, a bathroom with toilet and shower, modern kitchen, dining room, living room, and several bedrooms.

"Not finished yet," I put in.

"Looks like you're coming along good," he said. "That the

fireplace in the middle?"

"Yup. You fasten a sheep hide over the top to keep the heat in when the fire goes out. It also acts like a skylight."

"Nice idea."

"Stefansson's." Anton was not particularly an avid reader. "It'll look more like a house when I get the sod up."

"Right," he agreed. "Only one problem . . . " He coughed and dug his foot in the snow. "You'll never convince Kate to live here."

I glowered.

He chuckled, distancing himself. "Women are strange creatures, you know. No man I know can figure 'em out. They act sometimes like a different breed, don't want the same things a man does. You and me now, we don't mind sleeping on the ground, hunting, fishing, living rough. But a woman likes her place clean and pretty. Likes to have friends over, set a fancy table, and have things frilly and nice." He lifted his finger for emphasis, squinting as if from strain. "This would be even more true, I'd imagine, when they start havin' kids."

Too proud to force his views on a hard-headed friend, that was as close as Anton ever came to lecturing me. In the days that followed, I suspected Esther had put him up to it. But I never asked, and the subject never came up again.

THE VOICE

Besides our dwindling hard cash, we now faced a dwindling food cache, and it behooved me to rectify this soon. In March and April I often went hunting near town, usually climbing the Bluff first, from which I could always spot moose. But by the time I picked my way down and bushwhacked into their vicinity, the huge beasts always managed to vanish. I made so many failed stalks, I began to wonder how anything except a ghost ever snuck up on a moose. What I needed was the stealth of a canoe, but the lakes and rivers were still frozen.

One day in mid-May, Anton ran through our yard trumpeting: "THE ICE IS GOING OUT. THE ICE IS GOIN' OUT!"

Kate grabbed Billy, I Scott, and we followed Anton to the riverbank, where gigantic ice blocks were thundering past, rearing up and slamming against each other. "Look at the size of that!" Anton hollered, pointing to one as big as a cabin.

This was the event that spelled RELEASE to our winter-fettered spirits and would allow me to range quietly over the country again. We watched agog for over an hour, but at last Kate, Billy, and Esther drifted away. And Anton, Scott, and I followed soon after.

The procession of floes continued unabated for several days. Yet by the end of the week, the water rose, the ice dispersed and gradually gave way to a procession of driftwood—"sweepers" and "sleepers." Sweepers were live trees undercut by erosion, named while they hung over tributaries like giant brooms, now ripped loose and cast upon the torrent, their green leaves or needles lashing the air. Sleepers were old trees on a second or third journey, bark and branches stripped, trunks polished and silt-blasted, awash beneath the surface, named for their tendency to rise as if awakening when struck by a motorboat. A year's supply of firewood coursed past Eagle every day, but it might as well have been on the moon.

Besides, I needed meat, not wood. "Kate," I said, "I think I'll take Zeke and go hunting downstream."

She nodded, knowing it meant she'd have to keep house, cook, and take care of two kids alone. "But please don't bring home any bear meat! I can't stand the stuff."

I'd read Kate pages and pages of Stefansson, explained the arbitrariness of taste preferences by the hour. I couldn't understand why she still talked like that!

The next morning I hunched into my pack, swung my canoe up and set off with Zeke.

"Bring home a young moose!" she called from the door, thereby specifying not only what kind, but how old! What naiveté! What daintiness! What rigidity!

I laughed and waved. "You want me to bring you some boloney?"

Moose hunting wasn't even legal in the spring, but I'd lived in Alaska a year now, and as a resident qualified for the "subsistence" clause—if you're hungry, you can shoot it.

I slipped the canoe into the water, loaded my pack and rifles aboard, motioned Zeke into the bow, and shoved off.

I'd never lived beside water before, not even a pond or a stream, let alone a land-splitter like this mighty Yukon—half a mile wide at Eagle and over 2,000 miles long, from granite-pillared headwaters to the boundless oceans. To be sure, I'd studied the map and traced it upstream to Lake Labarge, Robert Service's setting for "The Cremation of Sam McGee." And I'd heard the old-timers tell of the Great Whirlpool near Circle, a "malestrom," they called it, a menace to canoes and kayaks; the Flats, where "mosquitoes can turn a stout man into a mummy in ten minutes," where "ducks outnumber even the mosquitoes," and "muskrats are as thick as hair on a dog's back"; the Delta near the ocean, where "the current runs backward" in a maze of false channels and cul de sacs. But maps and legends paled before actual experience.

After Kate's arrival in Eagle, the Merlys let us use one of their cabins, and though I'd bunked in town at Innes-Taylor's for a month, I spent the first week in that cabin just drinking in the scenery. Right on the riverbank and at the upstream edge of town, this cabin was afloat in a sea of scarlet—the blossoms of fireweed. Also, it was secluded, so that, for the first time since Berkeley, Kate and I enjoyed privacy.

The walls of this cabin were not tight: mosquitoes required continual swatting. We had no plumbing and the outhouse was in back of the garden. We had to lug all our water from the town wellhouse. Our diet consisted entirely of canned meat, fruits and vegetables, or dried milk, corn meal, flour, and vitamin pills. But we were happy.

We talked. We smooched. We kept house. We fussed over Scott. We washed diapers in the river. We cooked on a Coleman stove in the kitchen. We did our laundry by hand in a round galvanized tub and hung our clothes outdoors in the bright warm sun. Paying heed to our mutual need for cleanliness, we toted successive potfuls of hot water while our partner, head and feet akimbo, chased the soap in that same laundry tub. This was our first prolonged experience of true backwoods living.

Just beyond our front door was the Yukon River, and I often found myself languishing on our porch, mesmerized by its shimmering, roiling surface, moose ogling me from yonder willow flats, swallows swooping, sandpipers strutting, gulls gliding, and ravens check-marking the brilliant blue. A delight, a fascination, an unfathomable mystery, the river was a torrent of untold mass and pressure, tons upon tons of grit-freighted liquid, curling over and under and in upon itself as it churned inexorably toward the sea. But if I wandered down, immersed my hand, and restricted my gaze to the immediate vicinity, it became a bowl of tan soup.

The silt made a "Sh-h-h-h-h-h" on the canoe bottom as I paddled into the current, then relaxed and drifted. Zeke sniffed the breeze and pricked up her ears. It was a glorious morning—the sun warm, the air fresh, the hills green. I felt like singing.

A few miles below Eagle, a mother black bear and two cubs were grubbing ants atop a knoll. Sure, Kate had told me to ignore bears but she hadn't mentioned *cub*. For all I knew, they'd be the only game I'd see the whole trip. I drifted past, beached, grabbed my '06, put Zeke on her leash, and headed up the bearless side.

At the summit I rested until my breathing slowed, tied Zeke's leash to my belt, then crouched and inched over the rim. "Easy, Zeke," I whispered; she understood.

The bears were still there—a hundred yards distant, the mother schooling her tots in ant ways. A tranquil scene. But a hunter cannot be diverted by foolish sentimentality. I sat, elbows on knees, and brought my '06 up.

BOOM!

All the bears ran off. No squeals, no blood. I'd missed.

We ambled back down the knoll and shoved off, Kate's last words echoing in my head: "Bring home a young moose!"

During the next ten miles, I spotted half a dozen more black bears, all solo adults, all fresh from hibernation and intent on feeding. I'd never seen so many in such a short period.

"Bring home a young moose!"

We stopped again to probe a slough where giant ice blocks lay strewn in the shallows, a sparkling glacier palace with the sky for a ceiling, walls convoluted, sometimes rising to fifteen feet, narrow aisles opening into blue-tinted rooms—no current, no sound except the drip, drip, drip of meltwater, the air cool and dank like a cave, but bright. It was eerie.

A pair of mallards swam before us, the drake's iridescent green head beckoning to mc from the farthest bend. Zeke noticed them, too. We threaded our way between constricting walls, nearing a dead-end. Suddenly, the ducks took off toward us, squawking and flapping almost within reach. I forgot to shoot.

The corridor was so narrow I had to back out.

Five miles farther I saw a raft of pintails and floated to intercept them, .22 ready. When they spooked, I emptied the magazine into the flock. One fell, and I retrieved it from the canoe.

In another five miles we sighted Calico Bluff, a huge rocky promontory of variegated light-and-dark strata. We landed upstream and I toted my pack, rifles, and canoe up the bank.

At the top, a little way into the woods, was an old trapper's cabin, roof caved in, walls and floor sagging and dripping. What sort of a man built this, I wondered. Why had he come to Alaska? Why had he left? I scoured the premises for clues, but the place had already been ransacked.

Zeke and I moseyed back to the riverbank, flopped down, basked in the sun, and lunched.

Afterward, I took my rifles and canoe and portaged the half mile from the river to Ford Lake, which Anton had shown me on the map. Maybe Kate's moose was there.

I could hear the ruckus as we neared the water—thousands of quacking ducks, the males strutting, preening, and chasing females! Spring in Alaska! I slipped the canoe in, pushed away from the cattails, and immediately counted nine black bears on the surrounding hills.

"Bring home a young moose!"

We circled the lake and meandered among the ducks. I could've bagged dozens, but the shots might've frightened Kate's moose. He had to be here somewhere!

Returning to the trail head, we came upon a huge black bear, taller than a man, squinting at us, and swaying from side to side like a fur-coated swami dancer. With my '06 across my knees and just to see what he'd do, I eased the bow into the reeds, closer and closer—twenty, fifteen, ten feet—too close for Zeke. She beat a retreat to my feet while the bear gaped.

I back-paddled and let him be.

We landed, disembarked, and kept an ear cocked in the direction of that bear. I lashed the paddles across the thwarts as a yoke, but this time I balanced the canoe with one hand, kept my '06 in the other, in case that bear pounced.

Zeke and I made camp where we'd had lunch.

That evening a pair of what the Natives called black ducks were flying upstream and drifting past camp, flying up and drifting past, always the same pattern. I took my .22, hid behind an ice block, and fired as they came abreast. They leaped instantly into the air, but my fusillade dropped one and the current whisked it away. Pursuing, I called for Zeke. She plunged in for what first looked like a routine retrieve. But the duck was drifting away in faster water, while she was chasing it in slower. After a quarter mile she hadn't gained a foot. Finally I grew afraid she'd be swept around the Bluff. "Here, Zeke. Come on, girl! Forget the damn duck!" She hauled herself out, gasping and shaking, and we trudged empty-handed back to camp.

About an hour later a beaver paddled by. I killed him with one shot. Zeke swam out, grabbed his ear, and dragged him to shore. Half as big as she was, he somewhat compensated for the lost duck.

We now had one duck and one beaver, hardly enough to head home. I rolled out my poncho and sleeping bag and turned in. Bears kept me awake all night. I heard them everywhere and in my dreams; they loomed like *Tyrannosaurus rex*. Zeke growled constantly. The sun woke me early, and I arose grumpy. After a half-hearted breakfast, I started packing. Where to and what for? I hadn't decided. The smallest chore seemed an insurmountable obstacle. Half-awake, half-asleep, still beleaguered by Kate's last words, I thought I heard a "Voice."

"Go to Pickerel Slough."

Startled, I looked up. I was the only one in view and knew I hadn't spoken. It seemed to be an inner Voice—calm, flat, devoid of accent or inflection. Just the bald statement in my head: *Go to Pickerel Slough.*

Pickerel Slough was about a mile downriver and on the other side, a sandy swampy area named for its northern pike. I'd been there on a moose hunt last fall.

Hmm. "Hey, Zeke! Whadaya say?" She wagged her tail, put her feet on my chest and licked my chin. We loaded up and shoved off.

The Slough's clear brownish water vanished at its outlet into the silty Yukon. Turning upstream, I eased the prow onto the sand. Zeke, roped to the bow, jumped out and waited. I disembarked and hauled the canoe up. "Stay," I whispered. "Sit!" I patted the sand, she squatted, and I unknotted her leash. If I left her tied, she'd whine; she required freedom and trust. "Quiet," I murmured, putting my finger to my lips. "Stay here! Be quiet!" She understood. But the first shot would bring her scampering.

I gently eased a shell into the chamber and stalked along the edge of the slough, gesturing to Zeke with a finger to my lips as I rounded the bend. Then I slunk onward between dripping ice blocks.

Sensing me before I saw him, the moose bolted into the slough about fifty yards away. I leaned against an ice block and fired. He flinched. I fired again as Zeke flew past, barking. The moose wheeled and charged her. I fired. Again. Again. Again. He crumpled and fell.

We approached warily. He lay half in the water and half on the sand. Zeke sniffed, started, circled, and sniffed again. I prodded and kicked his back. His small antlers were still in the velvet. He'd go maybe 750 pounds—exactly what Kate had requested.

I lifted my arms over my head and whooped. Zeke yipped, jumped, and licked my face. I hugged her. She bounded, pranced, and wagged her whole body. I lifted my face to heaven and whooped some more. We danced around the moose. "How about that, Zeke! We did it, we did it! We got Kate a moose! We got Kate a moose!"

After a while, we traipsed back to the canoe to get butchering tools—knife, ax, and bucksaw.

I'd read how the Eskimos and other "primitive" people bless the spirit of an animal they kill for giving up its life. I knelt and did that. I also thanked the Voice.

Liver, heart, lungs, hide, hindquarters, forequarters, ribs, backbone, neck, and head—all had to be separated and packed to the canoe. This moose was small, but I was again astounded at his size. Butchering took hours.

I could have saved work by not administering an immediate coup de grace, letting him chase Zeke toward the Yukon and dropping him closer to the canoe. Maybe ... but he might have stomped Zeke or escaped.

Lugging the meat out, short-cutting through the slough, I spied the long sleek shadow of a huge northern pike, skulk-

ing in the shallows. It lunged for deep water at my approach.
Near the canoe I lashed up a pole rack to hang the meat,
keep flies off.

Without tackle, how could I catch those northerns? I took
my .22, went back to the slough, waded into deeper water,
sidled toward the shallows and stared until I spotted another northern. Aiming just under its head to allow for
refraction . . . BAM! The fish rolled and flopped on its side. I
heaved it on the sand and clobbered it with a stick. The bul-
let never broke the skin; its balance mechanism had been
bollixed by the shock.

I finally killed about a dozen, all between three- and four-
feet long, lunkers! and hung them on the rack next to the
moose.

By then it was growing dark and I was wiped out. I made
camp on the beach and built a huge driftwood fire. Zeke
and I feasted on moose liver, that scrumptuous hunter's
jackpot, gazed at the stars and rejoiced over a concert of
wolves in the hills. I stretched out on my down bag, propped
my head up with a soft log, and scratched Zeke's ears.

I thought of my father who commuted to Wall Street every weekday, my brother who seemed headed down the
same route, my high school and college friends, all committed to a life of tedium. And I wouldn't have traded places
with them for all the gold in Alaska.

I filled my cup with clear Slough water and proposed a
toast . . . to Pickerel Slough . . . to the moose . . . to the pike . . .
to the beaver . . . to the duck . . . to myself . . . to Zeke . . . and
to the Voice. Life seemed excruciatingly sweet. I could
hardly wait to tell Kate.

After a few hours, I awoke, loaded the canoe, and started
lining upstream.

We stayed on the Slough side until cliffs blocked our
progress, then crossed. I was afraid our added weight would
sink us. Not Zeke. She bounded atop the moose meat. "Get

down," I snapped. "On the floor! And hold still!"

With only a few inches of freeboard, I had to float the canoe out to knee depth and mince aboard. I knelt with my feet under the seat, swinging my paddle gingerly.

On the other side now, hauling through a shallow backwater, we drew abreast of a flock of geese on an island 200 yards out. The channel looked calm and fordable. I skinned the canoe onto smooth rocks and told Zeke to "Stay!"

I pumped a shell into the .22 and waded in. The footing was uneven, muck and rock, and the water was icy. I grimaced as it rose to my waist, then ribs, laying the rifle across the back of my neck to keep it dry. The water rose to my chest and snatched my breath away. I was about halfway across, still a hundred yards distant, when an old gander—the flock's lookout—twitched his head in alarm. "Just stay there, geese," I mumbled. All they could see was my head, arms, and rifle as the water rose to my shoulders, then to my chin and lips. I put the rifle on top of my head. If it got any deeper—one more inch! But it didn't. It dropped to my neck . . . my collarbone.

On numb feet and wobbly legs, step by shuffling step, I was inching across the uneven bottom when the old gander squawked and the whole flock exploded into the air. I had no chance. I about-faced and retraced my steps.

Zeke pranced and danced as I approached, glad to see me, with or without a goose.

I'd been in that ice water twenty minutes. My legs were blue, my teeth chattering, and my shivers threatening to turn into a death rattle. But I knew that metabolism and the sun would soon warm me up, so I grabbed the tow rope and started metabolizing.

We kept on the rest of the afternoon, past Joe Malcolm's fish camp, uninhabited this early in the year. Several times cliffs halted our progress and forced us to cross. Now and then we stopped to snack. Finally I sighted Eagle Bluff. By the time I reached it, it was dark, not pitch, but a deep dusk, as dark as it got at this season. I guessed it was about midnight.

We trudged past the sleeping town, crossed above Eagle Bluff, and landed near Mission Creek. I beached, unloaded my rifles and pack, dragged the canoe onto shore, covered the meat with my poncho, grunted into my pack, and hobbled home. That last mile seemed like ten.

I was surprised to find Kate awake and giving Billy a bottle.

"What you doin' back so soon? Give up?" she asked.

"Who me?" I grinned.

"You must've gotten a moose."

"A moose, a beaver, a duck, and a couple dozen whopper northerns."

"You've only been gone two days!"

"Two-and-a-half to be exact."

"Where's the moose now?"

"In the canoe."

"Shouldn't you bring it home?"

"Can't."

"Why?"

"Exhausted. I can hardly stand up."

"Aren't you afraid someone will see it?"

"Sure."

"What you gonna do?"

"Nothin'. That is, nothin' right now. Except sleep."

"Where'd you get the moose?"

"Pickerel Slough."

"That's pretty far down, isn't it?"

"Twenty-five miles."

"I didn't think you were going that far . . . "

"I heard a Voice."

"A what?"

"A Voice."

"What do you mean, 'a voice'?"

"I mean words in my head. They told me where go."

"Like when I tell you where to go?"

Always the joker, Kate.

"What did this 'voice' say?"

" 'Go to Pickerel Slough.' "

"That's all?" She tilted her head.

"That's all."

"And you went there and found the moose."

"Right."

She looked away. "You'd better be careful whom you tell this to."

I nodded.

"Maybe it was luck," she suggested.

"You got any idea of the odds against finding a moose, let alone a young moose, at any given moment, at any given spot in this whole immense territory of Alaska?"

"High."

"Astronomical," I corrected.

"Maybe you imagined it."

"I didn't imagine the moose."

She rocked Billy and looked away. Finally she said, "I'll be damned. I'll be absolutely damned." That was about as close as Kate ever came to cussing.

The next day I drove up the Taylor Highway to American Summit and filled two washtubs and the car trunk with snow. I packed the meat in the snow and stored it in the cellar until we finished canning—about a week. During that time, I thought often about this incident and brimmed over with questions:

Did I actually hear a Voice or just imagine it? And if I just imagined it, how did my imagination "know" where a moose was? How could it know something I couldn't? Did it have "eyes"? How could it see?

From where in my mind did the Voice arise? Was it merely

a hunch? An intuitive prompting? Had anyone else ever heard such a Voice? Was the moose there when I heard the Voice, or did the Voice also direct the moose? Whose Voice was it—mine, a spirit's, God's?

Or was it, after all, as Kate suggested, just luck?

Canning alternated with mirth, impromptu feasts, a special treat being canned northern pike, its fine, sharp bones rendered soft and palatable in the pressure cooker. A full cupboard and succulent treats produced good will in our house for the next month.

We had enough meat to last all summer, but after it was gone, it was all gone, and I made a crucial discovery: The real meat of the experience was the wonder and mystery of that Voice.

DOG DAYS

I wanted my wife to cherish my Hayfield, breathe in its wild flowers, bathe in its creek, salaam to its mountains, ogle its wild game, go nuts over my sodhouse. She couldn't do that while occupied daily with two squalling brats. But an opportunity arose with the return of the Hatchers, newly-weds from back East, who were spending their second summer in Eagle with the Episcopal church. For several weeks after their arrival, we gathered at the church's upright piano, chatting and singing while Carolyn played and Bob sang. They went wild over Billy, pumped us for all his birth details, and seemed genuinely delighted that a couple of similar age and background had settled in this far-flung outpost.

At my behest, Kate asked Carolyn to look after Billy, Esther to look after Scott, and when they both agreed, with packs in the canoe, Kate, Zeke, and I set off upriver.

Once past the Indian village, we crossed to Eagle Creek.

Before we were married, Kate and I had often enjoyed camping together. I hoped this trip would re-establish the unencumbered zest that had come so easy to us then. But as we neared the north shore, Kate turned, "I hope you aren't counting on me living in that sodhouse."

"Don't you want to see it before you make up your mind?"

"No! I'll never live there. Never! And this visit won't make the slightest difference."

I felt stung. But after having arranged baby-sitters and having come this far, I figured we might as well keep on.

We beached. I carried the canoe up the bank, set it under a bush. We donned our backpacks, then strode up Eagle Creek in cold silence.

Zeke, in heat again, stuck close, perhaps sensing what I knew: that female wolves had been known to track and kill female dogs in heat.

Arriving at the sodhouse, we made camp, sat around, watched the birds, took in the view, and spoke not one word. Zeke kept bringing me sticks, which I threw half-heartedly. We each made our own lunch.

I dragged out our plastic box camera and, while Kate was changing into more comfy clothes, after she had taken off her bra and was sitting there, topless, I snapped her picture.

CLICK.

She glared at me, finished dressing, and stood up, trembling, "All right. Give me that camera!"

My jaw went slack.

"I want that camera!" She started toward me. "Now!"

I backed away. "Why?"

She lunged, caught my shirt; I twisted away. She chased, I ran. She accelerated, I accelerated. She sprinted, I sprinted. She slowed, I slowed. She stopped, I stopped.

Her teeth were set and her eyes smoking.

"Come on, Kate. You can do it." I held the camera toward her.

Around and around we whirled again, to the raucous accompaniment of Zeke's barking and my jeering laughter.

Finally she sat. I rewound the film, put the cannister in my pocket and set the camera at her feet. "You win. Here."

She ignored it.

Finally I said, "I can't understand why you're so angry. All I did was take your picture."

"That wasn't just 'taking my picture.' "

She was right there.

"How would you like it if I took your picture without your pants?"

"Probably wouldn't. But I doubt if it'd make me berserk."

"I wasn't berserk; it's just that, well, I don't like being photographed when I'm not ready."

I clammed up. She was hedging, trying to make her fury sound innocuous. She'd been livid—I'd seen it in her eyes—as if I'd committed a heinous crime, not a slight error in timing or aesthetics. "Good. Let's try it again then. This time get ready!"

Our mood turned gray. We never did re-establish that old unencumbered zest I'd been hoping for . . . not that day . . . not that night . . . not any time on our way back to Eagle the next day.

Back in town with her two sons, with Esther and Carolyn close, Kate snapped out of it. But I felt we'd passed some intangible fork in the road. She'd just flat overruled me, guillotined my dream of living off the land, scorned my chosen life style without acknowledging its importance to me. "Go fish and hunt day by day . . . " Thoreau had urged. Those words had once electrified me; now they sounded hollow. My future had begun and ended with my sodhouse. True, this was a "genie in the bottle," but I felt as if I'd just been forced to eat it whole, starting with the bottle.

Meanwhile, Zeke had become a foxy lady. She escaped often from the house without me ever discovering how. The first few times she turned up with Banks and Wrango, Anton's malemutes, near the edge of our backyard. Later she grew cagier and roamed farther, always returning exhausted and caked with slaver.

One afternoon while she and I were meandering back

from an unsuccessful small-game hunt up the Taylor Highway, I spied a flick of motion in an open area beside the
road. I stopped. A wasp was dragging a dead spider up a
three-foot dune, clutching its booty in its jaws and front
legs—pushing, pulling, and yanking uphill. Half the size of
the spider, the wasp looked too small to accomplish it. Often it slipped and toppled back. But it kept at it.

From entomology I vaguely remembered a wasp that
stung spiders, buried them in a hole, and laid its eggs on
them—a "spider wasp," they called it.

"Stay back, Zeke."

At the top of the dune, it revved up its wings and lifted off
with the spider, like an overloaded helicopter, only to crash
at the base of the next dune, where it immediately began
tugging uphill again.

Up one dune and a crash landing on the next, up that
dune and a crash landing on the next, the wasp continued
across the desert until, after an hour, it arrived at its hole.
Next it pushed the carcass in, crawled in after it, struggled
out, in and out a dozen times, until (I presumed) it had laid
all its eggs. Then it filled the hole and began preening. Finally it flew away. That was it. Just flew away.

Where to, I wondered. What next?

The sun was low when Zeke and I headed home. In my
fascination, I'd lost track of time. Like me, the wasp was a
predator. It had done for its progeny what I'd done during
my trip to Pickerel Slough. It had killed the spider; I had
killed a moose. But it had what I'd lost since Kate had
spurned my sodhouse—purpose.

In the weeks that followed, still at loose ends, I started
hanging around with Bob Hatcher. He'd been a wrestler at
Williams, in fact, New England champ in his weight division and was now enrolled in med school. He'd been
charged by the church with developing recreational programs for the Native children. Perhaps I was attracted to his

sense of purpose. Perhaps he saw Zeke and me as potential assets to his mission, approved and sanctified by his church, which was, basically:

TO HAVE FUN.

Zeke knew how TO HAVE FUN.

"Hey, kids," I hollered one day as Bob's gang of redskin whippersnappers gathered near the river, "Watch this!"

Throwing a stick into the Yukon, I shouted, "Fetch!"

Zeke plunged in, paddled out, seized the stick, towed it to shore, dropped it, shook, picked it up, strutted back to me, teased, dodged, clamped down when I grabbed one end, and hung on for a tug of war, which she eventually let me win.

The kids soon took up the game themselves, laughing and hollering "Fetch!" until—after a time—the novelty wore thin, and one by one they sat down. Then Zeke would slobber their faces, drool on their arms, sop their bare legs, nudge with her cold nose, switch with her wet brush, pester and cajole until, howling and giggling, they'd get up and invite her to play again.

Besides "Fetch," Zeke also loved "Hang Dog," a game we'd invented where she gripped the center of an old rag and hung on while I lifted her off the ground. Or she'd grip it while I turned round and round, faster and faster until her body became airborne—THE FLYING DOG!—a wonder and a marvel to kids who'd never seen TV or watched a circus.

Zeke also had a collection of parlor tricks we'd learned while I was in the air force, just-for-fun stunts that could last maybe ten minutes if I threw in enough "Atta Girl's" and "Good Dog's." She could:

Sit.

Shake Hands.

Turn Around.

Lie Down.

Roll Over.

Play Dead.

Hup over My Outstretched Arm.

Gimme a Kiss.

Close the Door.

Speak (a sharp bark).

Whisper (a low growl).

Sing (a droll howl)—only possible if she weren't too excited, which imparted a discordant yip.

Hold a tidbit of food *on her nose* until I said "O.K.," then toss it, catch it, and gulp it.

Hold it *in her mouth* until I said "O.K."

And then . . .

The Grand Finale!

("Pay attention now!")

"CATCH AND HOLD!"

("You got that, Zeke?")

I'd throw. She'd catch and hold . . . I'd raise my hand . . . and . . . tidbit dangling . . . saliva dripping . . . body stiffening . . . our eyeballs locked . . . she'd hold . . .

until . . .

I'd drop my hand, say "O.K.!" and she'd gobble it.

That stopped those whippersnappers cold, made them giggle and jump up and down.

Of course, it looked to them as if all this was happening for the first time, as if Zeke could understand every word I said, would do anything I asked, eagerly, willingly. They had no idea of the weeks and months that had gone into perfecting our routine.

"Again, MaGeel! Do it again!"

Dad once mused in all seriousness: "I wonder how many *miles* that dog wags her tail in a *year.*"

Zeke knew how TO HAVE FUN.

I, on the other hand, was existing in a state of pretended animation, going through the motions without really being involved. Not knowing what to do with myself, I had stopped thinking about the future.

As Zeke became more obviously pregnant, her tummy and teats swelling, she began sneaking away. Once I discovered her in the cellar of a deserted house a hundred yards from ours. She'd squeezed through a broken window too small for me, intending to build a den, have her pups there, safe from human interference. But if I allowed it and she had trouble, I wouldn't be able to help.

I set up a bedding box in the living room, as I'd done for her other litters, but she spurned it. Returning from a walk, she'd beg to go to her den. I'd say, "No!" but she'd keep hounding me. After three or four rounds, I'd act mad, though I wasn't, and after two weeks I felt like an ogre. This, she kept telling me, was her ultimate purpose.

One day I saw her sneak off, followed, and found dirt flying out the window of her self-chosen den.

I returned with a flashlight and looked in. "Hi, Zeke."

The dirt stopped flying.

"It's O.K., girl. I know what you're doing. It's O.K., but you can't have your pups there. It's not smart. So come on out now and we'll go home."

She just glared.

"Zeke! Come here!"

She didn't budge.

"COME ON! Git your butt out of that hole!" I tried to sound angry.

She didn't budge.

Never in her whole life had she looked me straight in the eye with utter defiance.

But this was her den, her home, her private project, in effect her sodhouse. This was, she was telling me, none of my business. I knew how she felt. I turned and departed.

Back home, Kate said, "Where's Zeke?"

"In her den."

"You gonna just leave her there?"

"Have to. Can't get to her."

"She ready to have her pups yet?"

"Hope not."

Zeke came home in a few hours. Two days later she had nine pups on a blanket by the stove in our living room.

The next day, with a pup in her mouth, she scratched to go out.

"No, Zeke. You can't go outside. Those pups will be all right." From her half a dozen other litters, she'd never tried to take a pup out.

She glared at me accusingly, pathetically. She either didn't understand or didn't believe. She kept carrying the pup to the door and begging. "No!" I told her over and over. Each time she glared at me.

"Graham," Kate said one day at breakfast, "there's something I have to tell you."

"I'm listening."

"My period is two weeks overdue."

"Two weeks isn't much."

"Yes, but I'm starting to feel sick."

"Morning sickness?"

"I think so."

First Zeke and now Kate. I shoved my chair back, stood up and stalked from the table.

"I didn't accomplish it alone, you know!"

I marched out of the house. This development spelled THE END for me in Alaska. It meant I'd have to turn my back on my ideal of self-sufficiency and abandon my sodhouse, forget about surviving the nuclear holocaust, go elsewhere and get a regular job, tie myself permanently to the commercial treadmill.

I felt I'd just been kicked in the gut.

Why should I have to give up what I wanted, what I knew

to be best for all of us, because Kate, a Catholic, kept getting pregnant? It didn't seem fair. No matter how hard I chewed on it, from which angle I squinted at it, I couldn't make it seem fair. And yet the Merlys, my parents, Kate's parents, our whole damn society, expected me to be responsible.

But what was responsible? Was it forgetting about surviving a nuclear holocaust? I didn't think so.

One thing I did know, I couldn't afford another baby. We would have to leave Eagle. But where to go?

I could probably find work in Fairbanks, but where, with whom, on such short notice? I wasn't friendly with anyone in Alaska except the Merlys. This wasn't their problem; we weren't their family.

I needed time. I needed money. I felt scared and lost.

A week later we were sure Kate was pregnant. I went to the post office and, to Esther, dictated a telegram:

"DEAR DAD (STOP) KATE PREGNANT (STOP) MUST LEAVE ALASKA (STOP) NEED $1,000 (STOP) GRAHAM"

DEPARTURE

In 1960, $1,000 was what Mom later termed "a small for-
tune," but I was reasonably certain Dad would send it.
Meanwhile, I turned my attention to Zeke's nine puppies. I
could not transport them with me back to New York; customs would never let them through. So I tacked up a poster
on the post office bulletin board: "Free pups. Mother Zeke,
father Wrango." I wasn't sure Wrango was the only sire, but I
wagered he might help sell the pups. I displayed another
poster at the Northern Commercial Company and im-
plored Esther to spread the word. Also, I bragged about the
pups to everyone, stressing Zeke's smarts and Wrango's
strength.

Anton was not optimistic. Zeke was genetically an alien.
The Natives wanted sled dogs, not retrievers or clowns, he
said. And who, with winter near, would interrupt his autumn labors to bottle-feed an unweaned puppy?

As the weeks wore on and no one responded, I was forced
to consider the unthinkable. In California or New York, I'd
have called upon the vet or the dog shelter, refusing to involve my hands or my conscience. But in Alaska, death had
begun to seem a natural part of life, the other half of a total
process. And so it began to seem not unreasonable that I

consider some form of quick, painless sleep for these homeless waifs and not unreasonable that I administer it myself.

My first concern was for Zeke. She was five years old now; this was her seventh litter. She seemed able to get pregnant routinely, effortlessly. She always had at least eight pups, once thirteen. Several had been stillborn, and she'd disposed of them in the ancient way of all canines—by consuming the carcass—a wild, instinctual behavior which replenished her energy, but mortified some people.

Yet these pups were precious to Zeke, and this concerned me. If I stole them, would she hate me? Did she know each one, individually? Would her milk output adjust to lesser demands?

I picked one up one day. Zeke glowered. The next day I did the same. But her vigilance couldn't be constant; she had to go out. And this gave the thief his opening.

One by one, over the next two weeks, I whisked the puppies away, went out of sight and earshot, and rapped them once over the back of the head with a pipe—an instant and painless death, which nevertheless made me shudder beforehand and choke up afterward.

Soon there was only one pup left. Would its absence expose my horrendous crimes, shatter Zeke's trust? Until now, unless she'd learned to count, she had no reason to suspect a thing. But her last one? Finally, I stole it as I'd stolen the others and monitored her closely afterward.

She nosed around for it for a while, seemed perplexed, but appeared unconcerned the next day. As the weeks rolled by, she suffered no physical or psychological trauma that I could discern, didn't leak milk, nor seem in pain, didn't seem to fear or mistrust me, all of which possibilities had tortured me.

Meanwhile, Kate and I collected Northern Commercial Company boxes and began to pack.

Soon we became aware of a huge problem: how was Kate,

pregnant, going to get on and off airplanes with two heavy toddlers? Would the airline help? Once again, the Hatchers stepped in. On their way east to Bob's parents' house, they had to change planes at O'Hare. There they could give Billy to Kate's mother, thereby relieving Kate of half her burden.

Right on schedule, I received Dad's check for $1,000, which the Merlys cashed, a friendly gesture which saved me endless trouble. Mom's accompanying letter contained uncharacteristic sarcasm: "Do you think we own a money tree?"

So our plans were set. The Hatchers and Billy would fly out first, Eagle to Fairbanks, Fairbanks to O'Hare. Kate and Scott would follow soon after, same route. I would pack up and drive back via the Alaskan and the Trans-Canadian Highways.

Soon Bob, Carolyn, and Billy departed on the mail plane, leaving Kate, Scott, and me feeling depleted. But before I knew it, Kate and Scott also departed and I was alone.

I was surprised when I didn't feel depressed. The hollowness of the house affected only my ears. I felt relief from being treated as an adjunct to motherhood and from my pretense of cheerfulness. I could discard my husband mask. Suddenly, it was just me, my books, my typewriter, my canoe, and Zeke, as it had been in the air force. I could shout, cuss, spit, fart, piss in the yard! Do anything I damn well wanted without thinking about Kate.

With only a few chores left—cleaning the house, finishing the packing—I felt no particular rush. Precipitously, I was possessed of a delirious abundance of leisure. The chores would take only a day or two . . . then what? Just leave? No. I wanted one more wilderness fling, a good-by salute, a final bon voyage, one more casting myself upon the silty pulsing breast of that beautiful Mother of All Alaskan Rivers.

The next day, telling Esther my plans, I thought I detected

a suspicious squint. Had she tuned into my secret thoughts? Did she feel I might ditch my wife and children and become a wandering squaw man?

I slid my canoe into the current, and Zeke and I headed out.

Last fall at about this time I had floated this same route a mile behind the Hansens, they in their motorboat, towing an oil-drum barge with mining gear. I had been on my way to the Tatonduk or Sheep Crick to hunt Dall's sheep, about forty miles downriver. That we'd left together was strictly coincidence.

At that time the Hansens had beached below Pickerel Slough, and I had drifted over to say "howdy." Barney, Ole, and Jim were sprawled around a driftwood fire.

They all waved and shouted, "Hi, Graham."

"Fancy meetin' you here."

"Where you headed?"

"Thought I might float down to the Tatonduk and find me a sheep."

"Come on over and coffee up."

"Hopin' to make camp before dark. Nice of you to offer, though."

"Hell, camp here! The Tatonduk's just around that first bend. You city fellas're always in a hurry."

"Did you see those three moose on the willow flat about a mile back?" I asked.

"No."

"Two bulls and a cow. I'll bet they're still there."

"We were probably gabbin' when we went by. How big were the bulls?" Barney probed.

"Full height, small racks. Last year's calves, I think. The cow was smaller."

"Just right for eatin'."

"They get tough when they're too old," Ole put in.

Barney poked the fire. "Why don't you and Jim mosey

back and check 'em out?"

"Was plannin' on sheep."

"A moose in the hand's worth about four sheep in the bush."

"Already got half a moose on Junebee's license."

"Half a moose ain't much to see you through the winter," Barney noted. "Why don't you and Jim mosey back. Kill one bull on Jim's license and the other on mine. You keep one of 'em, Graham."

I was tempted.

"The Junebee boys told how you killed that moose off the highway at a quarter mile. Jim here's a pretty good shot, too."

"What'll I do with Zeke?"

"Leave her with me and Ole. When I hear shots, I'll bring the boat up. We can load up the moose and run 'em back to Eagle tomorrow."

"You mean I won't have to line my canoe back?" This was sounding *very* tempting.

"If those moose are still there . . . If they ain't, all you've lost is a few hours. Course, you city fellas're always in a hurry."

"Wouldn't it be out of your way to boat back to Eagle?"

"Sure, but what the hell. If we don't leave today, we'll leave tomorrow. If we don't leave tomorrow, we'll leave the day after. This trip is sort of a vacation."

"You Alaskans're always on vacation."

Zeke leaped out as the prow neared shore and jumped all over them. Barney and Jim fended her off; Ole shielded her face.

I handed my pack to Jim, snapped on Zeke's leash, surrendered the end to Barney, hitched up the canoe ropes, bade Zeke "Stay," and Jim and I lined upstream to the mouth of the Slough. We ferried across, hauled the canoe up, tucked our rifles under our arms and stepped out toward the willow flat, Jim in the lead.

He was about a decade younger, but taller, heavier, and generous in his opinion of himself. "How far d'ya think it is?"

"Maybe a mile."

"How'd you happen to see these moose?"

"Heard a branch snap. Canoe floats quiet, you know."

"We were probably gabbin' when we went by."

"So your dad said."

"Gettin' dark earlier now," Jim noted. "Chilly, too. Mist's already risin'."

Jim, though still in his teens, was born and brought up in Alaska, which, despite our age difference, made him the old-timer and me the chechako—a distinction that I thought rather overimpressed Jim, for he kept up a steady patter as we strode along, on bush life in general and moose behavior in particular. I didn't like being lectured, and the longer he jabbered, the less I liked it. This had happened to me all my life. People mistook my reticence for insecurity or sulkiness. Who did he think he was, anyway? Daniel Boone? Davy Crockett? How could I teach this juvenile some respect? Quote Stefansson? Give him the Bronx cheer?

At the same time I realized his attitude was provoked by the ancient yearning of all teens—to break from his family while lacking direction, to appear commanding while lacking confidence. So I bit my tongue.

In about fifteen minutes, we approached the flat. I touched his back. "Not far now, Jim."

He stopped; I stopped. "Where were the moose when you last saw them?"

"In the willows, there." I pointed.

"You think they're still there?"

"Who knows?"

"All right. Let's quit gabbin'."

Now he was gettin' the right idea!

"Be careful not to step on a stick, and don't step in the muck. It'll slurp when you pull your foot out," he whispered.

Oh, really!

We skulked along about a hundred yards farther when three moose emerged dead ahead, two bulls on either side of the cow.

We crouched.

"You take the one on your side, I'll take the one on mine," Jim murmured. "Fire when I say 'three.' "

We squatted and brought our rifles up, resting our forearms on our knees. "One," began Jim.

The temperature had dropped. Dew had collected on my '06 scope. Everything was blurred. "Two," he continued.

"Wait! Don't shoot!" I hissed. "My scope's fogged."

The moose ambled toward us, curious. I wiped the glass on my damp shirt.

"You ready?" I thought I detected a hint of sarcasm.

We brought our rifles up again. "One," said Jim.

I still couldn't see. "Two," he said.

"Hold it! Don't shoot!" Again I rubbed the lenses on my shirt. The three moose turned slightly, moving laterally, curiosity yielding to wariness, only fifty yards distant.

"We'd better shoot this time." The sarcasm was unmistakable. *Only city fellas use telescopic sights.* I could almost hear him say it.

"One," he said.

Unable to see cross-hairs, I put the fuzzy moose in the middle of the scope.

"Two," said Jim.

I exhaled slightly, held my breath, and let my finger touch the trigger. "Three." Our two rifles cracked almost simultaneously. "BOOM-BOOM!"

Jim's moose trotted off while mine collapsed as if pole-axed. Jim stood, reloaded, and fired again, "BOOM!" Again, "BOOM!" Again, "BOOM!" Finally his moose fell, too.

Mine, on the other hand, was lying on its side, half paralyzed.

"Great shot!" Jim said.

It was not a great shot: I'd been aiming for the chest; he'd been drilled between the eyes. But, still smarting over Jim's gabbiness, I decided he didn't need to know everything. So I put my thumb under my armpit, spat, and finished him off with one more shot. "Not bad for a city fella."

"I'm sure my first shot hit that moose," he insisted.

"Moose don't always die easy," I, the chechako, spoke.

Soon we heard Barney's boat.

I thought Jim laid it a mite too thick while telling his dad the details. We dressed out the moose by flashlight and gas lantern, loaded them into Barney's boat, picked up my canoe, and chug-chugged back to Eagle.

A few days later, in front of Jim and the Merlys, I confessed to aiming at the heart, but my reputation as a marksman was sealed. Barney, despite my protestations, accused me of flagrant modesty.

Kate and I canned moose for the next two weeks. The Hansens never did make it to Coal Creek that year. I never made it to the Tatonduk either.

Now, on this trip downriver, my bon voyage, those willow flats hid no moose. The early hunting season was already closed. Aspens and berry bushes splashed the hillsides with yellow and crimson. I was surprised at how little silt the Yukon carried now that the glaciers had refrozen. For all in Eagle it was a time of preparation, of girding for cold and darkness, for all except me.

At Pickerel Slough, the canoe brushed the sand and Zeke jumped out. I hauled it up, and, remembering the Voice, Kate's moose, the duck, the beaver, and the dozen northerns, retraced my stalk of last spring. Zeke pranced and danced, remembering, too, I thought.

I flipped the canoe over, propped up one side, anchored a tarp over it, I built a bonfire and cooked supper. A shallow-swimming dog salmon, driving upstream to spawn, made a bow-wave in the clear water. Then another and another. With a dip net I could've stood in the shallows and snagged as many as I wanted. I could've built a cabin back in the woods and, as Thoreau put it, "live the life of my dreams." I could've. But without Kate, Scott, and Billy, it seemed a dismal prospect.

Zeke and I headed home the next morning. With no reason to hurry, no story to tell, the miles and hours dragged by. I'd snared neither sustenance, nor adventure. No one depended on my return. I just put one foot in front of the other and stared listlessly at my moving knees. "Time is but the stream I go a-fishing in," Thoreau had written, " . . . whose bottom is pebbly with stars." A poetic phrase, I thought, yet a stream of backwaters, eddies, sloughs.

Once back in town I slept, had breakfast, threw my pack in my car, and gassed up. Anton had inspected my trailer in my absence and, deciding it was overloaded, reinforced it with two coil springs from his "junk" pile, a parting gesture which misted my eyes.

"Looks like you're leaving with more stuff than you came with." He grinned. I shook his hand, hugged and kissed Esther, fought back tears.

Then Zeke and I climbed into my old gray Chevy and headed out—first stop, Chicago. Then "home" to New York.

I, the city fella, had reverted to type.

BOOK II

Row, row, row your boat
Gently down the stream
Merrily, merrily, merrily, merrily
Life is but a dream
Children's round

POWER FOOD

After a reunion with Kate and my boys in Chicago and our arrival at The Farm, my parents' second home in Galway, twenty miles north of Schenectady in upstate New York, I began to realize I was part of a community. It included my parents, who were now supporting us; Kate, who, before my arrival in Chicago, had miscarried; and Scott and Billy, whom I was supposed to be supporting. Only one of us had been a jet fighter pilot. The others had never attended secret nuclear briefings, never dropped dummy H-bombs on imaginary Soviet targets. They were blissfully unconcerned, I thought, about our nation's MAD defense policy. Like ostriches with their heads in the sand, they conducted their lives as if their civilian half-truths were the whole truth, the only truth, and they expected me to acquiesce. Which I decided to do. At least for the time being. In the interest of family felicity.

Once we had settled in at the Farm, I drove to Ithaca for an interview as an airline pilot, and was invited to sign on immediately. But on the way home, I waffled. Most of my air force career had been spent boring holes in the sky. Boring holes, I'd discovered, was nothing if not boring. Flying a four-engined airliner would be more of the same.

Mom, who'd spent years writing short stories, had been ecstatic over the publication of "Impasse!" in *Field & Stream*. Beyond that, she thought I had talent, and Mom had spent her whole life helping others develop their talents. So why not ask her and Dad to subsidize me while I developed mine?

"But what are you going to write, Graham? You think you can just make up a story out of thin air?"

"No, Mom. I have an idea."

"You want to tell me about it?"

"Last week I discovered a book by Stefansson I hadn't read titled *The Fat of the Land*. It tells how Stef and his pal, Ole, convinced skeptical doctors that man can live on nothing but meat. They stayed on an all-meat diet for a year while the docs in New York City examined them. Why can't I, the author, go on an all-meat diet, cite examples from Stef and others, describe what it feels like, tell what I know about the Natives in Eagle, and show how a modern outdoorsman might benefit from trying it?"

"This diet won't make you sick?"

"No, Mom. I've done it Alaska. You could do it, too, if you wanted to bad enough."

"What about vegetables? Carbohydrates? Balance?"

"Medical propaganda."

"Says you."

"No, says Stefansson. Think about it. How can people who hunt and fish for a living possibly balance their diets?"

"Well, I couldn't be sure until I see how you handle it, but it sounds like you might have a saleable idea. Remember! If you get sick, I can't afford to send you to the doctor!"

Thus encouraged, I started in as I had for college term papers, filling twenty 3X5 cards with possible beginnings, thirty 3X5 cards with acceptable endings, and forty 3X5 cards with tidbits for the middle. But when I tried to put them together, I couldn't make the narrative gel. I was stuck.

Living downstate, Mom and Dad visited The Farm only on weekends during the school year, so we had the place pretty much to ourselves. That was fine with me; I didn't want to solicit their advice. But the more stuck I felt, the more stuck I became, until I seriously doubted that I could succeed.

At Wesleyan I'd studied liberal arts and had majored in forestry at Berkeley, but I'd never been a good student. I was not naturally charming or articulate. I often had difficulty saying, let alone writing, what I intended. My vocabulary was sparse, my sentence structure basic, and my spelling frequently inventive. When confronted with details, I easily became confused. I'd never felt called to go around bragging about my IQ. I loved listening to stories, but was not a gifted raconteur. I loved reading, but hated desks. And now I was expecting to launch myself into a new career on the strength of one published story, an event which, I was now certain, had been pure luck.

Mom had a pair of bookends—miniature editions of Rodin's "The Thinker," mirror images of a naked man with his chin on his fist. They made me grimace in recognition, for I, too, assuming that classic pose, had felt unclothed and metallic. True, I'd convinced my parents to let me try writing, but when it came to actually doing it, I suspected I was inept. Finally I left all my cards, pencils, and books strewn around the room, turned away, and didn't look back.

Part of my trouble, I knew, was trying to write at The Farm. Nothing here looked like, belonged to, or had anything to do with me. My typewriter and reference books were borrowed from Mom. My writing room had been Mom and Dad's bedroom. The closets were festooned with their clothes, the bathroom with their doodads, the living room with their knickknacks. Wolf-like, they'd marked their territory—perfumed powder in the bathroom, scented soap under the pillows, French silhouettes on the upstairs bathroom walls, booze bottles in the kitchen cabinet; in effect, transporting a corner of suburbia to upstate New York, and now expecting me to fit in, which meant mowing their lawn, washing their windows, vacuuming their rugs, mopping their floors, answering their phone, watching over all these tokens, badges, and prizes of a lifetime of success in 20th-century America.

I hated it.

The Farm was my parents' retirement home-to-be. They had installed a new septic system, an oil burner with hot air, running water, a modern kitchen, upstairs and downstairs bathrooms, a beautiful stone fireplace, and a huge picture window in the living room. With twenty-three acres of second-growth woodlot and a few acres of pasture near the house, they called it The Farm, but it wasn't, really. The trappings of comfort were its only produce—pansies, petunias, daffodils, irises, roses, phlox, and hollyhocks; a front garden with white picket fences, benches, and an arbor, where Dad often worked as Mom's handyman; an amusing patch of vegetables in the rear, where Mom often worked as Dad's handywoman, the flowers labeled "her" garden, the vegetables "his." They had a private backyard, forest paths, a trout stream, a pond with weeping willows and a resident muskrat, a three-stall garage, a split-rail fence, an entrance off a dirt road, and rural mail delivery. To their New Rochelle cronies, they bragged about Galway, the smallest incorporated village in New York State, its proximity to Saratoga, Great Sacandaga Lake, Lake George, and Adirondack State Park.

I hated it.

So far they'd only lived here in the summer and on weekends. They told us they needed someone to take care of it, protect it from vandals. They seemed to be sincerely trying to make us feel at home, even clearing out a downstairs bedroom for the boys, Dad hoisting Scott onto his broad shoulders, Mom helping Kate with the innumerable chores of motherhood. Both seemed happy as grandparents and proud of their new relatives. Kate, too, with access to supermarket, laundromat, and hospital, seemed relaxed and cheerful here.

I hated it.

One morning while I was ensconced in the breakfast nook, pining for Alaska, Mom, who with Dad was visiting for the weekend, entered. Clear blue eyes, white hair, triangular face, sharp chin, and rosy complexion, she didn't look sixty. She smiled, poured herself coffee and sat down opposite. "You know, Graham," her voice mellifluous, "I've told you before—we bought The Farm because your father wanted it, not me. It's his place really, not mine." She sipped her coffee. "I'm saying this again, now, because I want you to know it doesn't bother me that you're not happy here."

"I'm happy enough."

"Don't give me that! You're heart-sick. And I don't blame you!"

I gulped.

She patted my hand. "You forget whom you're talking to. I've known you a long time, remember?"

Mom had a way of seeing clearly what I wouldn't or couldn't admit, even to myself, and voicing what she saw as truth. If I didn't like it, well, that was my problem. I smiled in spite of myself.

"Why don't you like it here? That's what I want to know. Do you know?"

"I miss Alaska."

"Why? What's the matter with the Adirondacks? Potentially, I'd think, they're just as wild and beautiful as Alaska."

"No, Mom."

"Why not? They have deer and bear. Forests, lakes, rivers, and mountains. Trees, rocks, and swamps. Just like Alaska."

"No, Mom. Not like Alaska."

"How so?"

"No moose, caribou, wolves, or grizzlies. No Eskimos or Indians. No Yukon River. No salmon."

"That's quite a list!"

"And they're overdeveloped, too close to a bunch of cities."

"There must be places in the Adirondacks that aren't overdeveloped, that aren't close to a city. Aren't there?"

"Yes, but . . . " I sighed at the everlasting inadequacy of language, the incredible gulf of understanding Mom was expecting me to leap with words. How could I begin to explain this to a woman who'd never been north of Montreal?

"It must be something intangible?"

I nodded, swallowed.

"Well, Graham, you've expressed yourself well. Now I have some idea of why you feel the way you do about The Farm. But let's talk about your magazine story. You haven't mentioned it in weeks."

"I seem to be stuck."

"Seem to be? Or are?"

"I guess I am."

"Well, keep at it! I know you, Graham. You can do anything you set your mind to. Always remember that. Writing is not easy. But difficulties overcome yield a great sense of accomplishment"—she reached out and grabbed my chin—"when you finally get around to overcoming them." She chuckled.

By then the rest of the family was drifting down to breakfast, and our conversation shifted to other subjects, but several weeks later, after Mom and Dad had departed, I entered my writing room and began reading my notes. Some, I decided, were actually interesting. An idea came for an acceptable lead, so I rolled in a piece of paper and typed it out. Somehow I knew what should come next, so I wrote that out, too. Then I built those sentences into a whole paragraph, then more sentences, and second and third paragraphs. Almost before I realized what was happening, my fingers were rattling the keys, my mind rattling on magically ahead of my fingers. Somehow I was remembering my notes in a reasonable and logical sequence, almost as if I were not writing but watching, as if some smarter me had taken a firm hold. The story began to flow, and I relaxed and flowed with it, until it acquired shouts, strides, colors, melodies, scents, emotion, life—the very breath of life itself!—an unfathomable process which lasted until I became stuck again. But "I know you, Graham," Mom had said. "You can do anything you set your mind to!" So I simply returned to my notes, and somehow, by not struggling, by separating myself from the fear of failure, by opening myself to a wider vista, I kept on rattling the typewriter keys, sometimes referring back to my notes, once recuperating in the kitchen with a stiff cup of coffee. Finally, I pushed back my chair and stood up. I had finished! Lapsed time: three hours!

This was no reworked epistle, no flash in the pan. I'd dug up an idea, researched it, and carried it off, accomplishing what I'd envisioned and intended. And I was ecstatic!

Though I knew there might be rejections and delays, I also knew it was good. Somewhere someone out there would publish it.

Borrowing Dad's camera, I took pictures to illustrate it.

Field & Stream, Outdoor Life, and *Sports Afield* rejected it, but *True Magazine* paid me $300 and featured it in the 1961 *Hunting Yearbook* under my title, "Power Food."

Mom, Dad, and Kate popped their buttons. But $300 for three months' work would hardly support a family.

After this euphoria, groping around for another idea, I returned to the library, reperused Stefansson's works, but always came up empty-headed. My spark of inspiration had fizzled.

Remembering all those moose I'd seen from the top of

Eagle Bluff, the way they always vanished before I could hie myself close, I wondered if ideas, like moose, were wild, shy creatures, if maybe I just needed to slip my mental canoe in an imaginary Yukon and float after them.

INGENUITY FOR SALE

"Anyone home?" I called, entering Cole's house through the front door. The strobe and drone of his welder emanated from his shop. So I sashayed thence and found him squatting on a stool in the far corner, torso enveloped in sparks, face shielded by a full black mask, left hand steadying his right, flux rod vanishing in a circle of blue-white fire.

When the arc sizzled, I said, "Howdy, bub."

He raised the mask. "Hi, Mac. Just thinkin' 'bout you."

"I see you're busy."

"Who me? Busy? Now you oughta know better 'n that. I'm never busy in the commonly accepted sense. Unless you count contemplatin' my navel. What's on yer mind?"

"Lookin' for a story idea. Maybe I should come back later."

"Don't do that! Stick around! Go on in and make yourself some coffee. Be witchya in a jiff."

I nodded.

He dropped his mask and resumed welding.

I went in, started the percolator, and waited in the easy chair, my customary perch. When the pot sighed, he entered as if on cue, strode to the sink, washed his hands, poured two mugs, handed one to me, and installed himself

113

in a backward chair at the kitchen table, his customary perch.

Zeke greeted him. He scratched her ears. "Story idea, eh? Sounds like a matter of decision, determination, and perspiration."

"For you, maybe. For me it's inspiration. I have to find the *right* idea."

"What about one of your Alaskan huntin' yarns?"

"All fluff. No point. Can't get worked up about any of them."

"I don't mean a really-happened story. I mean fiction. Describe the event and setting from memory, and make up the characters and plot to say somethin' essential."

"Don't think I know how."

"Just takes practice."

"Don't have time for practice. My folks and Kate are getting antsy. Gotta write another saleable story or I'll hafta get a regular job."

"Haftas and gottas—that's yer trouble, Mac. You work too hard at it. You need space. You need to go at it like ya did in Alaska. Make it a game! Sit back! Relax! Have some more coffee! Writin's not like drivin' a steam roller, you know. As Zorro says, 'Ess more like fencin'.' "

"Fencing?"

"'You grip zee foil (or zee quill) like she is a canary— firmly, but delicately—like zees.' " He hooked his left arm over his head, mimicking Zorro. " 'Not too loose or she fly away, poof!' "—and there it went, out of his open hand; he watched it flutter around the room. " 'Not too tight or you squash zee canary.' " He gazed at the dead bird, truly remorseful.

"Good analogy," I admitted. "I still need an idea."

" '*An* idea!' Hell, Mac. You mean, ideas, plural. Why there's millions of 'em, jillions! In every book, magazine, and newspaper. We're manufacturin' 'em right now, releasin' 'em into the atmosphere. There goes one past your noggin' right now! Watch it! Don't let it get away!" He reached up and snatched air. "Gotcha!" he gloated.

"Dammit, Cole. This is serious."

"That's the point. It's *not* serious."

"Not to you, maybe."

"Maybe you oughta take a vacation, go huntin' with me and the gang this weekend," he glanced out the window, "which, incidentally, oughta be droppin' in any minute now."

"Being broke and taking a vacation won't sit well with Kate or my folks."

"You don't hafta tell 'em everything, you know. Tell 'em a deer will save a bundle at the butcher's, a buck in the freezer's worth lotsa bucks, plural, in your wallet." Cole chortled.

I appreciated Cole's practical views. He'd grown up in an Adirondack logging camp in Arietta; I in a middle-class suburb of Manhattan. His home was plain and unpolished; mine, or rather my parents', bulged with fripperies. His time was solitary and free, oriented around mechanical skills; mine was circumscribed by family and children, at the moment oriented around writing. His shingle proclaimed him part of his community: "North Broadalbin Machine Shop— Ingenuity for Sale," had earned him his nickname, "Ingenuity." I still felt like an addendum to my parents.

His place on the shore of the Great Sacandaga Lake was ten miles from my parents', but worlds away in life style and appearance. Scattered around his yard were innumerable broken items from which he was currently scrounging parts, discombobulated derelicts from which he'd already scrounged parts, various unrecognizable doohickeys, from which he was about to scrounge parts; several old cars of assorted years and species, including "the pride of the fleet," his father's cream-puff LaSalle with an aluminum body, "still practically in mint condition," now buried in the tall grass behind the house—"a damn junkyard," his neighbors complained; "precious antiques," Cole cooed.

At the core of this collection was Cole's shop, actually in two discrete sections—a three-sided shed adjoined his house and kept the rain off several table saws, a heavy-duty drill press, a chain hoist, and an oxyacetylene torch, dolly-mounted for easy portability. A side door led from the shed to the back porch with more machines and tools.

The living room also betrayed his uniqueness. On the wall hung two photos of women framed in toilet seats—"old acquaintances," he claimed. "Misogynist" was scrawled on a blackboard beside my chair—"woman-hater," he explained—the latest on his list of new words. Cole was writing about guys he'd known in combat, "real men," he called them, a book about World War II. But he wasn't ready to share it yet.

Also on the wall were a pencil sketch of a haggard GI with a hole in his helmet, three rifles, a bugle, and a full-sized but broken airplane propeller. Cole had been a waist-gunner on a B-26 and a Stearman banner-tow pilot after the war.

His sofa was draped with a horsehair blanket he said "used to be Fred," a pet from his Arietta boyhood. The other walls were bare boards covered with aluminum foil. Outdoor light was filtered through two small windows perpetually overcast with accumulated dust and smoke. Beside the front door was a homemade woodstove—two halves of an old boiler welded to heavy steel plates. His toaster worked only when thumped with a ball-peen hammer, stashed on the table for that purpose. His commode was a hand-carriable "honey-bucket" secreted in a closet beside the front door. His kitchen table was usually stacked with old magazines, miscellaneous papers, cartons of cigarettes, boxes of crackers, a trio of ash trays, and assorted machine parts.

Housekeeping wasn't high on Cole's priority list, but fixing things was—anything from a loggers' mammoth forklift to a kid's delicate water pistol.

I'd met Cole when, fresh out of the air force, I'd brought him a school bell Mom had bought at a garage sale. The pull-arm had been fractured. Cole not only fixed it, but called on Mom a week later, explaining that cast iron sometimes "took" a weld, sometimes didn't. "If it breaks again," he promised, "I'll fix it for nothing," an offer which endeared him to Mom, even though she never had to take him up on it.

First, we discovered we were used-to-be pilots and now would-be writers, which, despite externals, cemented a bond.

Cole's clear blue eyes were set off by smile wrinkles, overhung with a heavy brow and topped with a sparse crewcut, his face rectangular. His hands were thick and powerful, extentions of muscular arms and shoulders, yet possessed of startling agility, accentuating his patter like a conductor's baton, pointing up, toning down, tying together, and drawing conclusions; hands, I thought, that might crush a milk bottle. Or build a toothpick airplane inside it. He probably weighed an eighth of a ton.

Two cars pulled up. He peered through the window. "Here's my huntin' gang now."

Five raggedy youths rambled in and deposited themselves on makeshift surfaces around the room—an upside-down waste basket, a wooden milk crate turned on end, and the hastily cleared sofa. Cole's place was the woodchuck YMCA, the coffee-holic watering hole for the North Broadalbin teen set.

Zeke rose and sniffed.

"You guys know Mac and Zeke."

Actually we'd met only once. But they remembered Zeke.

"Just stopped in to make sure the hunt's still on for this

weekend," said the guy on the waste basket.

"Far as I know." Cole lit a cigarette. "You gentlemen mind if I bring a friend?" He nodded toward me. These loggers' sons and grandsons weren't known for their open-hearted acceptance of strangers.

"Mac here's been huntin' in Alaska, never in the Adirondacks. His education has thenceforth been examined and found woefully wanting. Most of our kills are made at fifty yards or less, so we use drivers and watchers."

"Drivers and watchers?" I raised an eyebrow.

"Half of us saunter through the woods noisily, in a line. The other half sit still and wait. Deer move away from the drivers and are surprised by the watchers. At least, that's the theory."

"So what you been up to lately?" prodded the guy on the sofa.

"Same old stuff. Weldin', cuttin', fixin'. I keep busy around the shop."

"Where we headed this time?" asked the guy on the milk crate.

"Same place. Can't think of a better." Cole was referring to Arietta where he'd grown up.

That decided, the guys stood up, stretched, and departed. Obviously, they admired Cole. I think they were hoping to catch him alone.

He and I chatted awhile, and then I left, too. The man sure had confidence and a passel of ideas, plural. But none that seemed suitable for me.

DEER HUNT

The more I got to thinking about hunting in a gang, the less I liked it. I didn't like sitting in one place, didn't like walking in a line of armed men, and didn't like splitting one deer six ways. But I'd said I'd go and would have, too. Except for the flu.

It began with sniffles and progressed to a throat so sore I could hardly talk.

I dropped in at Cole's place to croak, "Maybe next weekend."

Cole called me the Monday after, which was actually a great honor: he had to walk a quarter mile to a pay phone. "How's the cold?" he probed.

" 'bout da same."

"The gang's goin' again Saturday. Think you might make it?"

"Cole, ah'd love to . . . "

"You don't sound so good."

"Well . . . "

"Sure hope you feel better. If so, same time and place."

"Don't wait," I rasped.

"O.K." And we hung up.

I was still sick the next Saturday and the next one, too.

Secretly, I was glad for the excuse. My apologies had sounded hollow, even to me. Cole's replies were almost too polite. I began to wonder what he really thought. I had no way of proving my Alaskan hunting stories, all of which could sound far-fetched to an Adirondacker. For all he really knew, I'd never been hunting in my life. I was sure he thought I was a "four-flusher," as he put it, a bluffer, a guy who does his hunting with his mouth.

Three Saturdays in a row I backed out on Cole. But the next Monday, feeling better, I decided to go alone.

I stopped in at Cole's on the way north. "Guess I'll try it by myself."

"Wouldn't bother, if I were you. A man alone can't cover enough ground. Deer's ears and nose are too good."

"You wanna come along?"

"Got a rush job for my log-slashin' neighbor."

"Haftas and gottas."

"Touché." He grinned. "Wanna leave Zeke here?"

"I'll take her along."

"She'll spook the deer. Though I 'spose it won't matter. You ain't gonna see any anyway."

"She went everywhere with me in Alaska."

"Arietta ain't Alaska."

"I'll keep her leashed. She'll be all right."

"You'll be sorry."

"She's my pal, Cole."

He knew what I meant. I could see it in his eyes.

I drove to the base of State Brook Mountain, slung on a three-day backpack and my '06, snapped Zeke on her leash, and started bushwhacking uphill into the wind. I stalked west most of the day, taking my time, focusing on being quiet, not seeing deer but enjoying the musty smells of autumn and being outdoors. But these woods were no Hayfield, and the Adirondacks were no Alaska. The woods seemed empty except for us; I heard no shots. Now and then

I picked up bits of dry grass and dropped them to make sure I was still proceeding upwind.

Near dusk I put up two bucks. Both bolted before I could aim, but I whistled. I'd read somewhere that a shrill note will sometimes stop a deer. One did. I raised my '06 and fired. It dashed off, but dropped within fifty yards, shot through the heart.

I hung the carcass in a tree, built a fire, and Zeke and I shared deer liver, cheese, and nuts for supper. By then it was too dark to head home, so we made camp.

It had been so easy, I couldn't help remembering the Voice, and wondering what, if anything, had led me to this deer.

Later, I heard a creek some ways down the mountain and realized I was thirsty. I took my canteen and flashlight, reached the creek in about twenty minutes and headed back. I'd forgotten to mark my camp with a lit flashlight or a bright object on a branch. Now I was disoriented, in a worse fix than being thirsty. If I rested, I'd grow cold. If I kept fumbling in the dark, I'd become exhausted.

"Find camp, Zeke!" I put my hand on her back. "Where's our deer?"

A simple trick for her.

The next morning I dragged the deer down the mountain and loaded it in the trunk, stopping at Cole's on the way home.

"Back so soon?" he leered.

"Yup. Gave up." I strained to keep a straight face.

"I told you those deer were hard to spot."

"Sure are." My straight face cracked.

"You, bastard. You got one, didn't you?"

I grinned.

"Son-of-a-bitch! Where is it?"

"In the trunk. Come see!"

He hauled himself out of his chair and we traipsed together to the car.

"Spike horns are the best," he said. "No better eatin' in the world. Where'd you nail him?"

"In a saddle near the top of State Brook. You can have a haunch when I get it 'skun' out."

"Just might take you up on that." He beamed.

Mom, Dad, and Kate were pleased.

The gang went out several more times that year, but the quarter I gave Cole was the only venison they saw that year.

Now Cole knew I wasn't a four-flusher. But I still didn't have a story idea, which filled me with doubt about writing in my future.

BRUSH MAN

Mom spoke softly, but there was steel in her tone: "I'm very proud that you've sold two stories to major magazines. As you know, I've spent a good portion of my adult life trying to sell stories and haven't had as much success as you have in one year. But freelance writing is a hit-or-miss business. And it's not only me that says this; it's many, many full-time writers. No matter how good you are, you won't be able to make a living at it at first. You may manage with more experience. For now, your father and I want you to think about doing something else."

Or, in plain language: Son, get a real job!

Damn! What was the matter with those people! Couldn't they see I was doing my best! Routing the vandals! Keeping them stocked with venison! And them with two houses, two cars, and two paychecks! I fretted and sulked the rest of the day.

But a few days later my friend Bob Hinkle phoned. He described working as a Fuller Brush man in Greenwich, Conn. "It's a blast! All the housewives love me (chortle, chortle). I love them, too!" He loved being outdoors, being his own boss, and running his own business. Making good money, too! He slept home every night, and his wife helped with peripheral chores. After we hung up, I cogitated.

A week later it seemed almost an omen when I noted a "Help Wanted—Sales" ad in the paper.

Door-to-door selling in America in 1961 required no special qualification or education. Anyone who looked presentable, could smile, walk, and talk could get hired. But to excel required charisma, pizzazz—something extra— and to find out if you had it, you auditioned. This consisted of several days of you watching the district manager until you felt you'd gotten the hang of it, then the district manager watching you. Then the Fuller Brush Company presented you with a black snap-top carrying case for your merchandise, a plastic card with pictures of your free gifts, and your very own territory.

My territory was the whole city of Gloversville, generous for one man, I was assured, about twenty miles east of The Farm. My district manager, an upbeat exuberant fellow in his late twenties, met me for coffee at a diner at 8:30 one morning; we hit the streets at 9 sharp. He watched me for a few houses, passed on a few pointers from his vast experience, then, apparently satisfied, departed. This was my first solo.

"I'll meet you at my car in an hour," he promised.

As a salesman, your demonstration or "demo" was your key to success. When the door opened, you smiled, held up your card, and said, "Good morning, Fuller Brush. What would you like for your free gift—pastry brush, vegetable brush, or comb?" If she said, "I have those" or "Not today, thank you," you flipped the card over. "That's all right. How about a shoehorn, soap caddy, or spoon caddy? Choose one!"

Nearly everyone could use one of these handy gadgets, though they cost you only pennies. When she decided, you then said, "Fine. May I step in a moment and get it out of my case?" If she said, "No," a rare occurrence, you dug one out on the front stoop, hoping she'd ask you in the next time. If she said, "Yes," you thanked her on the way in, perhaps mentioned the weather, something nice about her house, or this week's specials. You asked if there was some place— "a table, a chair?"—where you could set your valise. Then you offered to let her sample a product—hand cream, air freshener, hair spray, furniture polish, tooth paste . . . ? Sometimes you volunteered to clean her oven. After each sample, you asked, "Would you like one?" Or "a couple"? Or "a dozen"? Depending. If she said yes, you pulled out your receipt book and wrote, thus closing the sale.

On the way out you offered another free gift—lipstick (many colors), perfume, or toilet water in a tiny bottle. You promised delivery "not this Saturday, but the next," left a catalog with your name, address, and phone number and departed with a smile and a "Thank you."

Now and then you encountered a man, and you demonstrated your more practical items—moth spray, degreaser, tooth brushes, pot scrubbers? Less constrained with their money, men were often big spenders.

Friendly. Simple.

On that first day in Gloversville, without the district manager, I got an answer at every door. All but two asked for free gifts, all but two asked me in, and all of those bought something. One lady said she'd been waiting to see the Fuller Brush Man for months; her bill totaled $23.57. Wow! Dispensing double free gifts, I felt like a door-to-door Santa.

When I met my district manager in an hour, he prodded, "How many houses did you visit?"

"Seven."

"Only seven? That's not near enough for an hour. How many sales?"

"Five."

"You're kidding! Let me see your receipt book."

"Start here," I prompted.

He flipped through the pages. "I'll be damned."

"Beginner's luck, eh?"

"Amazing! Terrific! I've taught a dozen guys the basics of this job. You're the only one who's ever batted over 500. Many sold nothing at all their first time alone."

I beamed.

We parted then, and I continued on my own for the rest of the day, which, though less astonishing than my whizbang initiation, nevertheless yielded a profit.

I thought, *Gosh! Maybe there's a place for me in this crazy world, after all!*

I soon discovered that the classic image of the gigolo Fuller Brush Man is a myth. He doesn't have time. After months on the job, I only met one housewife who, answering the door in her nightie, was apparently inclined. I departed posthaste.

The 9-to-5 workday was actually closer to 8-to-6 when you counted driving time, and in "off" hours I worried about how much and what kind of new products to order, stocking up on specials, keeping my inventory down, finding an honest delivery boy, and making sure the right goods were sent to the right customers. Sunday was supposed to be a day off, but the heavy workload often took a slice of it.

On the plus side was the chance to rub elbows with hardworking affable people. One couple whose dinner I'd obviously interrupted invited me to share it. Their big-heartedness shamed and touched me. Personally, I'd never have been that generous with a salesman. I thanked them profusely, but demurred.

Late one afternoon, despite my persistent ringing, no one answered the front door. I headed for the back. A police dog growled and charged at my approach. I halted. Nothing was making me do this; I had only to turn and leave. But this dog was chained, and chained dogs, I knew, often barked because they felt cornered. Maybe it was the way he held his ears, an ambiguous look in his eye, or my years of observing Zeke—I don't know. But I *knew* that this pooch would be a pushover. I opened the gate. "Good boy. It's O.K., boy. I won't hurt you." I shifted my satchel to his side, just in case, and pressed forward. What a hullabaloo! Enough to wake the dead!

The back door opened before my knock. I held up my card.

"How did you get past my dog?" the man demanded.

I looked over my shoulder. The dog was sitting quietly.

"Who? You mean lover boy?"

"No one gets past my dog."

"Really? Well, he seems calm now."

"Sure. You're already beyond his chain. And he sees us yakkin'."

I waved my card in his face. "What'd you like for your free gift? Pastry brush, vegetable brush, or comb?"

Shaking his head, he tapped the vegetable brush and invited me in. He kept shaking his head while I dragged out my samples, pattered, and gestured. By the time I left, he'd spent $7.83. Had he really needed any of it or just been flummoxed by me acing his guard dog? I didn't ask.

One night working late, I finished my day at the end of a dead-end street. The house was dark, but I trudged up the porch steps and pressed the bell. A dim light in the living room suggested a live body. I pressed the bell again. And again. Finally a hulk lumbered into view. The door cracked. No light came on. Man or woman, I couldn't tell. I smiled. "Good evening, Fuller Brush. What would you like for your free gift—pastry brush, vegetable brush, or comb?"

In answer, as if from a monster, I received a guttural growl. My breath caught; my eyes bugged; my hair prickled on the nape of my neck. I vaulted off the porch and fled.

Not till I was safe in my car did I realize that I'd confronted a laryngectomy victim, a man who'd had his voice box removed. The growl had emanated from a hole in his throat, the poor fellow's only way of communicating. I'd been panicked by the delay, the dark, and my vivid imagination. I felt stupid, insensitive, and embarrassed. But I didn't go back.

As spring came to the Northeast, I was amazed to find myself happy and prospering. I'd passed some unannounced test, it seemed, as a 20th-century breadwinner. My parents acted relieved, especially when Kate, the boys, and I moved out of The Farm and into a rented house in Galway.

The boys were growing like weeds, Scott getting into everything, Billy whooping and rattling the bars of his playpen. Often I helped Kate with the chores of motherhood, changing diapers, waking up and feeding someone in the middle of the night; baby-sitting Scott, taking him for piggyback rides around the house. Allowing herself to be used as a teddy bear, yet ever on the alert, Zeke acted as solicitous as if my boys were her own pups. Watching over my family, making innumerable sacrifices of time and energy, I was beginning to enjoy the pride and concern of being a father.

Then Robby Springer, air force fishing buddy, called from Alabama.

"Hey, Springer! Great to hear from you! Whatcha doin' with yourself?"

He'd started his own business, was heading a gang of driveway pavers. But he called to tell me about a magazine story that described "gold diving," he termed it. Gold divers needed no pick and shovel, as the Klondikers of 1898, nor dozers and sluice boxes as prospectors of today. They went under water into the creek itself and sucked gold directly from the bottom. Robby was intrigued.

"You run across any nuggety lookin' spots while you were in Alaska?"

"Sure did."

"You think this gold divin' idea might work up there?"

"Sounds interesting. Send me a copy of the article. I'll get back to you."

Robby was married now, also with children. Ever brash and impulsive, he'd sounded the same as when we'd both been single jet pilots. His voice reminded me of many great times a-fishin'.

"That was Robby Springer!" I told Kate later. "You remember him?"

I didn't mention Alaska.

ROBBY

For the next few days, until Robby's letter arrived, time stood still. But finally I had it.

The magazine story described gold diving: A gas engine pumped air to divers through "hookah" hoses and pumped water through high-pressure hoses to an aspirator in a dredge, which then sucked water and muck. One diver supported the dredge, the other moved the nozzle along the bottom. A removable riffle box at the back of the dredge collected gold.

I called him back and told him it sounded fine, great.

"You know any places in Alaska where we might try it?"

"Last Chance Creek," "Hard Luck Brook"—their names evoked a reverie. I said, "A bunch."

"Maybe you and I should think about going back together."

"If there were the slightest chance . . . "

"You've been there. I never have. What's it like?"

He was asking me this on the phone! Thinking of moose, the Hayfield, my sodhouse, I said, "I'll write you a letter."

As the days and weeks rolled by, I found that writing to Robby about Alaska was almost like being there, with one drawback: it made me hate selling.

One morning on my way to work, spotting a gaggle of geese near town, I stopped the car and gawked through the open window. Two hundred birds were diverging and converging in two wobbly "V's." Their wild cries pierced my heart. Goose bumps (literally) coursed up and down my spine. *I could be where they're going,* I thought, continuing on my way. All that day and for the next week, I recalled their music with sharp twinges of yearning.

Steeling myself to sell was requiring more and more effort. One morning, practically overcome by spring fever, I pulled off the road near Kennyetto Creek, spread out a blanket and, wishing Zeke were with me, flopped down in the sun.

What difference did it make in the incessant flow of human events whether or not I sold one more can of handcream? Why had my life become such a drag lately? Why did I feel so tense, frazzled? What was I really doing here? What, other than money, was I contributing to my family?

Enjoying the grass and the sun, and pondering thus, I dawdled by that creek all day, an unconscionable vagrancy that gouged into my earnings. But on a deep level I didn't care. I couldn't get worked up about profit. I was not, as my district manager believed, a highly motivated salesman. After piloting a jet fighter, this seemed like milk toast.

"Readjusting to civilian life," Mom called it. I called it weakness. Dependency. Living a lie. Pretending I didn't know what I really did—that we were all doomed! Every last one of us! Wholesale carnage. Total wipeout! No way to escape! All we had to do was keep building more H-bombs and intercontinental ballistic missiles, keep following the same path we'd been following since *Sputnik.* Keep shaking our national fist at the Soviets.

To me it seemed ridiculous to expect world peace to arise from mass terror tactics, as if humans were automatons, unencumbered with minds and emotions. But why couldn't others see this? Had we all, unanimously, signed a secret evasion pact? Or was the outcome too monstrous, too horrendous to contemplate?

That was one side. The other was my rancor at Kate, which at the moment I was stuffing. I resented having my sodhouse, my scheme for surviving this collective abomination, snatched from me by Kate's stubbornness, her religious proclivity for motherhood. We did not agree on ideals, on the basics; but she was insisting on having it her way. And so far I'd kept my "genie securely corked in his bottle."

Robby and I continued to conspire via the post, until by April, it had begun to look as if we had a workable plan. But when I announced this, my parents were appalled. Mom quickly branded it "irresponsible."

"You're not a bachelor anymore," she scolded. "You have a wife and family to take care of now."

"Oh, Mom. I'm not plotting abandonment!"

Not plotting, no! But Mom knew that I, her introvert son, sometimes felt like withdrawing from everyone.

She squinted at me sharply.

At first Kate sided with my parents. But I figured she wouldn't mind if I struck it rich. So I kept accentuating the gold angle. One snag: Robby wanted $1,200 for my share of our equipment. Without a solid credit rating, I had to borrow it from a loan shark. I never did mention this to my parents. By the time our plans were definite, Kate had softened her objections a bit.

At last the big day arrived! I quit my Fuller Brush job and started packing for Alaska!

First I dragged out my '06, cleaned and oiled it, and spent several evenings reloading surplus army casings with high-velocity charges, exactly what I'd done in Berkeley before my first trip. Weighing out powder, reinserting percussion caps, crimping in 150-grain bullets, the sweet smell of

Hoppes powder solvent—the familiar routine evoked waves of nostalgia.

I made pemmican from two quarters of beef and beef tallow, purchased wholesale with borrowed funds—slicing, drying, and pounding the jerky, trying the tallow, mixing and hardening it in cake pans. Then I sliced off squares and wrapped them in foil.

One May evening, Robby swaggered into our kitchen. Twinkling blue eyes, auburn hair, cowboy boots and stetson, no shave, he'd hauled his new eighteen-foot aluminum canoe all the way from Alabama to show off the Indian design he'd hand-painted on the gunwale.

After chatting several hours, I felt a certain strangeness. Where Robby was confident and sociable, I was quiet and reflective. Where he was jolly and expansive, I was cautious and critical. He had a way of directing his remarks to me, yet not excluding Kate. Now and then he requested my expertise on this or that subject, but I wondered . . . Out of necessity? Or a desire to seem nice?

Patiently but firmly, we answered Kate's questions.

"How is Cathy reacting to this?" Kate probed. Cathy was Robby's wife. She'd apparently assented to this trip, despite being pregnant. I was sure Kate was glad she wasn't.

"I'm here, ain't I?" Robby smiled.

"Alaskan rivers are cold." Kate spoke from experience. "How will you stay warm?"

"A quarter-inch wet suit and a thick skin." Robby stretched and yawned.

"What about food?" Kate brushed away a strand of blond hair.

"Salmon, moose meat, and blueberries. Sounds rough, don't it?"

"Sounds like you'll be hunting and fishing, not gold diving," Kate objected.

"You think we're doin' this for fun, lady?" Robby chortled.

"Wrong! We're gonna dive through the ice! But if we just happen to run across a little fun, enroute, so to speak, accidentally, so to speak, we probably won't try to avoid it."

"Actually, I've planned a pretty Spartan menu," I put in.

"Spartan, hell! Nothin' but dry meat and glacier drippin's. 'Power food,' he calls it. No bread, cheese, raisins, nuts, berries! He don't believe in enjoyin' his vittles."

Kate grimaced.

Robby shrugged. "Hey, if he thinks he can handle it, I reckon I can, too."

"What if you don't find gold?"

"That's the least of our worries. Prospectors been findin' sparkles in them rivers for decades. Got to be gold there. You'll see! It's denser than other soil matter. It percolates to bedrock."

The next day Robby and I went for a stroll. "Mac," he rubbed his chin. "I've spent $1,000 on equipment so far. We'll need another $2,000 for our diving rig. It's manufactured by an outfit in Los Angeles. We can pay for it and pick it up on the way."

"You think I'd let you come this far and then back out on you?"

"No. Just thought we oughta chat."

"Well, no sweat. I took care of the moolah problem before you arrived."

We stopped at Cole's to say so long. I asked him to keep an eye on Kate. He smiled. "That's bound to be one of the toughest assignments I've ever received."

The next morning, after I'd tossed my stuff into Robby's pickup, my family gathered in the front yard.

"Don't worry, I'll bring him back alive." Robby hugged Kate.

"You better. We need him," she quipped.

I fussed over my boys, tousled their hair, smoochled their necks.

Then Kate and I entwined each other in soon-to-be-empty arms and hugged, long and hard. Relaxing momentarily, I noticed moisture in her eyes. I touched her hair, her cheek. My throat had a lump in it as spiny as a pine cone.

At last Robby, Zeke, and I climbed into the cab.

"Say bye-bye." Kate waved Billy's tiny hand. Scott, holding onto her skirt, raised his arm.

"Find lots of gold," Kate called, not trying to hide the tears.

"See you in few months," I promised. The truck backed down the dirt driveway, turned south on Rt. 147, and headed out.

GOING FOR THE GOLD

As much as it seemed the long way around to be heading for Alaska by way of Alabama, I knew Robby had loose ends to tie up, not the least of which was my meeting Cathy. But beyond that, I now felt deliriously free. Timetables, schedules, and all such fetterings had been ditched back there in Galway. Neither Mom, nor Dad, nor Kate, nor Uncle Sam, nor the almighty buck were in charge of my life now. Only me. And I wouldn't have let out a peep if, before turning north, Robby had headed for southern Argentina.

We only stayed at his place a day, spent a couple of more swinging through L.A. to pick up our diving gear, and another testing our dredging equipment near Sacramento. Then we were on our way north.

The Alaska Highway began officially at Milepost O in Dawson Creek, B.C., where a totem pole lists distances: Whitehorse—918 miles, Fairbanks—1,523. Forty miles past Dawson Creek we passed Fort St. John and fifty miles past that the pavement quit. Then came the dust. It hung behind all cars and trucks like fog, and sifted through grommets, gaskets, and rolled-up windows as if they weren't there. Overtaking another vehicle or trailing some demented speeder, we continually spit brown. "Being left in the dust" acquired a new and asphyxiating meaning. But gradually the traffic thinned and the road flour grew less exasperating. "The best dirt road in the world" proved well-drained, hard-packed, wide, nicely banked and mostly smooth. We averaged about 40 m.p.h.

As our latitude decreased, gas prices increased. Sometimes it was hundreds of miles between log shacks—"That was a town?"—and 40 miles between petrol pumps. No one had to remind us that a breakdown could be catastrophic.

But as the moving finger traced our progress upward and leftward across the map, and having traced, moved on, I felt happier and freer. The weight of months as a successful salesman, of trying to live up to Kate's and my parents' expectations was lifting from my shoulders. This was the real me. This was the life I wanted—independent, free, full of adventure.

At last snow began appearing in dells beside the road and on distant peaks. At night we rolled up the windows and turned on the heater, then, farther north, did likewise during the days which grew ever longer, until, by the time we passed Lake Kluane, a glow was visible most of the night. Finally we cleared customs and entered Alaska.

Seventy-five miles later we turned right onto the Taylor Highway, passed Chicken, Jack Wade, and Liberty, then over American Summit and down the last grade to Eagle.

As we stumbled out in front of the post office, ducks and cranes yabbered overhead. The bracing air, the walloping view, the Yukon River, the trees, the smells, the hush. A grin, a deep sigh of "Thanks," I pounded the air with my fist and shouted—"I'M HOME!"

The astounded Merlys greeted me like a long-lost son.

"I thought you were still in New York!" Esther's screech punctuated her bear hug.

"I knew you couldn't stay away!" Anton pumped my hand and slapped my shoulder.

"Folks, I want you to meet Robby Springer." They traded "howdies."

Esther asked about Kate, Scott, and Billy.

"Oh, they're fine. Waitin' for me to return with a poke o' gold dust." Personally, I didn't much care about gold dust. I was just glad to be in Alaska.

Anton was immediately intrigued with our gold-diving gear, but skeptical: "I don't think you've got enough riffles in that dredge," he objected. "The old-timers around here used as many riffle boxes as they could beg, borrow, or steal. Arranged 'em in tiers, sometimes hundreds of feet long. Made 'em outa rough wood, sometimes carpeted with burlap. And when they were through minin', they burned every board. And still found gold in the ashes of their *last* boxes.

"Your rig has only one two-foot riffle box, and it's made outa galvanized," Anton continued. "No wood or burlap. Most of the fine gold will wash out the back."

Robby winced. My stomach knotted. If Anton was right, we'd just driven 7,000 miles, half of it on my borrowed money, for nothing.

"Are you sure?" I balked. "The water flows over the riffles in those old-style boxes like rapids. Our dredge works underwater. The wave action will be entirely different!"

He scratched his bald spot. "Hmm . . . Don't think it'll matter."

We fetched our magazine and pointed to pictures.

"You fellas don't know nothing about that photographer," Anton retorted. "Nothing! You don't know if he ever tried it or found gold with it. You can't even be sure he wasn't bribed!"

"No bribe," I parried. "The idea sounds reasonable."

"Not to me," Anton scoffed.

"It says right here they found gold," Robby challenged. "Even shows it!"

"Prospectors been saltin' gold claims for years." Anton

shook his finger. "Be mighty easy to salt a picture."

Robby looked jangled. "Well, we're here now. We can't just turn around and go home."

Anton pulled his ear. "I'm not sayin' you should turn around. Where you headin' anyway?"

"Up the Seventy Mile." I stuck out my chin.

"To The Falls? Good spot! But be careful. Water level changes quick. Lots of old-timers lost everything there. Don't leave your stuff lyin' around on the shore!"

Esther insisted on feeding us, which she did, but also on us settin' awhile, which we didn't. "They're too young for settin'," Anton explained.

We stopped our van atop the Yukon bank, portaged the canoe down, launched it, and started loading, a slow process with all our hardware. Zeke yipped and pranced. But finally we parked, locked the van behind Anton's house, and returned to the river. Zeke bounded aboard; Robby and I slid onto aluminum seats; we drifted away.

The Seventy Mile was named by Klondikers for its supposed river distance from Dawson. But that was before aerial maps. Actually it was 150 miles from Dawson and 35 downstream from Eagle.

Blue skies, warm sun, calm winds, and green hills—June in Alaska! Like me, Robby was struck by the sibilance of glacial slurry scouring the hull, and he'd never seen so many birds—gulls, terns, sandpipers, eagles, hawks, geese, ducks, ravens, swallows.

"Listen, the river sings!"

We stopped for a pemmican lunch at Pickerel Slough and a pemmican supper where the Seventy Mile fed into the Yukon.

I felt a profound release, a joy that went to the core of my being. "Simplify," Thoreau had advised. Being here, living in the wilderness as he did—this was about as simple as it got. But my friend was preoccupied.

"I been thinking a lot about what Anton said," Robby poked our campfire.

"Me, too."

"You think he's right about our riffle box?"

"Well, partly. At least about the fine dust. But I think we'll still find nuggets. All we gotta do is get down to bedrock, suck the silt outa the cracks. There's gotta be a bonanza in the veins under The Falls. No one has ever mined there."

Robby grunted. "This all we got to eat?"

"Listen, I spent weeks drying, pounding, and cooking that stuff. And months before that, researchin'. It's the best travel ration in the world. All the old trappers swore by it."

"Well, I'm swearin' *at* it."

"You'll get used to it after awhile."

We snuggled into our sleeping bags while Zeke kept watch. I dreamed of fish wheels and caribou herds.

It never did get completely dark. We judged morning by our growling stomachs and Robby's watch. After a late breakfast of pemmican, we broke camp and headed up the Seventy Mile, paddling an hour before escaping silt and another hour before noticing current. I breathed deep. It felt great to be outdoors and exercising after a week of confinement in the van.

The river was often too high and deep to permit wading. We had to paddle hard. But at last we encountered shoals. Zeke bounded onto dry ground as we eased our feet over the side.

Robby recoiled in mock horror. "You expectin' me to DIVE in this slush?"

"Sure! I'm gonna sit on the shore and watch. Somebody's gotta make sure you don't drown!"

"Whew! This feels like it just dripped off a glacier around that first bend."

We uncoiled our lines, steadied the canoe, and began picking our way across slippery rocks. First we'd scramble

GRAHAM McGILL   141

out, then in, out, in, out, in—a process which continually
shipped water. Eventually we had to bail.

Late that afternoon, not yet hardened to river rigors, we
camped early, munched pemmican for supper, and chewed
it again the next morning for breakfast.

"Yuk," Robby spat.

"It gets better," I insisted.

In and out of the water, back and forth across the river,
and upward, ever upward into the current, we skirted sand-
bars, cutbanks, sweepers, and flats. The heavy canoe
squatted in the water like a barge; to get anywhere, we had
to strain. I thought I was in good shape from lugging my
Fuller Brush case around all day, but every muscle in my
body burned. Robby, I presumed, was suffering as much.

About mid-afternoon we encountered a cow moose
chewing her cud. Head clearly visible above the weeds, she
didn't spook, didn't even glance our way, just lay there,
calmly chewing.

We hauled the canoe to the opposite bank and roped it to
a tree. I snapped on Zeke's leash.

Robby reached for his rifle. "Moose would taste mighty
good after all that pemmican." He levered a shell into the
chamber.

We crouched on a sandbar in mid-river, fifty feet away.
Suddenly she stood and faced us.

"If we shoot a moose now, it'll mean a heavier load.
There'll probably be lotsa moose at The Falls."

"If we don't shoot a moose now, we may wish we did. We
don't wanna spend time huntin' after we start diving."
Robby, a native Pennsylvanian, had hunted all his life.

"Well, I suppose it doesn't matter. There's hundreds of
moose around here, and no hunters anywhere, except us.
Reckon the Seventy Mile can spare one cow."

We killed the cow. Then saw her calf.

"Oh, no!" Robby moaned.

It's fur was soft and light tan, very different from its mahogany mother. Helpless and spraddle-legged like a new colt, it teetered toward us on wobbly legs and nuzzled our hands. If we abandoned it, it would be savaged by wolves or bears; or it would starve. If it followed us, well, we had no milk. There was only one merciful solution. I killed it with one shot to the head.

Robby, I thought, felt worse than I did. As the ranking old-timer, I was inured to the blood and violence by which Alaskan fauna sustained itself, including humans. To me, the cow and the calf were not so much individuals as expressions of the infinite forest. Years would pass before other men trekked here. By then, the niche once filled by this family unit would be filled by others. This wasn't a case of greed or wanton massacre, I knew. We'd killed that moose for food, no other reason. The calf had been an unfortunate accident. But we butchered in silence, then turned without a word and headed upstream.

A few miles later we came to a steep hill on the right with a beach and a flat beyond it. Exhausted, we prepared to camp. Zeke raced around, sniffing frantically.

"Mac! Come 'ere! You won't believe this! Wolf tracks! Hundreds of 'em!"

"Better keep an eye on Zeke."

We dumped our backpacks on the sand, built a stone fireplace, dragged a few logs up for stools and cooked the liver.

"Good, eh?" I scratched my stubble.

"Mmm," Robby muttered.

"The meat we left behind won't go to waste, you know."

He nodded. "Wolves, you mean."

We rinsed off our dishes, dug hip and shoulder holes under our ground cloth, checked our rifles, and turned in. Zeke settled down between us, ears up and eyes wide in the twilight. We drifted off instantly, but jerked awake a few hours later when Zeke, staring downriver, growled.

"There's a wolf!" Robby whispered.

"Where?"

"Comin' this way. About a hundred yards, just disappeared behind those rocks." Robby pointed.

"Don't see it."

"Still comin'." Robby grabbed my '06 and took a bead.

Finally I saw it—a gray ghost slinking along the shore where Zeke had walked. I put my hand on Zeke's back. "Easy. Shhh."

Robby shot it at about thirty yards—an old female in poor condition, muzzle white, teeth dull, coat matted. We guessed her weight at a hundred pounds and were struck by her length, height, and stench. She'd been rolling in carrion.

We skinned her, washed the potentially valuable pelt, spread it atop our duffel, and stood back to admire it.

"Hey, McGoo! Gaze at that rainbow!" Robby pointed downstream.

"Wow!" A dark cloud back-dropped the dazzling triple arch.

Robby threw his arms in the air. "You know what they find at the end of rainbows?"

I grinned.

"Right! And that's what we're gonna find at The Falls. Two pots o' gold! One each!"

But that rainbow was behind us, not ahead. I bit my tongue.

At three in the morning, the sun illuminated the landscape in mystical, other-worldly light. Despite only a few hours' sleep, we were too excited to rest. We bent to our tow line and splashed into the rapids.

Crossing and recrossing, now on one side, now on the other, immersed to our ankles or knees, occasionally to our waists, we pulled on all morning. Robby flipped out his harmonica, lipped "I'll Take You Home Again, Kathleen" for his wife, and "Row, Row, Row Your Boat," because it seemed pertinent. I tried "The Song of the Volga Boatmen" a cappella for its rousing "Heave Ho," making up in amplitude what I lacked in mellifluence. But our roistering suffered from lack of an audience.

About midday we entered a gorge, several hundred yards of serpentine labyrinth sculpted into black rock. Both sides were too steep and deep for wading, and the torrent often left us dangling instead of tugging. Our only recourse was to paddle furiously from one eddy to the next; or, after swimming, to catch a line from the opposite side and progress diagonally. Lips blue, teeth chattering, we finally exited the maze at the top.

Too early to camp, we dragged the canoe up the bank, burrowed into our bags, and conked like snuffed candles. Hours later, we roasted enough moose meat for three meals each and gobbled it all on the spot, not forgetting Zeke.

I offered Robby pemmican for dessert.

"Savin' all that for you," he parried.

That evening we stumbled onto Chester's Cabin, "Two-Mile Creek," a sign stated, but two miles from what? A homemade bucksaw with a broken blade guarded the door. We stooped, entered, and blinked in the dank gloom. Tendrils of sod dangled from the ceiling. Decayed floor joists squished beneath our feet. After our eyes adjusted, we spied fungi on the walls. In one corner a table was set, as if visitors were imminent, but the plate had corroded into a perimeter of rust. Moldy *National Geographics*, circa 1898, were stacked beside a bedraggled cot. Old letters in an indecipherable script were water-marked and smudged.

We hauled our gear up and spread out behind the cabin, intent on moose meat—fried, roasted, broiled, or boiled. I'd read that Eskimos, while journeying, jinked around the use of dishes by slicing off bites close to their lips. But such intimate sawing with keen steel proved intensely distracting.

We decided we didn't mind dishes.

During supper, hearing a strange "slosh, slosh," we raced to the riverbank. A bull moose was splashing up the channel, not crossing, but using it as a thoroughfare. For him the rushing torrent was no more annoying than a garden hose. But we didn't need more meat. Glowering over his shoulder at the barking Zeke, he plodded on.

Robby found some green rhubarb behind the cabin and ate too much. All night he groaned and passed gas.

In the morning we awoke to a misty rain. It continued on and off the rest of the day, soaking our backs as the river soaked our legs.

Around midday we came to a rickety cable car—an elongated bucket swinging from a rusty wire. I didn't trust that wire, but Robby wobbled up the dilapidated scaffolding, lurched into the bucket, and yanked on the crank. While he ratcheted himself over the water, the mechanism screeched, and Zeke and I cheered from below.

A few miles farther, we spotted the trail to Crooked Creek and Dick Bower's cabin. Barney Hansen, the last occupant, had suggested we stay there if we "happened to be in the area." It seemed like a good idea—we needed a break and it was still raining.

After hauling out our packs and rifles, we skidded the canoe up the bank, slid it back in the brush, covered it with a tarp, and headed up the trail.

A BREAK

Perched on a knoll overlooking the Seventy Mile valley, idyllic except for moonscape tailings, Dick Bower's cabin became our home for the next three days. Our stay was a perfect example of my favorite Zen maxim that one's reaction to stimuli depends largely on contrast, as the bare rocks accentuated the greenness of the surrounding sward. After all our tugging, slogging, and shivering, just hanging around became excruciatingly sweet. The simple day-to-day accomplishment of chores left us carefree and blithe. What more could anyone want, we wondered, than stoking the stove with the Hansens' firewood, hand-pumping spring water from Dick's well, washing our faces in Dick's basin, and flopping onto Dick's bunks. Ordinary glass windows seemed, clearly, a resplendent wonder. Four walls and a roof above left me so mellow I didn't even mind Robby shellacking me in a nearly continuous three-day game of checkers. Now protected, we pitied the citified multitude who never plumbed the intense marvels of existence because they never ventured beyond their back yards.

Regrettably, our host wasn't here to supervise our euphoria, since eventually we got slightly carried away. Poking around in his pantry, we found several boxes of pancake mix, which we first sampled, then obliterated. Then we discovered an opened jar of mustard, which made our unpalatable pemmican taste like scrumptious pepperoni. But there were a half dozen other jars, "and Dick won't miss just one little bottle, now. Will he?"

With nothing much better to do, I started quoting Robert Service—"The Rhyme of the Remittance Man"—as well as "The Call of the Wild," "The Cremation of Sam McGee," and "The Shooting of Dan McGrew." From the latter, a love-triangle/murder ballad, Robby seemed struck by:

> "And hunger not of the belly kind,
>   that's banished with bacon and beans,
> But the gnawing hunger of lonely men
>   for a home and all that it means;
> For a fireside far from the cares that are,
>   four walls and a roof above;
> But oh! so cramful of cozy joy,
>   and crowned with a woman's love—"

Afterward, he broke out his mouth organ and played, "Oh give me a home, where the caribou roam, where the moose and the grizzly bear play." And "Whoopee ti yi yo, git along little dogies. Don't you know that Alaska will be your new home."

Robby's motives for coming here were different from mine. He wanted his wife and family here with him, hence his focus on money; my wife had already decided not to live here. He saw himself as head of his family, part of a community; I thought of myself as a misfit, a rogue bull, beyond the need for community.

At last our emotional seesaw tipped away from ecstasy toward boredom, and we decided to depart. We gathered up our belongings, returned them to our packs, and, each in his own way, bid adieu to this holy place. Then closing the door, stepping gingerly over the stark tailings—sky bright, sun warm, nuggets calling—we followed the trail to the Seventy Mile.

There, we tobogganed our canoe into the water, bent our backs against the flood, and heave-hoed toward The Falls.

Around midafternoon, Zeke, following on the other side, cut toward the river to intercept us just ahead of a jagged cliff.

Mindful of her peril, I hollered, "NO, ZEKE! NO!"

But she plunged in, was swept toward the cliff and sucked under. We held our breath. Five, ten, fifteen seconds. Finally, imagining the worst, we raced back toward her. Was she now trapped against submerged crags, gasping for breath? No! She popped up; swam to shore, scrambled out, and shook herself off.

"That dog is amazing!" Robby yelled.

We hugged, petted, stroked, and fussed over her for ten minutes.

"Whatsa big deal, guys?" she seemed to say. "Didn't you know I could hold my breath?"

Under way again and catching snatches of what sounded like a cataract, we kept stopping and listening. Suddenly, we glimpsed it. But no! That couldn't be! In our imagination The Falls had become another Niagara, a veritable Victoria, a cascade of towering proportions.

Drawing close, we saw a series of standing waves, a mere overgrown rapids. We beached on the left bank, as far upstream as we could safely line the canoe, and clambered over boulders to The Fall's head. There, the river burgeoned into a slow pool, then spilled through a gap in the hills and tumbled through a canyon.

We pitched our tent on a flat twenty feet above water level, halfway up the canyon. We laced the trees with clotheslines and fashioned a rock fireplace. How long had it taken us to arrive here? A week? Two? We'd lost track of the days.

Assembling our fishing rods, we immediately caught a

grayling—jaunty dorsal fin, blue and silver sides, and soft, tiny mouth. We fried it for supper. Later, we boiled and ate them whole, as Eskimos did, but we used mustard, as if they were wieners. The flesh was pale and the bones sharp.

We soon discovered a drawback of camping near a waterfall. Mosquitoes loved its soggy moss and dripping trees. They trailed after us in skeins, gobs, clusters, trains, squadrons, hordes, and legions. The tent was a refuge, but it forced us to sit or lie down. After entering we spent five minutes swatting stragglers before daring to retire. All night we could hear them buzzing. Slap! Got one! Buzzzz. Oh, well . . .

In the morning, they were plastered against the netting, eager for exposed flesh.

"O.K., you sons-a-bitches!" Robby burst though the tent fly. "Come and get it!"

DEET—bought surplus and known then as bug dope, "guaranteed to repel biting insects for hours"—didn't even slow them down. They dove into it, swam in it, drowned in it, and eventually sopped up enough so their sisters could feast. DEETless, Zeke tagged after us, flapping her ears, pawing at her jowls, and sulking when she saw we planned to stay.

For breakfast, not daring to sit, we swatted amid the trees and nibbled pemmican, with mustard and mosquitoes on the side. To inhale was to ingest protein.

We unloaded our diving gear, distributed it along the shore, bolted the engine to its plywood base, inflated the oversized inner tube, fastened the base to the tube, laid out our wet suits, and prepared to get naked.

Naked?

Yes, naked.

This precarious step required planning and forethought, but standing around forethinking was accomplishing nothing.

Our next flurry required both speed—lest we be eaten

alive—and care—lest our fingers puncture the wet suits. We never quite achieved that balance.

Next we started the engine and, while it warmed, checked hoses, mouthpieces, and valves.

Then we smeared our face plates with saliva and sucked to test seal. Strapping on our weight belts, we stepped off the rocks into the frigid liquid—A TERRIBLE SHOCK!

Outward and downward we wrestled our dredge, gasping as the frigidity level rose to our thighs, waists, chests and necks. As our masks submerged, we stared through a top layer of micro-bubbles whipped up by The Falls. Lost in a symphony of raspy breath, we hoisted thumbs in a traditional "Let's proceed!"

Immediately our heads began filling with a thousand frets. How cold was it—32.1 degrees? Could our feet and hands withstand it? Would our masks fog? Would hoses stiffen? Kink? How long would the engine run on one tank of gas? If it quit, would we lose air suddenly? And where, on this whole vast corridor of a river bottom, was the best place to dredge?

We grappled the dredge erect and shoved it into the sand. Immediately, it began devouring muck and excreting silt. We kept shifting the nozzle back and forth, enlarging the concavity until it was two feet deep.

Soon shivering, I tapped Robby's shoulder and pointed up. Dragging the dredge, we sculled uphill, finally bursting into daylight—two black-skinned, one-eyed cyclops. We spit out mouthpieces, jerked off hoods, flopped on the stones, and wheezed.

"Kill that engine, will you?"

The ensuing silence was a relief.

"You wanna check the riffle box?"

"Later."

Teeth chattering, ears aching, we felt like perfect tyros. That dive had lasted ten minutes. If that was going to be our limit, we might as well quit!

We doffed diving duds, toweled off, donned dry togs, and scurried to our tent, the only mosquito-free sanctuary besides the river bottom. We nibbled pemmican and fell into a fitful sleep.

When we awoke, it was midafternoon and again raining. I glanced at Robby. "What's on the agenda?"

He opened one eye. "Whatever you feel like."

"Ready to try that river again?"

"No."

"Me either. Wanna go fishin'?"

"Nope." He rolled over.

"Huntin'?" "Nope." "What then?"

"Lemme think about it. I'll let you know."

Crawling out, I moseyed down to the dredge. Zeke followed. I opened the riffle box, dumped the contents into a gold pan and sloughed off the larger rocks and light sand. The residue was the usual black sand, garnets, and a few tiny rubies—worth nothing.

"Any color?" Robby called.

"Nope."

"That figures."

"Yeah. We barely scratched the surface. Wanna give it another go?"

"After awhile." But he didn't budge.

I fussed around, leaned against a spruce. "Listen, I think I'll climb that hill while you're wakin' up."

"Fine with me. I'll snag a few grayling for breakfast."

"Lunch," I said.

"Lunch. Dinner. Whatever."

I gathered up my binocs. Zeke and I jittered into the empty canoe, paddled across, and debarked on the other side. The hill was steep, but from the top I spied a shiny spot. "HEY, ROBBY," I shouted, "I SEE THAT AIRPLANE ANTON MENTIONED!"

He looked up from his fishing. "WHERE?"

I pointed.

Ex-pilots are usually interested in airplanes, especially wrecks. Zeke and I descended and recrossed the river.

"Where was that airplane, exactly?" Robby yawned.

"About a mile downstream, maybe a hundred yards back from the river." Anything to avoid that icy water.

"Well, let's go have a look."

It was a two-seater Cessna, the engine and instruments ransacked. Anton had told us that the pilot and his passenger, not badly injured, had hiked to Eagle after the crash and returned later as salvors.

As we returned to camp, a buck caribou stepped out of the brush at about fifty yards, shaking his head and snorting, his velvety rack the size of a stunted oak.

"You want him?" Robby unslung his rifle.

"Not me."

We still felt bad about the moose cow and calf.

The buck bounded into the forest. Robby put up his rifle.

We sat around our fire most of that day, but returned to dredging the next. Diving became easier each time. The newness and the fear wore off. My testes still shriveled, but my body seemed to acclimate to the awful cold. But we found no gold. After three days, Robby became discouraged. By the end of the week, he was disconsolate.

"Mac, I've been thinkin'."

"Yeah?"

"You know, Cathy is pregnant."

"She was pregnant when we left."

"Yeah. Well, I'm thinkin' I never should've left. I'm thinkin' I should go home."

I gulped.

"You wanna come with me?"

"No."

"You'd stay here alone?"

"Sure."

"You're a glutton for punishment."

"Not really. I just hate sameness. Can't stand too much security. I enjoy life most when it makes room for the unknown."

"O.K. Just wanted to let you know what was on my mind. We don't hafta decide now. Let's just keep divin' and mull it over."

We kept dredgin' all the next day. By that night we'd excavated a hole about four feet deep. It was hard work. The sand kept collapsing. And we still had no gold.

That night, sitting around the camp fire, Robby frowned. "Well, McGoo, I'm thinkin' I oughta be leavin' soon."

"When?"

"How 'bout tomorrow?"

"If that's what you really want . . . "

"I never should've left Cathy. I feel awful bad about it."

"It'll be much easier in August. The water drops. The mosquitoes thin out. The salmon run."

"You figure you'll stay then?"

"Gotta."

"O.K. I'll leave everything with you—canoe, diving gear, everything. You can have it all. But I'll hafta take the van. How will you get home?"

"Maybe I'll strike it rich, buy my own airplane."

Robby chuckled.

The next day he packed. Then he, Zeke, and I boarded the nearly empty canoe and headed downriver to Crooked Creek, and the overland trail to Eagle.

WASHOUT

After accompanying Robby to Eagle and returning to The Falls, I ducked into the tent, squirmed into the sleeping bag, and, with Zeke's head on my shoulder, zonkcd.

Sometime later, waking to the rumble of water, I slathered my hands and face with DEET, scrambled out, started a fire, and warmed my pemmican. That consumed, I corn-starched my wet suit so the rubber would slip on my damp skin, and wiggled into it.

My first dive showed what I was up against. I was only half of a team. With Robby holding the dredge, I had removed rocks and clogs from the nozzle. Now, I had to work around the rocks and shut down the dredge to remove clogs. Also, I couldn't let go of the dredge, ever, for fear it would tip and dump gold. I could only stand beside and aim it grossly.

After a half hour, I dragged the dredge shoreward, dumped the riffle box into the pan, and sloshed the residue. Nothing. I ate, slept, then dredged again. The next day the same—eating, sleeping, and dredging; eating, sleeping, and dredging— time unrolled in an unvarying routine. After each dive, I dumped the riffle box and inspected the residue—nothing. I consoled myself that I hadn't yet reached bedrock.

I really missed Robby, and not just the added safety factor, but his wiseacre quips. Alone, I was continually dancing on a knife-edge of fear.

After the tenth dive, I found a gold flake. Not much, just one flake. But my first! It gave me hope. And it showed that my riffle box wasn't a total washout.

Without a watch, I lost track of time; without a calendar, of days. But neither mattered, I figured, since I planned to stay until snow. The rain began gently and continued for several days, until my clothes and sleeping bag became damp and clammy. I hung them out between downpours, but it didn't do much good.

I kept dredging anyway. One day, I dredged until the engine ran out of gas, unhooked my weights, popped to the surface, swam to shore, refilled the tank, restarted the engine, hugged a rock, blub-blubbed back down, snapped on my weight belt, and kept at it. When I quit, it was almost dark. Lips blue, teeth chattering, and stiff with fatigue, I dragged the dredge to the shallows, dropped it, towed the engine to the shore, dropped it, hauled the gas cans up the bank, and dropped them. Then I wormed into my bag and plummeted into unconsciousness.

Sometime later—I couldn't tell how long—I thought I heard a "bong," very faint, very far away. Then another. It sounded as if I were at the bottom of a deep pit and the "bongs" were beyond the rim at the top. As I struggled to identify them, the bongs became "tinks"—intermittent, out-of-place. Was I dreaming? If so, why didn't they stop as I woke up? And if I weren't dreaming, what could they be? I staggered upright to investigate.

The water had risen six feet. My canoe was bonging against the shore. Gas cans, engine, dredge, hoses—everything was gone. If the canoe hadn't been tied, I'd have lost it, too.

I shouted, cussed, muttered, and paced.

"OH, NO! OH, GOD!"

The rain had stopped.

I called Zeke, jumped into the canoe, headed downstream, found the engine and gas cans hung up in eddies, and retrieved them. But I couldn't find my dredge and hoses. Searching was hopeless until the deluge subsided. Only God knew how long that would take.

"YOU JERK! YOU IDIOT!" I cursed myself as Zeke stared.

When the water level dropped and the deluge subsided, I donned mask and wet suit, and scoured the river bottom. Many yards downstream from my previous digs, I spied a glint in the sand, pried it up with my camp shovel, and uncovered my battered dredge—minus the riffle box and trailing a shredded hose. That was the end of my gold diving. I was done, washed up, finished.

I dragged back to the tent, ate, and slept.

Upon awakening, I pondered what to do. Head back to Eagle and my half-finished sodhouse? Stay here and explore? Maybe there was a nearby spot for another sodhouse. Maybe even a log cabin. There was plenty of time before winter.

Mulling over my alternatives, I decided to explore here. But my heart wasn't in it. Spotting game, I couldn't pull the trigger. Discovering a cabin site, I wondered "what for?" No matter which way I turned, what activity I pictured, I couldn't work up enthusiasm.

By process of elimination, it finally dawned on me.

I wanted to go *home*.

I could hardly believe it. Me. The great arctic hunter! The venerable proponent of Life's Great Unknowns! The chief espouser of steely eyed self-reliance!

I hated to admit it, but I was *lonely*. At this moment I felt lonelier than ever in my life. A bleakness, a blackness, a total vacuum of the hope of ever having a close friend. And in the face of that, even an imminent nuclear holocaust didn't seem very important.

Not that I suddenly agreed with Kate's dictatorial religious beliefs. Not that I felt responsible for her unplanned, unrestrained pregnancies. But, "for better or for worse," it seemed, a die had been cast. As my mother had reminded me, I was no longer a footloose bachelor, but a man with a family to love.

And viewing it coldly, selfishly, I knew I was afraid. Afraid that my energy, directed solely toward my own survival, that my happiness, pursued merely for its own sake, when all was said and done, would yield nothing but a lifelong harvest of rancid and bitter fruit.

"Hey, Zeke. Wanna go home?"

The familiar word brought a tear to my eye.

She wagged her tail and licked my cheek. Whatever I wanted was O.K. with her.

HOUSE HUSBAND

Within a few weeks after my return to Galway, I began to wonder if I'd done the right thing.

Rent was two months overdue. Dennison's grocery bill was spilling into the aisles. The phone and electric companies were threatening to pull the plug. The loan shark who'd financed my summer was clamoring for repayment. And I was unemployed.

Kate wanted me to find a job immediately, but my adventurous summer left me disoriented. I dreaded the prospect of a set routine. The approved pattern of credit, bills, and payments was to me a treadmill to oblivion. The normal aspirations of house, car, and bank surplus seemed an exercise in absurdity. My life had become inordinately complicated, I thought, for a disciple of Thoreau. Apparently, I did not fit in anywhere, did not particularly want to, and, as the Cold War intensified, again found myself brooding over humanity's collective tendency to mass murder. I had wrenched my body out of Alaska, but couldn't stop thinking about it. Yet Kate had staked a claim on me, and her right to do so was uniformly accepted.

Hanging around our rented house, I grieved for those wilderness activities I could perform in my sleep—hiking, climbing, canoeing, hunting, fishing, chopping, sawing, swimming. In Alaska I'd felt anointed, part of eternity, one with its timelessness. In Galway I was a face in the crowd, a displaced mountain man born a century too late.

When Kate and I met, I'd been an aviation cadet, on top of the world, literally and figuratively. The future had looked rosy then. Now, not knowing what I wanted, nor even how to find out, I felt ineffective, shot down, vanquished.

"All right, if you aren't ready to go to work," Kate snapped at me one night, snatching up a newspaper and turning to the want-ads, "then I will do it myself. But you'll have to stay home and baby-sit."

Kate was intelligent, poised, and idealistic. She made friends easily. Her love of the outdoors did not detract from her love of society. With a degree in social work, mingling came as natural to her as taking a breath. In my absence, it seemed, she'd managed disgustingly well, for which I both admired and envied her.

Kate had a realistic attitude toward money. I didn't seem to know how to get it, apparently did not care about it. Not that I felt it was "the root of all evil," just that I was confused by it, a repugnant and sinister confusion I was sure would catch up with me.

So Kate became a waitress in Schenectady. And I became a house husband.

My first task was to master the hundred-and-one chores all mothers accomplish with their eyes shut—cooking, serving meals, washing dishes, making beds, vacuuming, and mopping. This didn't come naturally, particularly diaper changing. Most wearisome, I found, was that never-ending nuisance of just keeping an eye peeled. But for this I had a full-time assistant—Zeke.

Scott and Billy loved warm, snuggly things; Zeke was both. They loved to throw; Zeke loved to fetch. Later, my boys were fascinated when she delivered a dozen pups. But we didn't have the pups long. I ran an ad, and every potential buyer, charmed by their mother, wanted one to take home. Which made Zeke a larger financial contributor to our family than I.

When the weather turned cold, we boys retreated to the living room, where I would ensconce myself on the sofa and, nose in a book, magic carpet away to literary realms, simultaneously keeping an ear cocked for trouble.

One afternoon while the boys were tossing magazines from the second-floor landing, and Zeke was barking her head off, Cole arrived, plopping onto his usual backward chair, not saying anything, just sitting quietly, grinning. It was unnerving.

I stuck my finger in my book. "What's so damn funny?"

"You really don't see it, do you? That makes it even funnier! Ha, ha."

"Clue me in." I frowned.

"Here you are, hee, hee, a new convert to *Summerhill*, tryin' your damndest not to criticize your boys. But you have three books balanced on every lampshade and you're living in pandemonium. The house is a shambles and you just asked me, 'What's so damn funny?' " He croaked between guffaws.

The book, *Summerhill*, urged parents to look for the good in their children, avoid criticism. I liked the idea; it's what the Eskimos had practiced.

I sat up. "I'll have you know this house is not a shambles!"

"Who says, you or Kate? Ho, ho."

"I suppose it could use a little tidyin' before she gets here."

"A little!"

"Sure. Won't take me an hour."

"Isn't she about due?"

"Well, let's see. I guess you're right." I stood and stretched. "O.K., boys. Knock it off. No more throwing!" (Oops! Don't forget *Summerhill!*) "We're going to play a new game— 'Let's-pick-it-up.' "

Scott and Billy weren't as wild about "Let's-pick-it-up" as they were about "Let's-mess-it-up," but by the time Kate arrived, I had everything under control, including dinner. She greeted us cheerily but retreated to the back bedroom, beckoning me to follow.

Kate was a gorgeous woman, especially undressed. Slipping into casual sweats, she whispered, "Did you ask Cole for supper?"

This was a touchy question. She and Cole had formed a bond while I'd been in Alaska. In fact, Mom had passed on a Galway rumor of late-night hanky-panky, which I'd summarily dismissed. Though he bathed often and kept scrupulously clean, Kate complained that he smelled like motor oil. Kate was a fastidious non-smoker, Cole an inveterate chain-smoker. Late nights I could imagine; hanky-panky I could not.

Cole, no doubt, was lonely, but he never rued it openly. If he ever hankered for a woman, he never talked about it. He always seemed busy doing for "the other guy." Generosity, loyalty, and friendship were his idols. He always carried a wrench and screwdriver in his pocket, the indefatigable Mr. Fix-It. Relationships between words and ideas, not sex organs, were what aroused him. He was apparently capable of sublimating his inner fires and of accepting it as his fate.

Answering Kate, I replied, "Well, I asked him, but he didn't say yes or no."

"Listen, I've had it with him yabbering on for half the night. All he wants to do is talk. I've mentioned it to him again and again, but he never takes me seriously. And he knows I have to get up early. You two guys can do what you want. I'm going to bed at eleven."

"Hell, honey, your bedtime is my bedtime."

"Tell it to Cole."

I returned to the kitchen, but Kate joined us before I brought it up.

I set the table and served. After dinner we sat and chatted in the living room. Topics ranged from flying, Alaska, and truck driving to waitressing, writing, and *Summerhill*. Putting the boys to bed and making and serving coffee were the primary interruptions. As usual, Cole did most of the talking. But precisely at 10:55, we heard a muffled alarm.

Cole grinned, produced a still-ringing clock from his jacket pocket, and held it aloft until it ran down. "Time sure has a way of evaporatin' around here," he explained. "Kate's gotta go to work in the mornin'. Mac's gotta figure out new ways to keep his house-wreckers amused. And I gotta go, right now!" He gulped his coffee, snubbed out his cigarette, scooted forward in his chair, hauled himself erect, and strode toward the door, thanking us for the meal. "See ya when I see ya."

"I'll be damned," Kate chuckled. "After all the nights I sat here squirming. I didn't think he was even aware of it."

"They don't call him 'Ingenuity' for nothing."

Cole, the writer, went unappreciated among his lumberjack cronies. He kept his literary ambitions veiled from them. Because we enjoyed discourse, he visited us often. But his enjoyment was probably more attributable to me than Kate.

Cole and I prized reading, especially good books, and sometimes we'd read them aloud. We also indulged each other's personal flying and wilderness anecdotes. One of mine Cole took home, embellished, and presented to me later.

"Great job!" I enthused over the opening third, making a few minor word changes. "God, don't stop to breathe. Just keep goin'!"

Middle third in hand, I applauded, "Stick with it, buddy! You're on a roll!"

The climax truly stunned me. "Whew! What you sitting here for? Go home, quick!, and type it up! Send it to the best magazine you can find!"

About 7,500 words, it had strong characters, snappy dialogue, suspense, humor, conflict, action, vivid setting, theme. Cole had weaved it from a mere skeleton; all I'd supplied was the incident. I was dumbstruck, especially when he sold it the first time out, with me listed as co-author.

Bluebook paid him $300 and changed his title from "The Eternal Fireball" to "Follow the Leader." But the editors deleted several paragraphs Cole had esteemed. Cole rattled off a fiery complaint. The editor rebutted. Cole zapped out another blitz, and a full-scale fusillade ensued. Finally incensed, the editor blackballed all future manuscripts by Holden and McGill.

I saw it as a tragic end to a foolish clash of egos. Cole had pushed too far, I thought. His anger had truncated what might have been a propitious relationship. But Cole took it casually. And *Bluebook* went out of business in the late '60s, when men's magazines slumped, so the blackballing had no practical effect.

Aside from his testiness, though, Cole, the author, amazed me. He made writing look so easy. Just tap, tap, tap on the typewriter. Sit awhile. Smoke a weed. Chug a little coffee. Tap some more. And presto! There was a story! If, as he'd once suggested, writing was like fencing, then I'd just been touched by a master.

No matter how much I read, wrote, or rewrote, I knew I'd never spin out a yarn as glibly as Cole. Develop an anecdote into a saleable saga? I didn't believe I could do it. But with "Follow the Leader" as a challenge, I felt I had to try. Arbitrarily, I chose one among Cole's multitude of yarns, picked up my pencil, and chewed the eraser.

Finally I strung it out for eight pages with dialogue and characterization, titled it "Shut Up, Please," and started it on its rounds. After several rejections, I concluded it wasn't worth the postage. By then Kate was having problems at the diner, and I was growing bored with house-husbanding.

It was time, I decided, to get a real job.

NEWSMAN

Looking for a job made me feel exposed and defensive. Someone had something I needed: it flew in the face of my self-sufficient fancies. Application might lead to supplication, then to subjugation. With Cyrano, I wanted: "To sing, to laugh, to dream,/ To walk in my own way and be alone . . ." Just thinking about looking for a job gave me the willies. But I screwed up my courage, gathered up my published stories, and went on the prowl.

Having already worked for the U.S. Air Force, the National Park Service, and Fuller Brush, and now wanting to write, I set my sights on our area's seven newspapers—*The Times Union, The Knickerbocker News, The Schenectady Gazette, The Union Star, The Amsterdam Recorder, The Gloversville Leader-Herald,* and *The Saratogian.* With no previous experience and no college degree, I felt I might have the best chance at *The Saratogian.*

Saratoga Springs, a.k.a. The Racing City, was the horse-racing capital of the Northeast. Its newspaper was located just down the hill from main street in a quarter-block two-story brick building. I vaulted up the half dozen steps to the front door, entered, and—two days before John Glenn orbited the earth—met Fred Eaton, managing editor.

Wiry, slight, with thick glasses, Fred murmured approval at my published stories, then produced his standard exam for newcomers—a who-what-where-when-and-how list of facts about a hypothetical incident. "Now we'll see what you know about journalism," he chortled, asking me to assemble these facts into a story. When I handed it back, he shook his head and grumbled. "News stories are written in inverted pyramid style—most important facts at the top. You've written this like an anecdote, important facts at the bottom."

He hired me anyway.

Kate, applauding my success, resigned as a waitress.

Fred seated me in a clump of desks with himself as news editor; Gordon LaSalles, state editor; and Landon Manning, sports editor. Fred was filling in because his last news editor had quit, a not uncommon event, as I learned later.

For the first few days he had me carry basketfuls of copy to the composing room foreman, a job usually reserved for a "copy boy." The foreman parceled out this copy to linotype operators, who set them in lead and gave them to makeup men, who, in turn, arranged them on steel page frames on heavy wheeled tables known as "stones." The composing room reeked of tobacco, sweat, printers' ink, hot oil, hot lead, and various volatile (and consumable) fluids. It rang with a staccato clunking of keys and levers and an undertone of male voices.

After a few days, Fred started me out on the police beat, but I didn't like cops, they didn't seem to like me, and my stories were dull. Next, he let me report on a city council meeting, but I lost salient details amid hasty and illegible scrawls. Then he had me scan competing papers to rewrite important items, but I hated news and lacked judgment. Therefore, I guess he figured, I'd make a perfect editor.

First, I had to learn how to spell—a skill which didn't come easily. The dictionary became my best friend.

Then I had to correct copy—⌐, stet, dele, ⊙ , ⊙ , Wed.), bf , ¶ , ⬚ , ⬚ , # , ∧ , ⌒ , —I had to learn what these marks meant.

Headlines came in many sizes and styles, but initially I was trusted only with those miniature ones which, if botched, would cause us the least embarrassment—one column, 12-point type; two columns, 20-point type. The three-, four-, five-, and six-column heads in large type—the ones everybody read—were reserved for Fred, Gordon, or Landon. But teaching took time, and Fred, with more important details to attend to, gradually foisted me off on Gordon.

Gordy was a slender, bespectacled, white-haired gentleman. He'd worked on newspapers all his life, had seen it all; or, if he hadn't seen it, had at least read about it. As state editor he covered news from the hinterlands, the outlying counties. Every day he faced mounds of drivel from barely literate stringers; every day he quietly made it readable. Though someone once described him as "a stickler for details," we hit it off immediately.

Nearing retirement, Gordy didn't take himself or others too seriously. No matter how misspelled, graceless, or garbled my creations, his response was invariably soft-spoken, encouraging and instructional. He never ridiculed, nor raised his voice. Whether about men or women, whites or blacks, rich or poor, bad or beautiful, each story was vital to Gordy, and he gave it his undivided attention. He seemed amused by humanity's foibles and saddened by its cruelties. Yet he was often pale and world-weary, and some considered him cold and ethereal. I worked like the dickens to please him. Under Gordy's watchful eye, I began to get the hang of it and glowed when he tossed me an occasional larger headline.

At the end of my third week, Fred suggested I use my Alaska experiences as a springboard for a weekly outdoor column. Titled "Wood Smoke," it started March 21, 1962, a month after I walked through the door. The first, devoted strictly to Alaska, brought me a three-cent post card from an apparently thrilled reader: "Congratulations on 'Wood Smoke.' You are off to a good start!" I couldn't stifle my grin.

My second and third columns were also about Alaska; my fourth, after Fred hinted at "too much Alaska," commented on local fishing problems; my fifth, about Cole, earned me much praise, even from Landon, who usually scowled over allotting me sports space.

After that, Fred named me "swing editor," which meant I filled in when someone was sick or vacationing, was responsible for Gordy's and Landon's pages when they were out, and the front page when Fred was out. But from this high point, my career took a nosedive.

Inadvertently I broke a release date on a story about a surprise retirement party, thus killing the surprise. Incensed, the party chairman berated me fiercely over the phone. I called Fred immediately and apologized; he was magnanimous: "Oh, Graham. Don't fret about it. Those things happen in the news business. I'll talk to the guy." Chagrined down to my socks, I was profoundly grateful.

"Wood Smoke" columns six and seven didn't go over well. My eighth, about Eskimos, bombed so universally that Fred asked me to desist.

Actually, I was relieved. I'd begun a weekly ritual of tearing my hair out for column fodder. I felt ill prepared for this new-found career and, as the weeks wore on, completely unprepared for Fred's cold shoulder.

Like most red-blooded Americans, Fred kept up with all the latest on The Race for the Moon. He knew, for instance, that Yuri Gagarin, Soviet cosmonaut, had orbited the earth ten months before Glenn, that Gherman Titov had made sixteen orbits six months before Glenn. From an initial sputtering, the U.S. space program was now getting off the ground, and when Glenn completed his flight, Fred reacted like many other Americans—with an arm in the air . . . but! The Soviets, Fred knew, were still several space shots ahead.

As a former jet pilot, I, too, was fascinated by this Race for the Moon, but I realized what many didn't—that rocket hardware was also used for ICBMs, and that hawks on both sides were tipping them with H-bombs and aiming them at civilians. This made me feel vulnerable, inconsequential, powerless.

In 1962 The Race for the Moon was between *us* and *them*—*us* the good guys, the white-hats, the freedom-lovers; *them* the bad guys, the black-hats, the Communists. I learned through the grapevine that my last column had made Fred suspect I might secretly be one of *them*.

I was stunned! Me? A former fighter pilot? Yet my last column had stated naively:

> "The individual Eskimo served the tribe. The tribe's needs came before his own. They shared food, lodging, and sometimes children and wives—almost everything except clothing, tools, and weapons. It might be called Communism, but it couldn't be compared to that in Russia today."

A week after my last column, M. Scott Carpenter completed three orbits in a Mercury capsule, landed safely, but 250 miles off target. Fred was shocked. Unless we could learn the secrets of pinpoint re-entry, the Communists might win. And that would mean the end of the free world, perhaps of the end of the entire world, the way Fred thought about it.

One June day a gorgeous, poised and tanned woman strode into the office. I couldn't help staring as she talked to Fred.

"Who was that?" I asked after she left.

"Anne LaBastille," Fred said. "Wanted us to run a weekly column about her living alone in the Adirondacks."

"Are we gonna?"

"Not enough local interest. Too specialized and too pricey. I told her to syndicate it."

I thought about her a lot after that—living alone up there in the Adirondacks. How was she able to do it, while I was tied securely to this desk? (I wondered if she needed company.) Later, she told how in her book, *Woodswoman,* and *National Geographic* articles.

When Fred hired a news editor who quit after two days, we chided Fred relentlessly. "Where'd he go, Fred?" "What didya do, Fred, say 'boo'!?" "Yup, that Fred Eaton's a mean hombre." "Hey, Fred, did that guy know somethin' I don't?" Yet, a current of envy ran through my jibes—that guy wasn't working here; I still was.

Saratoga's flat track opened in August, and I was named editor of *The Racing Sheet,* a pink tabloid of results published daily after the last race. *The Saratogian* paid me time-and-a half, and the McGills, now out of debt, needed it to stay afloat. But as Jaipur won the Travers Stakes, then slowed and walked to his stall, *The Racing Sheet* stalled, too, and so did my extra pay.

In September Kate and I decided it would save gas, cut travel time, and give her day-use of the car if we moved from Galway to Saratoga. We rented a house at 173 York St., a mile east and a block north of *The Saratogian,* just across the street from photographer, Bob Mayette.

As October began, Wally Shirra circled the earth six times and landed five miles off target. Fred was reassured.

But on Oct. 22 John F. Kennedy announced that the Soviets had installed offensive missiles in Cuba. Adlai Stevenson proved it with U-2 spy photos on television. And Kennedy ordered a U.S. naval blockade.

As page 1 editor that day, I ran a six-column banner with

a three-column photo of the nuclear-powered aircraft carrier USS *Enterprise* steaming toward the reader. No one complained about story judgment, heads, layout, or anything. "Good job," Fred said, but hired another guy as news editor.

Unlike the first, this guy didn't run away, and I soon saw why: he was meaner than Fred. In fact, he made Fred look like the tooth fairy; he also made my life miserable. Every one of my journalistic anthills he turned into a towering Vesuvius; he reprimanded me publicly for the slightest slip. Hardly a day went by without his hollering and my feeling like poking him in the teeth. Did he expect me to absorb his tirades like a stuffed pillow?

As an aviation cadet, I'd taken plenty of ass-chewings. Then it had been expected treatment, part of the program. But this mirthless tyrant was dead serious. He seemed to believe sincerely that his news room rank established his innate superiority.

Brooding and wishing I were back in Alaska, I began walking to work in the morning dark, then home again in the afternoon.

But he finally quit, too, and I thought Fred should let me have a crack at it, but he hired rotund, good-natured Howard Krieger, whom I learned to like.

Meanwhile, at home, I was cementing the bond I had formed with Scott and Billy. I taught them to rassle and play hide-and-seek. But in December Kate told me she was pregnant again, and the news threw me into a tizzy. I felt trapped, suffocated. Kate's Genie had escaped from the Bottle. My folks showered us with Christmas gifts, but it was small consolation.

In February, almost a year after I was hired, Fred took me to task in front of Gordy, Landon, and others for a spelling error on page 1. For the first time, also in front of others, I gave it back in kind. "Who do you think you are, Eaton, Mr.

Perfect?" He had the last word, but I composed a protest for the publisher.

The next day a sealed personal letter lay on my desk. I eyed it suspiciously. A grateful response? A polite explanation? No. These guys played hardball.

My employment with *The Saratogian*, it hereby informed me, was terminated forthwith.

LOST

To have been fired, sacked, cast into the streets by a man I admired made me feel like a bag of garbage. First I was angry, then depressed, then trapped in between. Even a sweet, personal letter from Gordy didn't help. The more I doubted myself, the more my pregnant wife doubted me, too. But the only way I could think of to pick up the pieces was to do what seemed like desertion to her: visit Cole.

Cole, an outcast, understood being cast out. An ex-flyboy, he knew about an airman's pride. An ex-Adirondacker, he'd harkened to the call of the wild. And having lived through his own anger, depression, and self-doubt, without pretending to tell me what to do with mine, he offered what I needed most—friendship.

So I became a steady caller at Cole's—sitting beside his woodstove, listening to his records, smoking his roll-yerowns, slurping his coffee, laughing at his jokes, and pretending his fibs were the straight scoop.

At Cole's I was no longer a gold-bricking no-account husband son-of-a-bitch who didn't know what to do with himself. I was a welcome guest, temporarily foundering perhaps, but still welcome. And to prove it, he welded me an exact replica of an Alaskan 55-gallon drum woodstove, but from a 20-gallon grease drum, and gave it to me for my birthday. "It'll remind you of Eagle," he beamed. "Keep you warm when you're in the doghouse with Kate. Take it home and set it up in your trailer."

Seeking seclusion, I parked the trailer in the backyard, ran a wire from the house for an electric light, stacked up a little woodpile, and created a cozy writer's den, with Zeke on one side, my new woodstove on the other, and a desk and typewriter in the middle. I spent many happy hours there, scribbling stories about Alaska. But my efforts paid no bills, and Mom, Dad, and Kate fussed. After a month, I went back to Fuller Brushing.

Saratoga and Gloversville were like night and day for a Fuller Brushman. Saratogians attended horse races, placed bets, and lived in the fast lane; Gloversvillians tanned skins, stitched leather, and manufactured usable products.

My delivery man was Victor Rhodes, retired black aristocrat—quiet, wry, twice as old and ten times as wise. Though crippled, he was more reliable than any other delivery boy I'd hired. One customer berated me for sending "a colored" around with his order; he never got the chance to place another.

One afternoon in early May, as I was about to move my car, my eye just happened to flick past my rear tire. Propped against it was a three-inch spike. I removed it, climbed in, and started. But I'd forgotten to look at my other tires. I shut off the engine, bailed out, and circled. As I suspected—three more spikes! If I'd rolled forward one inch! Four flats! Stranded! Work day shot! Needing a tow truck! Bank balance decimated! Scanning the area, I spotted the culprit ducking behind a hedge. But could I catch him and prove it?

If I hadn't just happened to glimpse that spike . . . Downcast at the thought of my barely avoided disaster, holding my head in my hands, too upset to visit another housewife,

I headed for Cole's house.

In late May Kate's mother, Emmy, arrived to help Kate with her last stages of pregnancy. Emmy stayed a month and, like all mothers-in-law, changed the character of our house. Beginning every day at breakfast, the two women would cluck and yammer like bitty hens. Every day I plied the streets and returned to a two-woman freeze-out. I spent many hours with Zeke in my trailer that month, spinning dreamy yarns about Alaska.

One afternoon Emmy caught Scott going pee-pee on the lawn. She snatched him up, whaled his butt, and dressed us down as if we'd perpetrated a felony. Remembering *Summerhill*, I challenged Kate: "Who does she think she is?

"Don't make a federal case out of it," Kate retorted. "She'll be gone soon."

As the weather warmed and the days turned sunny, I fell into a slump. I knew it was my attitude, but I couldn't seem to change it. Despite long hours and snatched lunches, I couldn't give my stuff away. At most houses, no one answered the door. When they did answer, they didn't want my free gift. When they did want my free gift, they didn't want to let me in. When they did let me in, they didn't want to buy anything. My slump deepened into a full-fledged funk.

I kept daydreaming about Eskimos, moose hunts, and fish camps.

The last straw fell when, making my rounds, I knocked and a woman's voice yelled, "Come in!" I entered and waited by the door. But seeing me inside, she screamed and came after me with a broom. I retreated to my car and sulked. What was I doing here? Why did I tolerate this hateful profession? Why wasn't I traipsing around Alaska?

Later, I learned that Saratoga's previous Fuller Brushman had raped a customer and been forced to leave town. By then it was too late.

Early the next morning I put my ax, adz, tent, sleeping bag, '06, and Zeke in my car and headed out . . . first stop: Cole's house.

FAILED HERMIT

Knowing Cole would be still asleep, I marched in anyway, greeted his two dogs, cleaned out his percolator, refilled the strainer, and plugged in the pot. It gurgled as I slouched in his easy chair and he sawed wood in the back bedroom. After it perked, I sipped java and riffled his magazines, until, coughing and cinching his bathrobe, Cole shuffled past me to the sink. "Hiya, Mac. Thought I heard someone out here. Ain't you workin' today?"

"Just quit. You're the first to know. Make you feel honored?"

He halted. "You've told Kate, of course."

"Nope, she thinks I'm in Saratoga." I grinned. He didn't.

He turned and splashed water on his face. "Fuller Brushes must be really rufflin' your fur."

"Yup. The housewives hate me, I'm sick of slammed doors, and I can't make a dime. But I have a plan."

"Oh?" He blinked at me over his towel.

"I've decided to become a hermit." I sounded sure, certain.

He snickered, but his eyes popped. "You're kiddin', of course."

"I'm *not* kiddin'. You're gonna drive me up the highway,

177

drop me off in the boonies, take the car back to Kate, and explain."

"Explain what?"

"I'm not coming back."

He ogled me. "Kate'll probably call the cops."

"So what? How'll they know where I am unless you tell?"

Cole rubbed his chin and coughed. "Whew! I ain't even awake yet." He sprawled on his backward chair, rested his hammy arms on its back, and stared at me. "Now let me get this straight. You want me to help you go AWOL, then come back and tell Kate."

"Right."

"You got ammo, chow, everything?"

I nodded.

"You wanna do this now, immediately? Whatsa matter with tomorrow?"

"I'm ready now."

"Tomorrow you might change your mind."

"Cole, I've been thinkin' about this for months." That wasn't quite true. I'd been thinking about Alaska, not the Adirondacks. It would have been more true to have told him I felt smothered by "genies in the bottle," that I needed Kate's attention.

"Hell! I'm not even dressed!" he growled.

"Well, get with it! I've still gotta check out the country, find a likely lookin' spot and camp. All before dark!"

"O.K., O.K. Let me rustle some stuff together. Be witcha in a jiff." He dropped the towel and clomped to the bedroom, dressed, ate, and was ready in half an hour—some kind of record for him, I figured. As he followed me to the car, I handed him the keys and motioned him into the driver's seat so we wouldn't have to switch when he let me out. Zeke, Silver and Sarge, her two grown pups, piled into the back. He steered west to Gloversville on Rt. 29A, then north up Rt. 10 toward Arietta. "Headin' this way out of habit, I guess.

Got any better ideas? Know where you wanna go, exactly?"

"Nope. Can't see as it makes much difference."

"Well, it might. You wanna be near water and not too far from deer. That probably means a lake."

"Yup."

"Dad's old huntin' camp on the back side of Little Trout would be ideal. Used to call it 'the pantry' 'cause it had so many deer. Creek for drinkin' is right handy, too."

"Suits me."

"Another thing. You're gonna be mighty glad for company after you've been there awhile. If I know where you are, I might just drop in now and then."

"You won't bring the cops, will you?"

"Who, me?" He beamed.

"Any trout in Little Trout Lake?"

"Used to be. All perch now."

No salmon, no northerns, no trout. I pursed my lips.

"Nothing wrong with perch if you catch enough. I've eaten 'em by the barrelful."

As we approached Arietta, Cole grew uncommonly quiet. Every other time we'd driven up here he'd run on like a carnival barker about his old stomping grounds—the amusement park and Sherman's dance hall at Caroga Lake, the house of this and that personage, the school, the logging roads, the lumber mill, the holding ponds, bridge building. I wasn't used to him speechless.

"What's a matter, buddy? You still sleepy?"

"No. I'm thinkin' about Kate. You've put me in one helluva position, in case you haven't realized it. She's gonna blow all her fuses."

"I doubt it. Half the time she doesn't act like she knows I exist."

At last we approached the river. "Hell, Cole, this is fine. Pull over anywhere along here."

He did and we stopped.

Zeke bounded out. We collared Silver and Sarge, then crawled out ourselves. Cole opened the trunk. I wrenched my pack up, steadied it on the bumper and hunched into the straps. Cole boosted, I hefted and wobbled under it till it settled into place. He closed the trunk and sat on the bumper.

"Helluva load you got there."

I held out my hand. "Tell Kate I'm sorry, will you?"

"Ain't gonna help."

"Sorry, too, to have rousted you out so early."

" 'Twon't kill me."

"Thanks for the lift."

"Where you headed?"

"Probably Little Trout."

He nodded.

I turned and trudged toward the forest.

"See ya when I see ya," Cole called.

From the woods, I heard his engine start and wheels crunch gravel. Then it was quiet.

I flopped on the duff, contemplating what I'd just done. Zeke and I felt at home in the woods. But where was my real home? In Eagle, where I'd left a sodhouse? In Galway, where my parents spent their summers? In Saratoga, where Kate and I rented? The only place I'd ever really felt at home was Alaska. Certainly not the Adirondacks.

Three weeks later, I'd killed and partially eaten an out-of-season doe, agonized over game wardens, built a lookout in a tree, and experienced the pits of loneliness. Thoreau had been my hero, but I couldn't stand solitaire. I was ready to go home.

Early one morning, Cole's rowboat appeared out of the fog. I grabbed his painter. "What gets you up at this hour?"

"You, of course." He stepped out. "Well, not you exactly. That she-male you abandoned back there in town. She's gettin' agitated."

"Well, come on over and sit. Fire's warm, water's hot."

"Fact is, I could use some coffee 'bout now. Just left your place a couple of hours ago. Haven't hit the hay yet."

"You must be dead."

"Hell, Mac. Kate wants you home. Now. Today. She misses you fierce. Can't stand it another minute."

"Been thinkin' along those lines myself."

"Eh? What? Will you please repeat that?"

"I know. I've been inconsistent. Can't seem to figure myself out lately. Been waiting to leave all week."

"You mean I won't have to hog-tie you? Rassle you in the dust? Put up with your rantin' and ravin'?"

"Oh, come on."

"Well, then let's do 'er. We ain't gettin' anywhere settin' here gabbin'."

We gulped our coffee and packed. I hid the doe parts in a duffel bag. By the time we'd finished and loaded, the fog had burned off and the sky was bright. We paused for a last look.

"Beautiful campsite." I leaned against a birch. Knowing myself, I figured I'd probably long for it once back in town. *Once back in town.* The words struck a chord of apprehension. What was I sticking my neck into this time, I wondered.

Cole untied the rope and shoved off. Zeke and Cole's two dogs plunged in and followed.

MOM TO THE RESCUE

Though I was pungent as a pickle and taut as a kindergarten kid when Cole dropped me off, Scott and Billy apparently didn't notice and fell all over me. And Kate seemed as calm as if I'd just dropped in for lunch. But I slunk off to the shower stall and returned an hour later, desmoked, degrimed and deodorized.

"Missed you." Kate smiled, easing my tension. I'd expected her to act distant, wounded.

"I missed you, too." I could not, at that moment, out loud, have revealed my soul-deep longing for her and our boys.

"I really appreciated your leaving me the car."

"I certainly had no use for it. How've you been feeling lately? Baby O.K.?"

She patted her belly. "Baby's fine. I'm feeling heavy, same as I always feel at this stage. But the doc rates us in the pink."

"Good."

"So, where'd you go, anyway? Have fun?"

Feeling relieved to have something to talk about, I described Holdens' camp at the back of Little Trout, my lookout tree, out-of-season doe slaughter, a spooked dog pack, and game warden hysteria. Cole would've added a lot as backup, but I was glad he wasn't there. Soon we adjourned to the kitchen for a venison dinner, where Kate, possibly charmed by my voice, or my masculine presence, or something, began to loosen up.

After dinner, I called my folks. They sounded relieved I was home—fearful for the future, but relieved.

In bed that night I asked, "See the folks often while I was gone?"

"Every weekend. They were very worried. Your Mom didn't think you were coming back. Which reminds me. Your Fuller Brush manager's been calling every day."

"I'll call him in the morning."

"What're you gonna do?"

"Quit."

"How'll we eat and pay the rent?"

"Maybe the folks'll let us move back to The Farm."

"We still need money."

"I know."

"I don't want to move back to The Farm. Your Mom doesn't like me."

It wasn't exactly that Mom didn't like Kate. It was more that Mom was making Kate feel unwelcome to protect herself against what she felt was the Catholic church's unfair treatment. At the time of our wedding, Mom had tried to dissuade me from signing the church's marriage stipulations—one in particular—not to practice any form of birth control, except rhythm. Four pregnancies and five-and-a-half years later—I could hardly blame Mom.

A few weeks later Kate went into labor and gave birth to Laura Beth, six pounds, four ounces, on June 15, 1963, at St. Mary's Hospital in Amsterdam. I picked them up a week later and moved them back to The Farm.

What was I going to do with myself? Where was I going to work next? I didn't have the faintest idea.

Then Mom, an avid reader, handed me *There Is a River*, a biography of Edgar Cayce. The book told how, as a young

traveling salesman in Hopkinsville, Ky., Cayce had lost his
voice and was unable to make a living. He visited several
doctors, to no avail. Hypnosis was all the rage in 1900, for
healing and entertainment, so he tried that. But it worked
only while he was entranced. Eventually, he sought help
from Al C. Layne, osteopath and neighbor. Layne suggested,
after hypnotizing Cayce, that he "see this body and prescribe for the trouble" himself. Cayce replied, "Yes, we can
see the body."

The trouble, Cayce explained, was poor circulation. He
advised Layne to suggest that the circulation increase;
Layne did. Cayce's throat turned red. Twenty minutes later,
Cayce proclaimed the condition improved. Layne suggested he awaken. And Cayce's voice was restored.

Intrigued, Layne persuaded Cayce to let him test his talent on himself, then his patients. The sleeper seemed able
to diagnose and prescribe for anyone, location notwith-
standing. Both were astounded.

The tale made me ponder the Voice, suspect that it wasn't
"just luck," that "something" in me had actually "seen" that
moose.

Cayce recalled nothing of this when he awoke, but gained
confidence over the years as he watched a long procession
of healed people. Eventually, he acquired a stenographer,
who wrote down everything. During his life he gave over
14,000 "readings."

Cayce's encounter with Arthur Lammers in 1923, a
wealthy printer from Dayton, Ohio, upset the apple cart.
Lammers asked him about life's deepest mysteries. Who are
we? Where do we come from? Where are we going? What is
life's purpose? The sleeping Cayce mapped out a divine plan
that included the Eastern concept of reincarnation,
whereby "an entity" kept returning to earth until it developed enough virtue to escape. Another book, *Many
Mansions,* discussed karma, a sort of law of divine justice. It

described suffering as a present-life opportunity for over-coming past-life transgressions.

I could see why Mom was enthused—Cayce's ideas seemed to embrace both Kate's Catholicism and our agnosticism. What one professed, in Cayce's view, was irrelevant. The application of ideals, what one did with what one believed, was what ultimately mattered.

When we'd both finished reading, Mom, a new Cayce fan herself, sought our reaction.

"Very interesting," Kate insisted. "Reincarnation sounds so plausible. I can't see why the church doesn't teach it."

My jaw dropped. I'd expected her to scoff. I reached out and squeezed her shoulder. Her openmindedness, her eagerness made me want to hug her. For the first time in our lives, we'd found a meeting ground, a place where we could come together, hold hands, let our "genies out of the bottle."

But on another level, I felt qualms. The story, reincarnation, karma, Cayce's insistence on an ideal—it all sounded reasonable to me. But I was still faced with the same me. I still longed to be in Alaska. Still didn't care about money. Still felt lackadaisical. Was still unemployed. I needed some ill-defined, amorphous brand of help, now. And Cayce was dead. "O.K., Mom," I wanted to ask, "now what?"

After returning to New Rochelle, perhaps sensing this, Mom set off on another tack.

She called me long distance. "There's a man in New York I want you to meet."

"Oh?"

"Name's Jack Cooper. A psychiatrist who's studied Cayce. Has a nice voice on the phone. I think you'll like him."

"No, Mom, I don't need a damn shrink!"

"Dr. Cooper believes in reincarnation. Can you believe it?"

"You think I'm crazy?"

"No. But I want you to meet this man."

"Why?"

"Why not?"

"It's a long drive. It'll be a royal pain."

"What else're you doing, right now, that's so awfully important?"

I bit my lip.

"Well?"

"Nothing, I guess."

"O.K., then. That's why I want you to meet Dr. Cooper."

"He gonna get me a job?"

"No. He might help you in other ways."

"Ilow?"

"You never know. I want you to do this, Graham. Please. Just because I asked you."

"It'll be expensive."

"Call it a contribution to your continuing education."

"Aw, Mom," I sighed.

"Just once."

"O.K. Just once. I guarantee I won't like him."

The cheeky woman had already made the appointment. And I knew she was right: I wasn't doing anything more important. So two weeks later, leaving Kate home with the kids, I drove to New Rochelle, met Dr. Cooper the next day at his office in New York City, and drove back to Galway the next day—a lot of miles for a one-hour chat, I thought. But Mom was mollified. Dr. Cooper was easygoing, direct, and droll, and somehow, against my better judgment, had talked me into a second appointment.

In the meantime, life went on at The Farm. Kate continued her regular attendance at church, as was her wont. Dad and Mom, as was their wont, continued paying our bills. Zeke came in heat again, as was her wont, attracting her usual coterie of panters. Planting and weeding, as was my wont, allowed me to look busy. And a first!—Kate and I had something in common to talk about, some hope for a fundamental accord. We were actually laughing together, cooing, and yakking it up.

Cole gave me a "doodlebug," a homemade tractor cobbled together from junk trucks. It had no springs, huge cleated rear tires, heavy chains, and a wicked low gear. After a crank start it would drag almost anything I hooked it to. Immediately, I began cutting and skidding dead elms back to the yard, an activity which reminded me of Alaska and gave me, though financially decrepit, a sensation of unstoppable power. True, it didn't put immediate cash in our pockets, but every stick reduced our winter fuel bill.

Now retired, Mom continued searching out other avenues for "my continuing education." One weekend at The Farm, while we four adults were sitting around the living room, Mom asked, "How would you and Kate like your own life readings?"

"What's a life reading?" I raised an eyebrow.

"You remember from *There Is a River.* Cayce gave life readings. It discusses your current life situation in terms of past lives."

"Who from?"

"I have friends." She smiled enigmatically.

Kate said, "Sounds interesting."

Dad stared at the wall.

"What friends?" I scratched my ear.

"Exceptional people. The only ones I know in the country who do this. They live in California." Mom wasn't smiling now.

"Do what, exactly?"

"They're husband and wife, a team. She goes into a trance, and he conducts the reading. She acts as a medium for a spirit named Jered. Similar to Cayce."

"Cayce didn't use spirits. Warned against it, in fact."

"Well, this works for my friends. They're very popular. There's a long waiting list. If I make a request now, it'll take months."

"What do you think, Dad?"

"This is your Mom's project." He kept staring at the wall. "Don't know a thing about it."

"You must have an opinion," I prodded.

He chuckled, "No, I don't, actually. Your Mom and I don't share everything, you know. And we don't always agree either. I don't even know who she's talking about."

"Could be fascinating," Kate put in. "I'm excited."

Mom nodded. "O.K. with you, Graham?"

I shrugged.

"Then I'll request two readings as soon as we get back to New Rochelle."

ANOTHER VOICE

The tape version of my life reading arrived in Galway in October, 1963.

It had been recorded by the Van der Slykes in a hotel room while they were traveling around the country, talking to groups about life after death and mediumship. Mom, Kate, and I had supplied them with background information and a list of questions.

I set our tape player on the kitchen table, placed the spool on its pin, and fed the tape around rollers and through the pickup mechanism. Mom and Kate waited. Dad opted out.

I pressed PLAY and Fred began:

"Our Father in heaven, we come now in deep earnestness in behalf of thy servants, the McGills, who certainly are in an unusual life situation, trying and testing each one involved.

"And Father, from the perspective and from the line of vision of earth, we cannot see much of an answer. We do not see the forces at work, we do not see the purposes at work.

"And so, from a vantage point higher than our own . . . " Fred ended the prayer, then counted backward from ten while Gwen entered her trance. Then Fred said, "Is Jered here? We ask for Jered."

A deep masculine voice superimposed itself on Gwen's alto. "Yes. I am here."

It was a voice from another world, from the land of the dead. Or was it? If she were faking, it was a remarkable performance. The hair prickled on the back of my neck.

Jered/Gwen: "Now let's get right into the major problems and questions he has . . .

"He is a young soul in earth-living, basically a feminine soul in a dominantly feminine life cycle but with masculine lives introduced, so that, as this soul goes along in earth-living, it may keep fairly balanced in development between the feminine side of its being and the masculine side.

"Now his great love for the out-of-doors, his intense feeling of at-homeness in the North, is the result of a strong carry-over from the past life, the lifetime immediately prior to this, which was in the 1800s and very early 1900s—at which time he was in the Yukon Territory."

I pressed STOP. "There's no such place as the Yukon Territory. It's the Northwest Territories, or the Yukon."

"Never mind, Graham," Mom clucked. "He's a spirit, not a geographer. Give him a little leeway, will you?"

I pressed PLAY.

Fred: "Yes . . . Now what was the racial strain of that incarnation?"

Jered/Gwen: "He was in the Eskimo tribe."

I pressed STOP. "The Eskimos are a race, not a tribe."

Mom scowled. "Oh, Graham!"

I pressed PLAY.

Jered/Gwen: "Now he was in the feminine valence at that time. The girl had a brother, a twin, and this twin was the soul mate of this one. This, you see, gave them a very close lovebond, and the girl in a particular way admired her brother. She often expressed the wish that she had been born his brother, rather than his sister because there were many things he could do that she as a woman could not do. He had freedom to go out, to roam the woods, to hunt, to fish; her duties were at home, but she longed to be with him, to be his companion. And many times she said, 'If I were a man, I would live my life just like my brother.' "

I pressed STOP. "Two things: There are no 'woods' where the Eskimos live. It's all ice, snow, and tundra. Also, Eskimo women do almost everything their men do, except hunt walrus and whales. It's a hard life. They have to!"

"Will you please let Jered have his say." Mom swirled the ice in her martini.

I pressed PLAY.

Jered/Gwen: "Now this identification with her brother colored her whole life. He had this great love of the out-of-doors and a sense of freedom that did not encourage a feeling in him for marriage, nor did it encourage any young woman who got to know him very well. So he did not marry. What he did was take his sister with him and go off on long hunting trips. He would install her in a little camp with the provisions, and then he would go and hunt. And she was very happy; she accepted this. She loved this kind of life. And repeatedly there was the declaration that, 'If I could be a man, I would live my life as my brother lives.'"

Fred: "Really setting quite a pattern, then, in the subconscious."

Jered/Gwen continued, "This young soul was brought into masculine living to experience the power of the will to pattern an earth life. The beloved brother is not in this lifetime. But the peace, the sense of completeness that Graham finds [in the North] are very real. They are not counterfeits, not compensations."

I grunted my assent. Mom and Kate looked rapt.

Jered/Gwen said, "It is the purpose of a feminine soul coming into masculine living to take hold of the circumstances in the time and the culture into which the soul incarnates, but progress has been short-circuited by this strong self-will carried over. Now the question arises, what to do about this?"

Fred: "RIGHT!"

Jered/Gwen: "The forces set in motion by the former life personality have got to be met and either fulfilled through expression or have drawn from them the content of emotions . . . The quickest way is for Graham to go North and give himself a quite extended period of time experiencing the kind of life he pictures for himself . . . This cannot be done in six months or a year. It would probably take two or three years. Now this poses problems because Graham has a wife and three children. They are not going to be the losers. If anyone is the loser, it will be Graham. He could lose his wife and children. But this desire on Graham's part is not a whim. It is not due to psychological forces of the present lifetime.

"Now there is an alternative. It is not impossible for Graham to make the choice that the sacrifice of family is too great and, therefore, he by sheer will power will put away, put from him, and himself turn away from these deep desires. But this procedure can seemingly tear him to pieces. It would be a mighty struggle. Frankly, we do not recommend it."

Fred: "Has he had any previous masculine lives?"

Jered/Gwen: "No. Actually, the personality is the victim in this lifetime. It is the victim of the strong forces feeding in from the soul. We would suggest that he make his plans and go North for a period of two or three years. Cut his ties."

Go North! Return to Alaska! But I'd already tried that, twice! Smirking and shaking my head, I seriously doubted the wisdom of this so-called spirit guide.

Jered/Gwen continued: "Now we cannot say which would be right from the point of view of the Divine Plan, because this is Graham's decision. Actually, either way is right. The force from the past will be met and either fulfilled by giving expression to it, or it will be conquered by a decision of the will. His ongoing pattern, the divine pattern for him, will follow the path he chooses."

Fred then recapped, seeking assurance that he understood. Next he asked about past-life relationships.

Jered/Gwen claimed that Mom had been my grandmother in an Italian life in the 1400s. Cole was said to have been my husband in that same life. And Robby had allegedly been a friend of my Eskimo brother in the last life. That was all. Jered/Gwen said I'd had no previous relationships with my father, brother, wife, or children. According to Jered/Gwen, I was here practically alone, with nothing to work out with anybody!

Fred: "Well, this covers what Graham has asked that this reading cover . . . Is there a final word for Graham at this time?"

Jered/Gwen: "We want to emphasize that from the soul point of view there is no right and wrong choice. God's plan for him can take one of two directions equally well. And so there should be no condemnation by himself *of* himself, or by others close to him, of him, for either decision."

Fred: "Thank you very much, Jered. And thanks to all those who had a part in bringing this through. I will now bring Gwen back. Ten, nine, eight, seven, six, five, four, three, two, one. Here you are. Hello."

In her normal alto, Gwen answered, "Hello."

I pressed STOP and REWIND, as Mom and Kate chatted.

"Wasn't that interesting?" Kate stretched.

"It certainly was," Mom nodded.

Mimicking Jered, Kate spoke in her lowest register. "That spirit certainly has a deep voice."

Mom chortled.

Kate rested her chin on her hand. "I wonder who *he* was in past lifetimes."

"He hasn't been incarnate for a thousand years," Mom explained. "He's past the need, according to their brochure." She measured me. "What'd you think about it, Graham?"

"A crock," I snapped. "The biggest pile of crap I ever heard."

Mom grimaced. "You think it was fake?"

"Just wrong!"

"How?"

"Just wrong. In a hundred ways. But who am I? Not a spirit guide! I certainly can't prove it!"

She reeled back. "Then the whole thing was a waste of money."

"That's the truest statement I've heard since this tape started. I'm goin' for a walk." I stalked out the back door, Zeke at my heels.

One thing I noted: my feelings for Alaska had not been belittled. " . . . very real . . . not counterfeits, not compensations," the spirit had said. I felt grateful for that, but still belittled.

" . . . not due to psychological forces of the present lifetime," the spirit had said—and that was not true. I'd nurtured my love for Alaska by reading, thinking, and traveling there. Jered/Gwen hadn't mentioned the traits that had attracted me to the Eskimos—humor, playfulness, courage, ingenuity, cleverness and stolidity in the face of hardships, their reverence for each other, for the land and the animals. And my fear that we'd all be incinerated in an impending holocaust—the fear that had mesmerized American consciousness for a decade—the spirit hadn't even alluded to that, as if it weren't important. Maybe when you were dead, you didn't care.

Angrier by the minute, I stormed through the woods, grousing and ignoring Zeke's stares.

What did he mean by "valence"?—I was not a damned molecule. What did he mean, "a young soul"? According to Cayce, all souls were created at once. How could one be younger or older? I didn't feel like any cosmic kid. What did he mean, "basically a feminine soul"? I certainly was no woman! What did he mean I'd had no past lives as a man?—didn't he know I'd been an officer and a gentleman, an air force jet jock, one of the bewinged elite?

I gave that spirit my most obscene mental finger, muttered "bull" a dozen times, as if the repetition would salve my bruised ego, then punctuated my tirade with a real-life middle finger, jabbed into the air where I hoped that spirit was sitting. But he seemed as isolated from consequences as a wind-breaking bypasser at Grand Central Station.

That night in bed, still chewing: Why no past-life ties with my father, brother, wife, or kids? Was that true? How could I know? Cayce often saw groups, especially relatives, returning together. He often outlined patterns where an "entity" had fallen short and returned to serve those he'd wronged. Wanting to run off to Alaska, that pattern seemed to apply to me. But if it hadn't been for my family, I wouldn't have had a reason to come back!

For the next few days, Kate and Mom talked as if they'd bought the whole thing—lock, stock, and barrel. They seemed to have embraced it totally, arm-in-arm in lockstep—bosom buddies, a pair, a united twosome—like Kate and Esther, and Kate and Emmy before them. I remained the holdout, the doubter, ostracized. I felt emasculated.

Then Dad listened to the tape and took me aside, "I don't believe a word of it, Graham, and I don't blame you for being ticked. All that past-life malarkey! Hokum! Poppycock! How could you ever prove it? For all we know, it's a clever scam. I simply can't see you as a 'young feminine soul.' Compared to whom, I want to know. If I were you, I'd forget it and quit brooding. And the sooner the better."

That raised my spirits, but I still didn't have a job, didn't feel like getting one, and spent most of my time at Cole's engaged in chit-chat.

About this time the Van der Slykes made a brief visit to New York City. Kate, learning of this through Mom and now armed with hindsight and curiosity about the actual trance process, went to their hotel to witness her private reading. I remained home with Scott, Billy, and Laura Beth.

A week later, after the Van der Slykes had had time to make a copy from their master tape and type up a transcript, Kate's reading arrived in the mail. First Kate reviewed it in private, then put it on the player. Again, Dad opted out.

Kate's reading began like mine, with Fred and Gwen praying aloud, and immediately piquing my suspicion with that presumptuous phrase: " . . . from a realm and a vantage point *higher than* our own . . . " Who said it was higher? Fred and Jered/Gwen?—I didn't believe it. For hadn't Cayce said we were all spirits, and that the dead didn't necessarily know more than the living?

Kate's reading asserted that she was the basically masculine half of the soul; that she was older and more advanced than I was; that she had had many lifetimes as both a man and a woman; that she'd shared lifetimes with all our children, but not with me; that she'd been a playboy in Italy in the 1600s, had sown wild oats, and had died of alcoholism at 42; that she'd been a French nun in a Canadian religious order in the last life.

I wouldn't have bet a penny on any of it.

When Fred said, "Kate feels that Graham's reading really spoke truly of him," I got up and stalked out. How could Kate possibly think my reading spoke truly of me? What could I, a spirit encased in a body, possibly say to counter the pronouncements of a ghost? How could two human beings—Kate and myself—hearing the same testimony, come to such conflicting conclusions? Boycott was the only way I knew to express myself.

But that night, with Mom and Kate yammering about what I'd missed, I finally listened to the rest of Kate's tape.

Jered/Gwen continued: "Well, now here we will speak very frankly and it is probably a good thing that that personality [Graham] is not present at this time . . . " Kate, in sharing, apparently didn't see the need for exclusivity.

Jered/Gwen said that Kate was brought in to open up to me "quite a different path of living, which will bring much needed growth in a different direction." After restating the belief that I should return to Alaska, Jered/Gwen said, "Now he may find through that experience that that is not at ALL the type of life he wants, not at ALL. And he may very gladly and very eagerly, and very successfully then, take hold of this other pattern of life already established for him, already gotten a start through his marriage to Kate."

This sounded like a bald-faced turnaround. My reading had stated that this might "tear him to pieces . . . would be a mighty struggle," and "we do not recommend it."

Jered/Gwen asked, "Now why is Kate in the picture from her point of view?

"Well, in part it is karmic—not in detail; but it is a balancing of that Italian lifetime which refused to take responsibility, refused to settle down, refused marriage and children, and refused making a success of life. The soul didn't do it in masculine expression." That made sense, if I understood karma.

Fred said, "It has been pointed out that essentially the unit is Kate and the three children, at least for now, as the present picture seems to unfold. Looking further ahead, if Graham decides to stay in Alaska, would it be good for the children to have another father-figure come in, and would it be good for Kate to remarry?"

Jered/Gwen: "Very definitely, yes."

Neither Kate nor I had mentioned divorce. And here they were discussing Kate's remarriage! Wasn't that a little premature?

My anger rose to cold fury, the colder for being futile. Oh, to throttle that spectral meddler! That interfering piece of smoke! But it was not here, not anywhere! I raised my frustrated fingers to heaven.

Finally, I pushed PLAY and listened to the rest of Kate's tape.

When Fred asked the location of my last lifetime, a query relayed through Kate from me, Jered/Gwen refused to give it, asserting that, if he did, I'd be tempted to go there, settle down and "the growth of this lifetime would be finished." Or, to put it another way, we know but won't tell. As if I had to be protected from my own worst impulses. I spat!

Then Fred asked, "How can Kate best help Graham, now and in the future?" and Jered/Gwen's answer smoothed my ruffled feathers: "The most helpfulness will be for her to cultivate and express toward him an utter self-givingness, a BIGNESS of spirit which expresses understanding of him; and a willingness to, in a sense, sacrifice, give up her pattern of life for his."

Well, now that's more like it! I thought.

Fred closed the reading as he'd closed mine, counting Gwen back to consciousness.

"Genies in the bottle." Everywhere. I shut off the machine and stalked upstairs to bed.

ANOTHER WORLD

After Mom and Dad departed, I detected subtle changes in Kate—a snap in the easy sway of her walk, a click in her usually musical brogue, an extra millimeter in the out-thrust of her chin. Where once she might have hesitated, now she tended to interrupt. Where once she might've discussed, now she was disposed to direct. Where once she might've flirted, now she leaned toward ridicule. Her normal geniality developed a brittle edge, as if some inner battle had been decided. Yet hadn't she just been informed—from a "vantage point *higher than*" her own—that she was my spiritual superior? Yet, at times I decided I was imagining the whole thing, because she wasn't consistent.

The Van der Slykes were to speak at the Unity Church in lower Manhattan at the end of November, 1963, and Mom, hailing it as "the chance of a lifetime," invited us to attend at her expense. I hated being dependent on my parents. As an air force pilot, I'd known the joy of breaking free even from the earth. Shekels, marks, liras, francs, yens, pesos, lucre, dough, bread, greenbacks, spondulics—whatever you called it—this was the means by which civilian rank was decided: those who had it ruled, those who didn't served. Having no sense for it, no knowledge of how to manage it,

I'd let my savings slip through my fingers and now faced the penalties of indigence.

I still had no job, could think of nothing I wanted to do, except escape to Alaska, and felt more depressed each day. Rather than helping, the life readings had exacerbated my dilemma.

They contained specific information aimed directly at me! And while I scoffed at most of it, I didn't know now what else to believe. Cayce made sense, but was too religious, too general. The concept of reincarnation seemed reasonable—but a young, naive, feminine soul? That really grated.

Jered/Gwen had interpreted my desire for self-sufficiency in terms of need and ineptitude. Courage, will power, self-reliance, confidence, and persistence—what I thought my masculine strengths—they had ignored. I was not weaker, nor unmanly for having left the military and ventured to Alaska. And the one person who seemed to understand this was Cole.

Cole, while praising Edgar Cayce, distanced himself from the Van der Slykes, an attitude which helped preserve my sanity. One summer evening he began what became a tradition at The Farm, starting a fire against a huge elm stump in the side yard. Then we dragged up lawn chairs and arranged ourselves around it in a semicircle, slurping coffee and swapping lies. The next night the same, and the next and the next. The six-foot thick stump only reached heat-reflecting perfection after a dozen blazes had sculpted it hollow. The next stage left it a charcoal crescent, then a few flimsy uprights which eventually crumbled into ashes, thus initiating a hunt for new stumps.

Cole did most of the talking at these stump fires, and Scott and Billy loved it. They gaped as sparks streaked toward the twinkling cupola of stars—Sirius, Castor, Pollox, Deneb, Capella, Vega—and constellations—the Dippers, Lyra, Cygnus, Arcturus, Aquilla, Scorpio, and Sagittarius—

stage lights for a symphony of owls, whippoorwills, night-
hawks, crickets, frogs, occasional jets, and now and then a
far-off truck. But eventually my boys, nodding off, would
need to be trundled into the house, where Kate, tarrying,
would remain, while Cole and I gabbed endlessly into the
night.

I often spent all day with Scott and Billy, looping a rope
around an elm branch to make a swing, accompanying
them on romps in the woods, helping them on rainy days
to find boy-sized nooks and crannies for hide-and-seek,
and stranding fish in the pond's outlet. But fish reminded
me of Alaska, which I seldom mentioned to them; it was too
painful.

Meanwhile, every other week, I was driving to New Rochelle and back, keeping appointments with Dr. Cooper. He
had studied our life readings, and I didn't trust his reaction.
At times he seemed understanding and wise, at others, critical. Like Mom and Kate, he apparently accepted the life
readings at face value. Did he interpret my skepticism as
false pride? I suspected so.

On one downstate visit in late November, Mom
screamed, "Graham, come quick! Kennedy has been shot!"
All afternoon and into the night, we watched television re-
runs of the president's assassination, while the nation
recoiled in horror. On the way to Galway the next day, desperately wishing I were in Alaska, I was sure it was a Soviet
plot and that nuclear war was upon us. My mind reeled.

A week later, Kate and I left food and water for Zeke, who
had a den for her three new pups under Mom's reading cottage, then, with Scott, Billy, and Laura Beth in tow, headed
downstate to hear the Van der Slykes.

The Unity church was a quaint, old brownstone building, satiny oak woodwork, and many stained-glass
windows. Red leatherette cushions softened the asceticism
of its hardwood pews. About forty of us, including Dr. Coo-

per, gathered; Kate and I sat four rows back in the middle. The pastor introduced his guests. Fred spoke about a book he'd written. Then Gwen approached the lectern to lead us in prayer. The lights were dimmed, candles lit.

"First," she said, "recall someone you've encountered in religious literature—Jesus or Moses or Buddha or Muhammed—and ask them to pray for you." I thought of Jesus. Next she said, "Remember someone you've loved and who has loved you, but has now passed over—and ask them to pray for you." I thought of my Grandma Lownsbury, who used to take me for walks in the New Rochelle Nature Woods. Then, she said, "Think of someone you've loved and who has loved you, but who's not now incarnate, and ask them to pray for you."

Closing my eyes and bowing my head, I recalled my alleged Eskimo brother, and thought, *O.K., brother, if you are real, not a figment of somebody's imagination, I need your help. My life is a mess. I don't know what to do about it. I am lost, drowning, failing everyone around me—Mom. Dad. Kate; even my children, Scotty, Billy, and Laura Beth, who are still too young to understand. Please help us. Help me.*

Grief, intense and overwhelming, surges through me like a wave, a veil lifts inside, and I see colors, faint and flickering, then steady and bright. Lavender. For moments I stare before recognizing it as a sunset, snow and ice stretching in every direction as far as my eye can see.

A woman crawls out of an igloo fifty feet to my left and strolls up a low ice hummock toward me.

I know this place.

Her Eskimo face is dark and lined, but familiar. In fact, she looks like me, I think, suddenly knowing she *is* me, and in that instant of knowingness I merge with her, become her. *How strange,* I think, *to be a woman,* while knowing I am still a man, still me. Yet I feel no different.

Noting the softness of my fur parka against my face and

the pervasive aroma of fish, my last meal, I squint seaward in hopes of spying my brother. He's been gone many moons and my belly is aching with loneliness. For the last five days I've been unable to watch for him because the wind has been riddling the air with ice crystals. I wonder where he is. Huddled under caribou robes, as I have been? Or frozen? Dead?

But today, far out in the unbroken whiteness of the pack ice, there is a speck. A bear? A seal? No. It is erect and moving toward me purposefully. Though still too distant to recognize, I know it is my brother. My eyes fill with tears.

He approaches. Now I *see* he is my brother, and *see* that he sees me. We do not wave; we do not run. He walks toward me, I walk toward him and weep. He stands beside me and, laughing, enfolds me in his furry arms. I feel the muscular breadth and thickness of him beneath his parka. We press foreheads and rub noses, his sun- and wind-burned, mine moist with tears. But his laughter is musical.

"You silly woman," he says in a familiar tongue, which I know is Eskimo and understand perfectly, "I have only been gone a few moons, hunting and fishing, and here you are, weeping, though you can see I am safely back with you." The joy of his teasing only evokes more tears. I speak his name, "Kobuk."

Then he leans back, grinning, and I lean back, weeping. And I see him with my wet eyes, and he sees me with his laughing eyes. And beyond him I see the sky, all glowing and lavender. And around him. And above him. The light dims. The veil descends. And far away, somewhere very far away, I hear another voice.

BOOK III

"*There is always a way of redemption, but there is no way to dodge responsibilities which the soul has, itself, undertaken. Thus a life is a way of developing, a preparation for the cleansing of the soul, though it may be a hard path at times for the physical consciousness and the physical body.*"

From the book, *123 Questions and Answers,* citing Edgar Cayce reading 440-5.

FAREWELL TO A FRIEND

Gwen's voice, the altar, the pews, the stained-glass windows—gradually I came to.

"You all right?" Kate stared at my tear-streaked face.

I nodded.

"What happened?" She handed me a tissue.

I mopped my eyes.

The pastor returned to the lectern, thanked his guests, and closed the service.

As we filed up the aisle, Kate repeated, "What happened?"

"A . . . " I cleared my throat. "A dream." It had seemed so real!

"What?"

"I had a dream."

On the way out we paid our respects to Fred and Gwen. Recognizing Kate, Gwen said, "I hope you enjoyed the service."

Kate said, "Graham had a dream."

Gwen regarded me. "How wonderful, Graham! Of what?"

I coughed. "My Eskimo brother."

She pressed her hand to her throat. "We're so glad when we can be channels for the Divine. How marvelous for you!"

I hoped my forced smile didn't reflect my agitation over

207

the readings or my horror at Mom's and Kate's unanimous acclaim.

When Kate and I descended into the street, I reeled back from the hubbub of traffic. What a contrast to the snowy stillness of my dream.

Once in our car, Kate pressed me for details. I complied as well as I could.

An hour later at my folks' apartment, Mom querried, "How'd it go?" I said, "A, er, ah . . . " Kate responded, "Graham had a dream."

Later, in private, Mom inquired again, and I did my best to describe it. She hugged me. "Wow, Graham! Beautiful! But you were awake. That wasn't a dream; it was a vision. Very few have visions. It's a mark of high calling."

Fearing Dad's response, I didn't mention it to him. His philosophy didn't include reincarnation. Trying to fit it into conventional pigeonholes, he'd want to analyze, define, categorize, and reduce it. He might ask, "What was it, *really*?"

Would you believe a past-life recall? No, Dad wouldn't.

But that night, mulling it over in bed, I couldn't see what else it could be. How could I have invented the name of my Eskimo brother? Or conjured up an instant familiarity with an unknown tongue? Or been suggested into "becoming" a female after that term had been linked to my weaknesses. Yet it had seemed more real than so-called "reality," and it had simply . . . happened.

I hadn't willed it; therefore, it transcended intent. I hadn't wanted it; therefore, it transcended desire. I hadn't conceived it; therefore, it transcended intellect. I hadn't originated it; therefore, it transcended ego. Which left it emanating from the soul. Which meant I had one. Or as Cayce put it, *was* one. And if I was a soul, death wasn't as important as I had thought. Worrying about survival was dumb, because, as I'd just experienced, survival was axiomatic, a foregone conclusion. Life was a continuous process, as Cayce insisted. And reincarnation was not an abstract theory, to believe in or not as I fancied, but a fact. Our life on earth was like other natural cycles—days alternating with nights, the waxing and waning of the moon, the changing of the seasons. No matter where I lived—Manhattan, New Rochelle, Galway, Alaska—I couldn't escape myself.

Months ago, while reading *There Is a River,* I'd asked, "How does this apply to me, specifically?" Now I had at least part of an answer. And it had zapped me to the roots of my being.

What was it, really? Well, Dad, I couldn't yet say for sure, but it felt mind-boggling. Whatever it was, I realized, it had occurred to me and to me alone. I could tell others about it, but could not impart the experience. I could describe it, but could not instill belief. I could toss it up, squeeze it, twist it, sniff it, taste it, squint at it, stomp on it, but could not convey the feeling of it. In this sense, it was singularly, individually mine. As would be its interpretation.

The next morning, while Kate, Scotty, Billy, Laura Beth, and I were preparing to return to Galway, a line from "Amazing Grace" kept running through my head—"Was blind but now I see." I felt that God had stretched forth His hand and touched me on the eyes.

Arriving at The Farm on that Thanksgiving weekend, 1963, feeling truly thankful, I did not immediately see Zeke. Alarmed, I hastened to her den, bent down, and peeked in.

"Zeke?"

She didn't move. My heart stopped.

"ZEKE!"

I crawled in and put my hand on her rump. She was cold. She didn't move.

My head slumped. *What could have happened? What had I done?*

Two of her pups were dead, but a third was still alive. I picked it up, backed out, cradled it in my hands and bore it into the house.

Kate drifted over. "Is Zeke all right?"

"She's dead." I choked.

Kate pressed her hand to her lips. "Oh, no!"

"One pup is alive."

"Oh, Graham!"

I turned up the thermostat, heard the oil burner rumble. Not daring to set down my burden, noticing that "it" was a she, I opened my shirt, pressed her against my warm belly. She snuggled and whimpered. I stroked her rigid body, wiped the dried mucus from her still-closed eyes, and shifted her to warmer skin. A tiny, cuddly furball, she was my only remnant of Zeke.

Billy looked up at me. "Daddy, is Zeke dead?"

"Yes, Billy." This was not the time to discuss philosophy.

Billy laid his head on the sofa next to the pup. "I loved her, Daddy. I don't want Zeke to be dead."

"I know, Billy." I caressed his head. Tears flowed from both our eyes.

Crying, Scotty sat beside me. "Why is Zeke dead, Daddy?"

I hugged him. "I don't know, Scott. Maybe she was sick."

She was only eight. I wondered what could have happened. I'd been so preoccupied. I felt racked with guilt that she had died alone, with no one to help. Why hadn't I left her in the house? Why hadn't I made sure she would be warm? And yet, 40° F. and drizzling, was that too cold for a dog?

My final tribute would be to finish what she'd started—take care of her pup.

Scott and Billy kept her warm while I found an eyedropper and heated some evaporated milk. She slurped it eagerly, then slept.

Kate hugged Laura Beth against her diaper-draped shoulder. "Wonder how it happened."

"Don't know. Maybe she was sick, maybe unborn pups."

"Cute puppy. Gonna keep her?"

"I guess. Will you watch her while I say 'good-by' to Zeke?"
Kate nodded; Laura Beth burped.

I crawled under Mom's reading cottage, slid Zeke's body
out, cradled her in my arms, the way I used to cradle her
when she was a pup, murmuring to her, hoping that,
though unable to respond now, she'd somehow hear and
understand. "I'm sorry, girl. I didn't mean to let you die."
Tears spilled as I bore her body to the site of our last stump
fire and gently set it down.

This shell is not Zeke, I thought. *Zeke is gone.* Humans
have souls, Cayce had said. We have a body. No one could
tell me it was otherwise for my dog.

I returned to the den, fetched the pups, gathered and
heaped up a pile of kindling, stacked elm logs, arranged the
bodies, bracketed them with more logs, tossed on a cup of
kerosene, lit a match and stepped back.

I knew Zeke wasn't really dead, just passed over into that
realm I'd glimpsed yesterday for the first time, but right now
it didn't matter. She'd been my pal, my constant companion, my beloved Zeke through thick and thin. Her eyes, her
ears, her fur, her tail, her voice, her playfulness, her joy—her
just being with—were gone from my life forever.

For a long time I stood there, remembering, as the flames
carried her body up. "I'll miss you, girl." It was the first time
I could remember weeping my heart out two days in a row,
first for a brother I hadn't believed I had, second for a dog I
thought I still had.

It was dark when I returned to the house. I named the
pup "Karma," and for the next month took on a full-time
job as her nursemaid.

Despite my vision apparently confirming my Eskimo incarnation, I seriously doubted the Overall Plan as presented
by the Van der Slykes' reading. Souls, they contended, were
continually being created, like an assembly line, which
would seem to make them replaceable. Cayce asserted we

were all created at once, eons ago, before The Beginning. No one was replaceable; each had singular gifts, each was able to contribute in unique ways, each was part of the Whole, the Oneness. Proof of either assertion was, of course, beyond reach, but I liked the feel of Cayce. His life showed an appealing goodness, a willingness to give self, a modesty, a humility. Despite personal hardship, he had concentrated on service, setting concerns for self aside.

I began reading everything I could find about him. One book, *The World Within* by Dr. Gina Cerminara, explored the deeper ramifications of reincarnation, as outlined by Cayce:

> "It affirms that each human soul is on a journey of return to its Source, which is God; that this journey of perfection cannot be accomplished in one short life span ... and that definite laws ... operate to determine progressively the circumstances of every lifetime ... "
> (p. 6)

By "laws" she meant karma, under which my present thoughts and actions would "determine the circumstances" of my next life. Or, to get down to brass tacks, my longing for Alaska had been short-circuiting my ability to fulfill my this-life's obligations. Now that I understood that, I was obliged to correct it.

Jered/Gwen had asserted that my returning to Alaska would involve "no right or wrong choice." I thought Cayce would have disagreed. Abandoning my family, I felt he would have advised me, would be a wrong choice.

In a chapter titled, "The Way Out," discussing information from mediums, Dr. Cerminara asked:

> "Are there *causal sequences* ... that show ... how to correct . . . past errors in the present . . . ?" (p. 201; author's emphasis)

Jered/Gwen had not mentioned "causal sequences . . . that show how to correct past errors . . . " Neither to me, nor to Kate. They had not set forth goals for us to work toward, ideals for us to ponder, or a spiritual framework for us to cherish. Rather than pointing us toward a latent higher ground, they offered invidious comparisons, pitted us against each other.

That had not been Cayce's style. In thousands of life readings, he'd insisted consistently that "The Way Out" was through love.

Like my beloved Zeke, I intended to love, not abandon, my family.

MAKING AMENDS

The problem was I didn't know how to articulate these thoughts to Kate. They were all too new, too vague. Kate also read *The World Within,* but she was often busy with our three urchins or preoccupied with other reading, so we never got around to discussing it.

One day, attempting to open communications, I said: "According to the life readings, I am a 'young, feminine soul,' right? Well, what I'd like to know is: why did I have a vision? Visions aren't exactly commonplace among humans. Maybe it suggests something unique."

"Who knows why you had a vision?" she shot back. "I guess God can grant His grace to anyone." Which I thought true, but beside the point. A "genie-in-the-bottle" reply.

By this remark I assumed she had interpreted my vision as corroborating my entire life reading—the whole thing. And I didn't see how to refute that; it had certainly corroborated the gist of it. Or she was still hanging onto a conception of me as an anti-social neurotic, which by all appearances I was. But to me my vision was a blessing, a soul awakening.

Gradually, I was learning to trust my own perspective. My fear of a holocaust had grown from a belief that death was the end, which I now knew it was not. My longing for Alaska had grown from a past-life "lovebond," which I wanted to put behind me. Cayce saw both fear and longing as symptoms of disharmony with God. He prescribed Search for God study groups.

Finding that none existed in our area, Kate and I started one with a few interested friends, among whom were Ruth and Elsie Shaver of Schenectady, whose sister, Jesse Jones, was a psychic; and Doris and Fritz Schaus, whose farmhouse near Galway became our first meeting place. Robert Clapp of Virginia Beach arrived to help get us off the ground.

Our group fizzled after a few months, but it had seemed to bring Kate and me together on theological issues, and it had given me hope for our eventual accord. It had also taught me a larger definition for "cooperation"—making my will one with God's—the first step of which, I was sure, was finding a steady job.

As if on cue, my friend, Howard Krieger, hired at *The Saratogian* just before I was fired, stopped in at The Farm, and offered to intercede for me with his previous boss at the Schenectady *Gazette.* The sooner the better, I told him. A month later, on May 12, 1964, I was hired as a copy editor, with hours from 4:30 p.m. to 1 a.m.

Schenectady was thirty minutes from The Farm—south on Rt. 29 through Galway to Scotia, east on Rt. 5 across the Western Gateway Bridge to "The City That Lights and Hauls the World"—"lights" for General Electric, where progress was their most important product, and "hauls" for the then-closing American Locomotive Company. A former Erie Canal waystop, the town had burgeoned into a metropolis through the wizardry of Thomas Alva Edison and Charles Proteus Steinmetz. As I arrived, it was locking up, heading home, making room for the night folk.

The *Gazette* occupied two adjoining brick buildings in the middle of town. Its nerve center was the hectic, second-

floor City Room—a place of jangling phones, clacking type-
writers, mumbling reporters and frantic editors. It reeked of
tobacco, rubber glue, cedar pencil shavings, halitosis, perspiration, stale coffee, catsup, mustard, and other sauces,
including soy.

Eye appeal had been an obvious afterthought. Plaster
walls wore succeeding coats of dingy tan. Gray asphalt tile
floors bore black heel-mark stains. The ceiling was festooned with I-beams, bare pipes, and harsh fluorescent
bulbs. Grimy windows peeked out upon State Street and
grubby railroad tracks. The men's room, whose thin wooden
door resounded with purgative acoustics, was tucked into
one corner; the copy desk, where I engaged in the symbolic
purgative act known as editing, in the opposite corner.

It was a larger, wealthier establishment than *The
Saratogian*, with the more relaxed atmosphere of a morning paper.

Two weeks after I started there, Cole stopped in at The
Farm to express condolences over my hard-and-fast routine. Coffee in hand, we sat around a stump fire. "So how's it
goin'?" He tilted his mug.

"Not bad. About as well as you might expect. So far I'm
not mouthing off to the boss."

"What's he like, anyway?"

"Friendly, but authoritarian. Like most bosses. Name's
Joe Armstrong."

"Have your own desk?"

"No. I sit at the copy desk. It's horseshoe-shaped, about
ten feet in diameter. Joe sits in 'the slot,' hence they call him
'the slot man.' Copy editors sit around the perimeter, hence
'rim men.' "

"Sounds cozy," he grunted. "How many rim men?"

"Well, let's see. Right now five, including me. They tell me
it varies."

"Whadaya do, exactly?"

"Read every story that gets in the paper. Check for clarity, continuity, readability, factuality, good taste, grammar, spelling, style, and punctuation; then write a headline."

"Sounds persnickety."

"No more than running a lathe."

"Don't you get a fierce hankerin' for Alaska, sittin' all night?"

"Some. But you know, since my vision . . . "

He nodded.

" . . . I'm convinced it was an authentic past-life recall, a genuine soul memory. No other theory seems to fit. This means reincarnation and karma are facts. Cayce says our goal is to return to our Source. If that's so, why should I go back to Alaska? I did that already."

"Must make Kate and your folks feel better."

"Mom, yes. I haven't discussed this with Dad. Kate, well, we don't get around to talking much, about anything. She's very busy with the kids. I think she believes the Van der Slyke readings. She seems lost in her own world lately."

No doubt Kate felt more secure about my steady job, but I was sure she didn't trust me yet. And why should she? I had so often bolted and run. It was a time, I thought, to let my actions speak. Or, as Cayce had put it, not by precept alone, but also by example. And if precept doesn't work, then by example alone.

Weekends and afternoons I spent free hours with my children. Laura Beth was now charging all over the house, grunting in the sheer joy of mobility, whimpering when she fell onto furniture or the floor. "Whatsa matter, baby? You fall down an' go boom?" I picked her up and consoled her. The top of her head smelled honeydew-sweet, especially after her bath. She loved it when I enclosed her in my arms and hugged her tiny body, or let her dangle from my thumbs, or pressed my lips against her neck and blew— "smoochles," my dad called them. Or when I marched my two fingers up her arm, chanting, "Here comes 'Pooh' and 'Piglet,' lookin' for a weasel," higher and higher, until "There's a weasel! There's a weasel!" I'd mount a full-scale attack as she dissolved in laughter. Another game I'd learned from Dad.

Billy, when playing hide-and-seek, had a unique ability; he could remain calm and motionless for the longest time in the tightest crevice. He loved being taken outside, held by his waist, tossed up and caught in my arms, the higher the better; it provoked us both to giggle fits. Once when my brother Don and I were taking the boys for a walk in the woods, I tossed Billy over a frozen creek to Don. At the last instant, Billy grabbed my jacket, tumbled into the water, and, wringing wet, needed a pellmell piggy-back race to the fireside. With me he seemed completely trusting. With everyone he was an instant charmer, a pint-sized heart-throb. Patting his blond hair, gazing into his blue eyes, returning his cheery smile, I thought I'd sired a cherub.

Scotty, a year older, loved being tossed up, too. But he was more of a handful. Also less tractable. You had to watch him constantly. Turn your back, and he was immediately into no-no land. His intense brown eyes, under his silky crewcut, could appear alternately sensitive and rebellious. I often sat with him, alone, and played games, or showed him how to catch fish from the pond, or took him into the woods and demonstrated basic woodcraft. He had inherited my knack, it seemed. And my bent for mischief, too. His daddy's boy, for sure.

Where had they come from, my children, I wondered. Who had they been in past lives? At last, I was allowing myself to bask in the joys and wonders of fatherhood.

When my parents visited, Mom took Kate under her wing on the pretext of teaching her oil painting. And the two of them would commune in the kitchen, while Mom regaled Kate with a seemingly endless repertoire of stories about me. The time when I, at two, snuck out of our yard, wandered toward the high school, slipped onto the football field during a game, and led the band au natural. The time when, before church, Mom asked me, at five, to water her flowers, begged me to put down the hose, got drenched, paddled me good, and stayed home from church. Hilarious to Mom, embarrassing to me, and boring to Kate, I was sure.

Possibly Mom was just trying to make Kate feel at home. Or perhaps she sensed that the life readings had created a rift and hoped she might dissolve it. Or maybe she hoped she could help Kate love and understand me again, the way she, my mother, did. But Mom had begun drinking a lot lately. She wasn't her usual irresistible self. And whatever her motives, she was only creating more tension.

TOMMY

In January, 1965, Kate took a job as a social worker in Schenectady. I didn't see the sense of it. I thought my salary was sufficient, and said so, but Kate was insistent. So I baby-sat when Kate left for work, and we hired Kate's girlfriend between my leaving and Kate's returning from work. I complained bitterly, but didn't try to overrule Kate. I still felt guilty about Alaska and wanted to give Kate the benefit of the doubt. If she felt I was still unreliable or might still want to desert her, I wouldn't have blamed her. So, quietly, without fanfare, I kept trying to make amends.

In March, at Kate's urging, Tommy, a wayward youth from Schenectady, moved in with us. A good-looking kid of fifteen, he showed his appreciation by avoiding me and hovering around Kate, an incitement she did nothing to discourage. On the contrary, one morning when I came down for coffee, she was resting her bare foot on Tom's knee; several other times I spied her arm around his neck; outdoors, she often held his hand. All of which, I felt, overreached the obligations of social work. But if I had protested, I felt Kate would only have stressed Tom's boyishness, professed her own innocence, and accused me of becoming a jealous husband. Still, I brooded about them sharing a house, alone, while I worked at night.

Tom surprised me one afternoon by assuming the prone position in the living room and showing me his push-ups. He flexed his spine a lot and didn't raise his hips. *Distinctly unmilitary,* I thought. "How many?" I asked when he finished.

"Forty-one. How many can you do?" he challenged.

"Most I've ever managed is in the twenties."

"Go ahead! Try it!"

"Hell, I just ate."

"I just ate, too. Whatsa matter, you chicken?"

I backed up. *You've got a mouth on you, jerk,* I thought, *but what the hell. Maybe I can show you a real push-up.*

Back a ramrod and nose bouncing off the boards, I eeked out twenty-seven, then collapsed.

Tom swaggered off.

Several weeks later, with Tom watching from the bottom, Kate and I were arguing at the top of the stairs. I don't even remember the subject, but we gradually ratcheted up the verbal register. Finally I roared, "Oh, kiss my butt, will you!"

Tom bounded up and yelled in my face: "DON'T YOU TALK TO HER LIKE THAT!"

I grabbed his shirt. Kate stepped in. I shoved her back and shook my fist under his nose. "LISTEN, YOU SON-OF-A-BITCH! THIS IS BETWEEN ME AND KATE! IT'S NONE OF YOUR DAMN BUSINESS! NOW YOU GET YOUR ASS BACK DOWN THOSE STAIRS BEFORE I THROW YOU DOWN!" My heart was pounding, my face flushed.

Kate retreated to the bedroom and slammed the door. I stalked outside. I don't know where Tom went, but he and Kate were sipping coffee and chuckling in the kitchen when I returned. I headed for Cole's house.

Several weeks later, Kate called me at work. "I have terrible news. Are you sitting down?"

"Just tell me, will you, please?"

"There's been a fire in the garage."

"What do you mean—'a fire'?"

"I mean it burned."

"Oh, no!"

"The firemen have it out now. They're still here."

"How'd it happen?"

"Tom was working in the shop. Started a fire in your woodstove. I guess it got too hot and ignited the wall."

"I never told him he could work in my shop."

"I did."

"You never asked ME!"

"Didn't figure I had to."

I bit my tongue.

"He's very sorry."

"I'll bet."

"You don't have to get sarcastic. He just needs affection. Will you call your dad and explain?"

"Hell, no! You call him! This was your idea."

"He'll be furious."

"I wouldn't blame him. He just had that garage built."

"Does he have insurance?"

"Probably. O.K. I'll call him when we hang up."

On the way home, the odor of smoke hit me a quarter mile from the house. Heart in my mouth, I turned in the driveway and stared at what had been an attractive two-story building. The entire second floor on the shop side was gone, as if a monster had taken a bite. Tongues of soot smeared the white paint. Charred rafters slashed the sky in stark ebony angles. Tendrils of steam wafted up. Water oozed and seeped. I stepped out of the car and into a puddle. The driveway was a swamp. Shards of glass glinted everywhere.

Dad had spent thousands building that garage, and I'd spent months building that shop. Now it was ruined, gone! Shaking my fists, clenching my teeth, I fought a losing battle with anger.

Contrary to custom, Kate was waiting up for me.

I plopped down at the kitchen table. "Hell of a mess out there."

"I know. You call Dad?"

"Yes."

"What'd he say?"

"Not much."

"Sound pissed?"

"No, he was too shocked."

"Did he have insurance?"

"Yes. Firemen here long?"

"Last one left a while ago."

"There's water everywhere."

"They pumped it out of the pond."

"Where's Tom?"

"Asleep."

"Figures."

"You never have a nice thing to say about that poor kid."

"Poor kid" were hardly the words I'd have chosen for Tom at that moment.

The next day on the phone, Dad suggested that Tom leave. Kate balked, but soon moved him elsewhere.

After his departure, the cold shoulder I was already getting from Kate became solid rancor. Her sense of humor evaporated. Her face locked itself into a perpetual scowl. The majority of her remarks were curt and hostile. She began reading *The Feminine Mystique,* a book extolling the superiority of women, and waved at me like Joan of Arc's banner. What about *Summerhill,* I wondered. Our hand-in-hand Search for God? Both forgotten.

When she wasn't spending time with the children, she spent it with her girlfriend across the street. She never seemed to find the desire or excuse to be with me. When I came home at night, she'd be asleep; when I awoke in the morning, she'd be at work. Our sex life, sporadic at best, regressed to nonexistent.

I felt abandoned, betrayed.

What are your ideals, Cayce had asked. Physical, mental, spiritual—organize them. Sit down and ponder. What was my ideal? To love, and not abandon my family, yes. But beyond that . . . ? It was all too new, too sudden. If I had an ideal, it felt like a new pair of shoes. And I was walking on eggs.

I didn't believe it was my place to tell Kate how to treat me or that she'd listen if I did, so I devoted myself to trying to be a good father, doing odd jobs for Dad around The Farm, keeping my nose to the grindstone, and staying out of Kate's way.

She had her own car, though, and without offering an explanation or me asking for one, she began driving herself to Boston to see "a psychic."

One day she exclaimed: "I want you to stop seeing Cole."

"What!"

"You heard me. You stop seeing Cole. I don't want him hanging around here anymore!"

"Why, for God's sakes?"

"I have my reasons."

"You mean you're gonna stand here and tell me I can't see my best friend and not even say why? Come on, Kate! What the hell is this?"

"I don't expect you to understand, but I'll tell you this: he's a dangerous person."

"Who, Cole?"

"He hates me!"

"Nonsense!"

"He's plotting my murder!"

I snorted. "Ridiculous!"

"It's true!"

"Kate! He adores you! Always has! How can you say that!"

"You don't know what I know. I'm warning you! If you don't tell him to stay away, I'm leaving!" She seemed close to hysteria.

"All right, all right. But what makes you think he's planning murder? Of all the outlandish . . . "

"This psychic I'm seeing in Boston. She had no reason to lie."

"You think that guarantees truth?"

"Well, I believe her. And unless you don't want me around anymore, you better tell Cole to stay away."

I turned and stalked off, muttering, but visited Cole the next day.

Cutting torch in hand, face masked against sparks, he didn't see or hear my approach, but my car-door slam made him look up. I raised my hand. "Howdy, bub."

He grinned. "Howdy, yourself."

"Can you knock off a few minutes and come inside and chat?"

"Sure. Go on in. 'Bout time I took a break."

Inside I greeted Karma, Zeke's last pup. I'd given her to Cole because one of his dogs had disappeared, the other had been killed. Also, still grieving over Zeke, I wasn't ready for another pooch. I filled my mug with coffee and sat. Five minutes later, Cole clomped in, washed his hands, and filled his mug. "What gives?"

"Cole . . . " No matter how I said this I knew it would sound stupid. The whole situation felt unreal, melodramatic, like a scene from a B movie. Someone else's. "I don't know how to tell you this . . . "

"I can see that . . . " he grinned.

"Kate says you're not welcome at our house anymore."

"What'd I do, stay too late one night?" He chuckled.

"She means it. She sent me over here to tell you she doesn't want you dropping in anymore."

"You can't be serious!"

"She's been seeing some psychic in Boston. Damn lady told her—of all the cockeyed things—that you're plotting her murder."

"You said, 'murder'?"

"Kate believes it."

"Well, of all the . . . " Cole spat.

"I know! It's absurd! Kate doesn't want me coming over here, either. Said I had to break it off with you, or she'd move out."

"Come on. Cut the crap." He looked as if I'd just slapped his face.

"She's apparently scared witless."

"Mac, this is idiotic!" Cole threw up his hands and rolled his eyes to the ceiling.

"I know, I know . . . "

"When did this happen? What in hell did this 'psychic' tell her?" He grimaced in disbelief.

"Don't know for sure. Kate just told me. But I gather she said you were plotting mayhem."

"Did I ever do anything to make Kate believe that?"

"How the hell should I know?"

"This so-called psychic, did she discuss motives?"

"Kate didn't mention motives."

"Well ask her, will you? I'd be damn interested!"

"I will. But don't expect a sensible answer."

"I mean, Mac, never mind plotting, never mind murder, why would I want to harm Kate?"

"Big mystery. I think it has more to do with her than you."

Cole shook his head in shock. "Well I'll be go-to-hell. If this don't beat anything that ever happened in my whole friggin' life. Women! My God, what will they think of next?"

I stood.

Head shaking, he stood and put his hand on my shoulder.

I grabbed his other hand. "Listen. This isn't good-by. It's just a feint to pacify Kate until she comes to her senses. Mark my words, it can't last long."

A week later, Cole delivered his response at The Farm's back door. A homemade billy club about two-feet long, turned on his lathe, varnished to a perfect sheen, its head skewered with a twelve-inch spike, a garish blood-stain painted under it, a note wired to the handle—"To Kate, With Love, As always, Cole." Just a standard boudoir trinket from your standard would-be murderer.

I laughed, but it made me want to bawl. Inappropriate and grotesque, it was his way of defying infinite asininity. I knew it had been fashioned from unwept tears and bitter disillusionment. Many men called Cole friend, but Kate was currently the only woman.

Kate wouldn't come near it. "You see! Look what he sends me!"

"It was meant to mock your fear, Kate. Can't you see that?"

She ground her teeth and stormed off.

First thing every morning, still trying to hang on to Cayce, I'd been recording my dreams, and asking Scott and Billy to tell me theirs. Billy said, "Daddy. I dreamed of seven golden candlesticks."

I expressed mild doubt. "Billy, I didn't know you could count that high."

"Oh, yes I can! One, two, three, four, five, six, seven. I can go as high as ten. Wanna hear me, Daddy?"

"Sure, Billy. Let me hear you." I patted his head.

Later I looked up seven golden candlesticks in my concordance. From The Revelation, chapter 1:

12 And I turned to see the voice that spake with me. And being turned, I saw seven golden candlesticks;
13 And in the midst of the seven candlesticks one like unto the Son of man . . .
20 . . . and the seven candlesticks which thou sawest are the seven churches.

The next day Doris Schaus, friend from our Study Group

effort, phoned to warn me Kate was planning to leave.

This hit me like a coal sack. I felt devastated that Kate had told Doris, even if inadvertently, but not ME. As if I were a third party, remote and indifferent. Also, I felt numb, powerless. I was only Kate's husband, not her conscience. It was not my responsibility to make Kate's decisions, nor to try to mold her after my image. "As ye sow, so shall ye reap"—that was the law. Whatever happened was my own doing. From my own past shortcomings, I realized, I had created this situation and would have to deal with my reactions. If I accepted whatever happened with humility, I could turn it into an opportunity. Karma, Cayce called it.

I thanked Doris, but kept my own counsel with Kate.

Three days later I came home from work to an empty house. Kate had taken the children and departed. Her car, the pots and pans, the dishes, my sleeping bag—all of it was gone. On my pillow a two-word note: "Will call."

On the kitchen table was Gibran's *The Prophet* open to:

> "Your children are not your children,
> They are the sons and daughters of Life's longing
> for itself."

I never saw Billy again.

BEREFT

Flailing the bed, twirling the sheets into ropes, blood-shot eyes boring holes in the dark, I trolled my head for a clue to my plight. Everything seemed to have come apart at once. The life readings, my vision, Zeke dying, an aborted Search for God, the *Gazette*, Kate's working, then Tommy. The turning point, I thought, was my vision, the confidence it instilled. Kate had stopped loving me then, I decided, because she no longer could pity. And that was the charm of Tommy; him she could pity. But to flee without talking? To take everything and run?

Anger, guilt, sorrow, confusion, and at the same time relief. The relief of being alone again, having Kate out of my hair, a cessation of the constant strain of trying to smile while feeling betrayed.

Sweat-soaked, I finally arose and stared out the window. A day off. I'd better call my folks.

"I'll never see my grandchildren again," Mom sniffed.

"Sure you will, Mom. There's such a thing as 'visitation rights.' "

"You have more faith in that woman than I do, Graham."

"Well, let's wait and see, shall we? Maybe we will patch it up."

"Will you stay in Galway?"

"I think I'll just try to hold still for awhile till I get my bearings. At least I have a good job here."

"All right. But this is a time for a family to stick together. You're welcome to stay at The Farm as long as you like."

"Thanks, Mom."

Next I called Doris. She expressed her sorrow, told me that Kate had told her that the Boston psychic had told Kate that not just Cole, but also *I* planned to murder Kate.

It seemed so ridiculous! So out of left field! How could Kate let herself be duped by such hokum!

If she'd come to me with honest doubts and fears, we might have worked it out. But to consult a psychic secretly, then invite a remote, alien judgment to supplant her own—that terrified me! I wondered if Kate had flipped out!

Was she fit to be the mother of my children?

I headed for Cole's house and barged in. He was up, staring into space, smoking. "What the hell you doin' here at this hour? Thought Kate had you roped to the sink."

"She's gone."

"Whaddya mean?"

"I mean, GONE. Took everything—car, kids, dishes."

When he got over his shock, he stared out the window. "Sounds like she 'burned her bridges.' "

"Eh?"

"Old GI expression—'burn your bridges behind you.' You do that when you retreat in a hurry, don't intend to come back." He puffed his cigarette, "Man, I'm really gonna miss that lady. What I wanna know is: Why? What happened?"

"Kate's believing that psychic in Boston didn't help us a bit. Lady told her I was planning to kill her, too."

"You! She said that about *you*! What in the living hell would make Kate fall for such crap?"

"Who knows? But listen, I also came over to tear down Kate's 'posted' sign. Drop in any time! Bring Karma! Only

right now I gotta grab some shuteye." I staggered to my feet.
"O.K., Mac." He followed me to the door. "I'm sorry as hell
about this."

At home I nibbled at breakfast and hit the sack. But the
house was cavernous, cadaverous. No wife, no kids, no dog.
I missed my usual weekend romps with Scotty and Billy.
Missed Laura Beth worst of all. Even changing her diaper!
Sunday I went back to work. Wednesday I received a let-
ter, postmarked Chicago:

5/17/65

Dear Graham,
    I realize my departure must have come as a shock,
but have decided that it is best for all that we live
apart just now.
    I have no return address yet because I don't know
where I'll be staying. In the meantime, you can write
to me at my parents'. They have agreed to forward
my mail.
    The trip out was tiring—trying to take care of
Laura Beth while driving. The car ran fine. We are all
O.K. More soon.

Love,
Kate

The next morning, keeping a tight rein on my anger, I
wrote back, revealing my knowledge of her alleged psychic's
extended pox. I denied plotting her murder, rebuked her for
believing nonsense, and asked where she was staying.
    Not receiving an immediate reply, I called her folks.
Emmy insisted Kate wasn't there. When I asked where she
was, Emmy said with her aunt in Wisconsin. When I requested the number, Emmy said there was none. When I
asked when she'd be back, Emmy said she didn't know.

I called back in a few days. Emmy said Kate was home now, but was "too terrified" to talk. I threw up my hands. Since I'd never lifted a finger against Kate, except for that shove when she'd tried to step between me and Tommy, I couldn't see how—after seven years of marriage and three children—she could honestly feel that. We were only connected by a wire! We were a thousand miles apart! What was this "too terrified" hooey?

A month later, still getting the run-around by letter and phone and figuring "her aunt" was really her sister Martha in St. Louis, I took a week's vacation and flew to St. Louis. But Martha, whom I called from the airport, said Kate was actually in Chicago. Then I made a crucial mistake: I called Kate's folks in Chicago. Emmy answered. I told her I was in St. Louis and wanted to see Kate. She told me Kate wasn't in Chicago, but that I was welcome to visit. So I took the train to Chicago, and Kate's father met me at the station.

He was congenial, gracious, but helpless, he said. Staying there two days, I was not permitted to see Kate or my children. Her father claimed Kate was unstrung, said she'd fled to her aunt's house the moment she heard I was in town. Depressed, deflated, riding the train back to Schenectady, I gave up all hope of reconciliation.

Back at The Farm, seeking meaning and solace, I pored over every Cayce source I could find:

> "For many an individual entity those things that are of sorrow are the greater helps for unfoldment... "
> (3209-2)

> "And each individual has the choice, which no one has the *right* to supersede—even God does not!"
> (254-102)

Kate's next letter asked if I would contest a divorce. I replied, no, but thought we should talk about it.

She wrote: "You have no past-life ties with either me or the children—what is there to talk about?"

"Past-life ties! What about this life? I am your husband, their father!"

We corresponded for a couple of months, with me reminding Kate of our Study Group ideals, the Oneness, and reminding myself to be kind and gentle. Since she had once upheld him as an inspiration, presumably still did, I often quoted Cayce:

> "It is true for the entity, and for most individual souls manifesting in the earth, that nothing, no meeting comes by chance. These are a design or pattern."
>
> (2620-2)

> "Each soul has its share not only of responsibility one toward the other, but of dependency one upon the other. Let both ever strive in their relationships, then, to become more and more a complement one to the other." (849-12)

Kate affirmed in each reply that she positively wanted a divorce. Then my letters went unanswered.

Meanwhile, rattling around in the huge farmhouse, missing Zeke, my children, and Kate, too, I wondered, had I rejected a lonely life in Alaska only to return to one of enforced loneliness in New York? I felt I must've done something in a past life to be suffering thus. Seeking support, I began studying the Bible, hoping to make up in a few months for my previous neglect.

Cole and Karma dropped in one day. I fixed coffee as we chatted in the breakfast nook.

"Whaddya hear from Kate?"

"Still wants a divorce."

"Isn't that against her religion?"

"Well, yes, but I am a non-Catholic. When a Catholic marries a non-Catholic, there are loopholes."

"For who, the kids?"

"No, the pontifical lawmakers. Helps 'em feel better about givin' you the shaft."

"How're things at the *Gazette*? You must be fightin' a wicked yen for Alaska."

"No. Actually I'm glad to have a steady job. It's sort of an anchor. Keeps my mind off my troubles."

"So what else you been up to?"

"Reading the Bible. Finding it really interesting. Jesus never made much sense until I believed in reincarnation."

"Jesus still doesn't make much sense to me."

"Remember those books on Cayce I loaned you?"

"*There Is a River* and *Many Mansions*? Yup. Reincarnation explains a lot about relationships that otherwise just seems random. Brings order to apparent chaos."

"I know. I wish Cayce had been alive to give Kate and me life readings. Might've changed everything."

"Frankly, I thought your life readings were pure malarkey."

I laughed. "Well, Cole, here's an alternative. Suppose they weren't *pure* malarkey, just partly. Suppose a fact or two got mixed in with the malarkey."

"You're talkin' about your vision."

"Sure. Also, Kate's reported alcoholic lifetime in Italy in the 1600s. That makes sense to me."

"She's no drunk now."

"No, but she has blind spots."

"Oh?"

"Believing that psychic in Boston. Also, accepting the Van der Slyke readings at face value, never seeing their fatal flaw."

"Which is?"

"Never mentioning a purpose for our marriage, never giving Kate and me a reason to stay together. They never discussed ultimate purposes, philosophical frameworks, moral imperatives, or definitive life goals. What's the point of living and suffering again and again? They never address that!"

"I've wondered about ultimate purposes."

I moseyed to the coffee pot and refilled our mugs.

"Cayce is very specific about it. He says it's: 'To know thyself to be thyself, yet one with God.' "

"Gobbledegook."

" 'Know thyself' is simple enough. Socrates said it long before Cayce."

"Right. It's the 'one-with-God' part that throws me."

"God is the Life Force, right? Well, suppose a man becomes aware of an aspect of himself that corresponds with the Life Force. You mentioned order in apparent chaos; order is an aspect of the Life Force; becoming aware of it, then acting on it makes it part of yourself. I seem to have become aware of a continuity, a part of myself that persists between lives. Well, suppose a human loses or attracts to his or her awareness aspects of this Life Force, according to one's behavior, losing or gaining from lifetime to lifetime."

"You mean karma. Cerminara discusses that."

"And suppose this learning process continues until we attain more and more Christ Consciousness, then no longer have to incarnate."

Cole massaged his stubble. "Wait a minute. Jesus never mentioned reincarnation."

"Cayce says Jesus taught reincarnation."

"How in hell could you prove that?"

"Not proof, but evidence. I'll give it to you as I read it in *Many Mansions*."

"O.K. I'm listenin'."

"One of the gospels says that, after Moses and Elias appeared with Jesus on the mountain, the three disciples asked Jesus: Why do the scribes say that Elias, meaning Elijah, must come before the Messiah? Jesus replied that Elias had already come and they did to him whatever they listed. The disciples understood He meant John the Baptist."

"So you're saying that Cayce says that Jesus was saying that John the Baptist was Elijah reincarnated."

"Right."

"That oughta make the churchy folks squawk."

"It all goes back to prerecorded history, back to the dawn of creation. Jesus didn't immediately spring into the earth, fully prepared to be the Christ, Cayce says. He grew into it, step by step, just like the rest of us. He, too, had to learn obedience to God's will. And He, too, had other incarnations. As Joseph, of the robe of many colors. Before that Joshua and Melchizedek. Before that Adam. But even before Adam, spirits pushed themselves into matter, became entangled in plants and animals, lost themselves in the pleasures of procreation and the struggle for survival, no longer aware that they were spirits who possessed bodies, not just bodies alone. So God asked for volunteers, and Adam, or Amilius, led the Children of the Law of One, the Israelites, into the earth on a rescue mission."

"Interesting. I'm not sure I believe it."

"Here's another reference from *Many Mansions*. Somewhere in the gospels the disciples ask Jesus, 'Who did sin, this man or his parents, that he was born blind?' Very interesting, if you stop to think about it. Cerminara says that to sin before birth presupposes a previous life, reincarnation. So Jesus and the disciples must have believed in it."

"How come the Bible isn't more explicit? Why only these vague references?"

"Cayce says the explicit references were expunged by the early popes. They were afraid a belief in it would make the riffraff uncontrollable."

"All right. Suppose Jesus did teach reincarnation, so what?"

"To create anything, you have to understand the principles, right? To create an airplane, the Wright brothers had to understand aeronautics. To create a doodlebug, you had to understand mechanics."

"So?"

"Cayce says the privilege of each soul is to co-create with God. But our first and foremost co-creation is ourselves. God establishes the principles—aeronautics, mechanics, biology, psychology—and we co-create."

"What's this got to do with Jesus?"

"Jesus said, 'Turn the other cheek, resist not evil.' "

"You try that, you're gonna collect some lumps."

"Right! Lots of people balk at that. That's why we're embroiled in the arms race. But Jesus said, do it anyway! Collect your lumps! And yet, co-creating according to Jesus must somehow be a benefit."

Cole smirked. "Pray tell, how?"

"It has to do with awareness. When you apply Jesus' principles, you become more aware of aspects of yourself that correspond with the Life Force. Application is the key."

"You ever discuss these ideas with Kate?"

"Nope. Hadn't thought about it until after she left."

Cole nodded.

I went on, "Funny how life works out. You know, Mom says I loved Eskimos from the time I was a kid. She says I was fascinated by their pictures in the *National Geographic* before I could even read."

"You were probably admirin' their boobies." He leered.

I laughed. "Come on, Cole, I was too young!"

"Not you. You were born horny."

"Dammit, Cole!"

He glanced at his watch. "Listen, I actually dropped in just to check up on you. Bachelors need someone to do that.

But I gotta be gittin'. Was supposed to meet a guy at my place ten minutes ago." He scooted sideways on the bench. Karma and I rose in anticipation.

"Great to see ya. Enjoyed the chat."

A burglar entered my house while I was at work that summer, dumped all my dresser drawers on the floor, and stole my typewriter and binoculars. Furious, but trying to integrate Cayce's ideas into my life, I prayed for him.

A few weeks later, Robby called from Alabama, wanted to know if I had a dog.

"Not at the moment."

"Want one?"

"Maybe."

"Name's Sergeant. Helluva dog. I hate to part with him."

"Why are you?"

"Sarge's sorta prejudiced against other dogs, won't let 'em in his yard. Damn poodle next door challenged him, and, well, good-by, poodle! Neighbors are up in arms. So, Mac, it's either you or the dog pound."

"He vicious?"

"No. He's great with kids, dotes on Cathy, has never even snarled at anyone in the family. He just hates other dogs."

"What's he look like?"

"An overgrown teddy bear. Black and brown, a fuzzy-wuzzy German shepherd. Throwback to the Heidleberg wolf of Pennsylvania, they tell me. Has a massive coat, makes him invincible in a fight. All that fur is like armor. Other dogs can't penetrate it. Also, he's big. Goes about a hundred. Helluva good *watchdog*."

Without knowing about my burglary, Robby had said the magic word. "Hell, Robby, bring him up."

Recalling that Eskimo women usually tended the sled dogs, I thought, *Must be good karma.*

A few days later Robby delivered Sergeant from Alabama.

"Shake hands with your new master, Sarge."

Robby quizzed me about Kate, but when the focus shifted to Alaska, we got into remembering the Seventy Mile, stayed up too late, and slept until the next afternoon. Saying "bye" to Sarge, he blinked back the tears.

That evening I poured Sarge a bowl of the dog food Robby had left, sat on the linoleum, and watched his jaw muscles as he munched. Robby was right: he was BIG. When I eased too close to his food dish, he growled.

"Come on, Sarge. I don't want your damn dog food." I slapped his rump. His tail wagged. I knew we'd be friends. *Be great to have a dog around the place again,* I thought.

As the maples and aspens turned red and yellow in a brilliant upstate display, I felt lonelier than ever in my life. The nullity, the pointlessness were worse than gold-diving alone. I still had a family then. Now I had nobody. But there was a difference. I wasn't just trying to survive. I had had a vision, a glimpse of the world within.

The *Gazette's* front pages that summer, 1965, had screamed of the nonstop bombing of North Vietnam, the first U.S. space walk by Ed White, and the fatal Watts riots in Los Angeles. Big stories. Yet I'd sniffed out a news flash that made them all sound like grange meetings. Sometimes I felt like bounding onto the copy desk and screaming: "Ex-Alaskan Recalls Past Life as Eskimo," "New Rochelle Boy Has Vision from Beyond Grave," "Yukon Reprise," "Bridey Murphy Revisited." Just thinking about it made me feel paranoid. And if I'd hinted at it openly, my cohorts would've sent me up the river.

As a rank newcomer, thinking Cayce was established evidence for reincarnation, I had stumped the office with an array of paperbacks. The response was invariably frosty.

Yet Cayce himself had been snubbed, even by Mort Blumenthal, who'd financed the hospital before the Great

Depression. Jesus, too, had been rejected by the disciples before the crucifixion. It was the way, the tao, the path to expanded awareness. I was achieving a perspective. My loneliness was acquiring a meaning.

Then I received a note from Amy, the youngest of Kate's four sisters:

                                                       9/13/65
Dear Graham,
    Kate is telling everyone you beat her up. I know it's a lie. You'd never do that.
    I remember when we used to go fishing and riding your motorcycle in California.
    It's not fair that she should be saying these things when you aren't even here.
    If there's anything I can do, please let me know.
                                    Love,
                                    Amy

Kind words had been missing from my life for months. To receive them unbidden was a priceless gift. To receive them from Kate's sister was a warm embrace.

I wasn't too surprised at Kate's charge of brutality. She had to tell her family something.

I left Amy's note on the kitchen table and read it every time I walked past. "Fishing and riding your motorcycle . . . " I had no idea Amy remembered that. Her note made my heart flop and my eyes seep. I read it so often I wondered why I didn't wear it out.

The next day I sat down with my own pen and stationery and began: "Dear Amy . . . "

REMEMBERING AMY

Amy and I had been friends since that summer eight years ago, when her father booted her out of the house. Amy had stolen the company Cadillac from the family garage and driven it into a ditch. Damage was minor, but so was Amy. Furious, her father ordered her to stay in her room or go live with Kate for an entire year. Devastated, Amy boarded the train in Chicago and wept all the way to Sacramento.

Kate, to whom I was then engaged, had found a rented room for Amy with an older couple who'd lost their only son in an auto accident. They lived on Winding Way in Fair Oaks, a mile from Kate's rented apartment in one direction and a mile from my rented cottage in the other. But Kate was social working in Sacramento all day, while I flew out of McClellan Air Force Base only two days a week. So it fell to me "when I wasn't doing anything else," as Kate put it, to "sort of look out for Amy."

Amy loved riding on the back of my Harley. One day we took a fifty-mile jaunt around Folsom Reservoir, stopping for lunch at a roadside cafe. On the way back, I slowed to let a string of Herefords cross. But slow wasn't enough for one thick-necked bull. He wheeled to face us. I slammed on the brakes, tires squealed, and we sat helpless while he pawed the asphalt twenty feet away. Pilot, yes; matador, no. My knuckles turned white. My heart pounded in my throat. For an interminable moment, the bull glared and snorted, then trotted off with the herd.

Relief washed over me as I let out the clutch. "Whew!"

"Did you think he was going to charge?" Amy laughed and hugged tight as I shifted and the wind tugged at our hair.

How wonderful to be so dauntless and blasé, I thought.

Kate on my bike was stiff and tense, grasping the sides of my jacket, leaning away from the curves, head up, eyes front, alert for the first miscue. But Amy was unconcerned. On her first trip she wrapped her arms around me and laid her cheek against my back in an ecstasy of abandon. Riding with her was a kinesthetic sensual experience. Sometimes when I turned to speak, she'd be so lost in the sweet, kaleidoscope of California aromas she wouldn't even answer, or her voice would come up husky, as if from a dream. Other times she'd be excited, aroused, high on the swaying, weaving fluidity of our two-wheeled, rolling display of balance.

One brilliant July day I took Amy to my favorite fishin' and swimmin' hole, just far away and hard enough to reach to have remained, in 1957, pristine and private. First, we drove to the bridge by car, launched the canoe in the river, paddled upstream a mile, trudged over rocks a half a mile, and changed behind separate boulders.

Amy wasn't as pretty as Kate. Her nose was too big, and she had a mole under her right eye. Her bikini-clad figure was still boyish.

Just under low cliffs on the other side, the river formed a deep pool, but the cliffs were accessible only to swimmers, and the water was cold. Amy didn't feel like swimming.

"What *do* you feel like?"

"Would it be O.K. if I fished?"

"Sure. But you probably won't catch anything. Fish usually lay low in the middle of the day."

"Doesn't matter. It'll be fun."

"You sure?"

"It's O.K. Really!"

"All right. You fish, I'll swim, and we'll eat later."

I'd brought two rods—a fly rod and a spinning rod—and a bare minimum of tackle. I handed Amy the spinning rod.

"Ever use one of these?"

"No."

I tied on a great feathery brown fly on a double-aught hook which I never used, but was heavy enough for spin casting. To my eye, it resembled a gob of brown pillow feathers; God only knew what provoked me to buy it. Certain Amy would never see a fish, I showed her how to flick it upstream, let it float until the line dragged, then reel in. She caught on quick.

"What do I do if I catch a fish?" she asked.

I thought, *Don't worry, you won't,* but said, "Grab this handle here, and reel in. Nothing to it. You see?"

"I think so."

"You gonna be all right, then?"

She nodded and took the rod.

"O.K. You fish along this shore. I'll swim." I plunged in, swam across, found hand- and foot-holds at water level and clambered up the fifteen-foot rock face to the top.

"How's the water?" Amy called.

"O.K., once you're in." I did a layout swan, let my momentum carry me to the bottom, returned to the crag without resurfacing, regained the top; did a flip, climbed again, then a layout back.

"Nice! Beautiful!" Amy cheered.

Repertoire exhausted, I lay on the sun-baked granite and rested my head in the crook of my arm to watch Amy. She was working her way upstream, the feathery brown lure painting monofilament arcs against the sparkling blue water. Finally dry and warm, I stood and gazed at the river.

Elongated shadows finned against white sand in the depths—lunker bass. In craggy crannies at the base of the cliffs, schools of minnows jinked and flitted. Periscope-eyed crawdads prowled backward in murky shallows. Plump gray water ouzels bobbed and weaved along rocky shores. A duck whistled past. A great blue heron, with "S" neck and stilts for landing gear, dawdled by on umbrella wings. Turkey vultures and red-tails hovered over the canyon. Everywhere deer tracks cross-hatched the sand. Camped all night on the other side, I'd once seen a coyote, a fox, a muskrat, and a beaver; great horned owls had hooted in the dark. This was my world, the world I loved and belonged in, though still exiled from it by a few more months in lockstep with Uncle Sam.

Suddenly my attention was drawn to the tail of the pool by a splash. I squinted against dazzling reflections to identify it. It was a steelhead that had just run the rapids and was now lolling upstream.

"HEY, AMY!" I hollered. "REEL IN AND COME BACK THIS WAY. I SEE A HUGE FISH!"

She started reeling.

"HURRY!"

"I'm hurrying!" Lure retrieved, she picked her way over the stones in bare feet.

"OVER THERE!" I pointed.

The fish, now abreast of me, looked a yard long—the largest steelie I'd ever seen. It just might see Amy's grotesque lure as a tempting tidbit.

"THIS WAY, AMY!"

"I'm coming! I'm coming!" She minced over the rocks.

"A LITTLE FARTHER!"

Amy stumbled.

"O.K. Stay there! He's headed your way. Let him come to you."

"Where is he?"

"Downstream. To your right. Look where I'm pointing. See him?"

"No!"

"You will!"

"What do I do?"

"Cast about ten feet in front and let the current carry your lure to him. See him yet?"

"No!"

"Right there! Where I'm pointing! You can see his fin."

"There?" She pointed.

"Yes!"

"What do I do?"

"Cast straight across and let the lure float to him. Stay low! Don't cast too close or you'll scare him!"

She cast, but not far enough. The current dragged the line, but he didn't spook. "REEL IN! TRY AGAIN! HURRY! CAST STRAIGHT ACROSS! LET THE CURRENT CARRY IT!"

On her next cast, the fly, floating high like a dead sparrow, converged with the fish. Three feet . . . two feet . . . one foot . . . the fish engulfed it. "O.K.! SET THE HOOK!"

Amy jerked the rod up, and the steelie, feeling real steel, dove for the bottom, turned, and shot straight up, head shaking, body flailing, hanging in the air almost at my level as if he had wings, then drifting down in a rainbow of spray.

What a whopper!

"ROD TIP UP! HOLD THE ROD UP!" I'd forgotten to mention that!

It dove and leaped, dove and leaped, each time farther upstream as I bounced, flailed, and whooped on the cliff top. At last I dove in, sprinted to the other side and touched sand.

Amy's rod was straight, the line slack. "He got away!" Amy cried.

I thought she was about to bawl. "Never mind, Amy. It's all right."

"I'm sorry. I'm so sorry."

I hauled out of the water and hugged her. "Sorry for what? It wasn't your fault."

"It *was* my fault!" Tears welled.

"Wasn't that the first time you ever used a spinning rod?"

"Yes."

"Wasn't that the first fish you ever hooked?"

"Yes."

"O.K., then. Actually, it was my fault. I forgot to tell you to hold the rod tip up."

"Whaddya mean?"

"Up straight, like this. See? The rod is springy. It helps take the shock off the line when the fish jerks."

"He was so BIG! So gorgeous!"

"I know."

We strolled back toward our clothes and lunch, holding hands.

"You think the hook will hurt his mouth?"

"No. It'll rust out."

"I mean, do you think it hurts?"

"Probably. Some."

"Will he be all right?"

"Hope so."

"I feel sorry for the fish."

"Me, too."

We opened our lunches, found our sandwiches and slouched on a flat rock.

Amy was smiling now. "I almost caught him, didn't I?"

"You almost did!"

"If I had, what would we have done?"

"Had him for supper."

'What's it taste like?"

"Better than anything you ever tasted in your life."

"Darn it! I wanted that fish!" She laughed and gritted her teeth.

"Listen, things like that happen when you fish. I never expected you to catch anything, but you hooked the largest steelhead I've ever seen. Actually, we should celebrate."

"Celebrate!"

"Sure. This way you'll have that fish the rest of your life."

"I don't get it."

"When you catch a fish, you eat it and that's it. When you don't catch it, you think about it. You wonder why. You wonder what you should have done. You marvel at the fish's power and spirit, and muse about what happened. You're glad for its sake that it got away, but sorry for yourself that you can't eat it. The experience gets a chance to etch itself on your brain, and etchings last longer than fish. That steelie gettin' away sorta makes this trip bittersweet. Like life itself."

Amy cocked her head, almost purred, I thought.

I put my arm around her and gave her a squeeze. Like hugging a sister, I thought.

Back home in Fair Oaks, Amy cackled and chortled as she told Kate about the whopper that got away.

A few months later, October, 1957, my air force hitch ended, and I became a civilian. Kate and I were married in Chicago two months after that.

Amy finished the school year in California.

But that had been eight years ago. Amy had been fifteen then, and I had been twenty-four. Now Amy was twenty-three and a woman; I was thirty-two and alone.

AMY'S SONG

"Dear Amy . . . "
I crumpled that sheet and started over.

Dearest Amy,

Motorcycling and swimming with you in California—those days come back to me like a dream. I amaze myself with how well I remember. The river where you hooked that steelhead, the crystal blue water, the sweet, wild sounds—it's a refuge in my imagination. You were really fun to be with.

I've read your letter, here beside me on the table now, a hundred times.

You're right, I never beat up Kate. Thanks for believing in me. Thanks for being you.

Tell me about yourself. What are you doing now? Going to school? Being somebody's girlfriend?

Love,
Graham

Our recollections stemmed from my air force days when I had money and social status. Amy had looked up to me, and, she insisted as we continued to write, still did. She claimed I'd once saved her life—which I thought an exaggeration. She'd slipped into a Sierra stream while backpacking, I'd raced ahead and offered her my foot. She'd grabbed it and climbed out. No big deal. What was a big deal—eight years later—was to have Amy still believing in me.

Amy's letters were beautiful. Not filtered through a typewriter, her words came to me in a precise and legible script, characters neat but tight, curves sharp, with straightforward up-and-down movements, like the tremblings of a seismograph. Generally unguarded about her troubles and shortcomings, Amy wore her heart guilelessly on her postal sleeve. Her vulnerability and naivete evoked the shielder and protector in me. She loved animals, music, poems, and stories and had a flare for the catchy phrase. She always seemed to know what to say.

Though eight years younger, she seemed much older and wiser. While I'd been lashed snugly to her sister Kate, Amy had been having adventures. Sometimes I felt she knew more about me than I did.

But the days dragged on, and I often felt abandoned, lonely, and sorry for myself. Somewhere, sometime, I believed, I'd done something to deserve this. As I understood karma, "an entity" who'd stumbled in a past life could press forward in the present through self-knowledge, attunement, and service. At the moment, I was serving humanity through my work at the *Gazette*. And in my spare time, I embarked on a program of prayer, meditation, exercise, and reading.

In the first chapter of Carl G. Jung's *Man and His Symbols,* "Approaching the Unconscious," an aerial photo of New York City was juxtaposed over Hiroshima after the A-bomb, reminding me of my fear of mass annihilation. A key Jungian idea was that modern man—through overvaluing the intellect—had lost his soul. He was no longer connected to the deep patterns of meaning that once gave him energy.

But these patterns, or "archetypes," were still available through dreams. In this way he could renew his ties to Nature. Remember your dreams, he admonished. Write them down! Pay attention to your personal symbols! Cayce said the same thing.

The last moments of consciousness before sleep could loft the soul toward other realms, Cayce had said, and to reach them he advised pre-sleep suggestions. So I picked out a Bible passage he recommended—John 14-17, Jesus' sermon at the Last Supper—read it onto tape, and played it to myself as my head hit the pillow. I hoped this would inspire other-worldly images, more past-life recalls perhaps. Maybe mandalas, as reported by Jung. But I was disappointed:

8/12/65

I'm flying a light plane over woods and lakes. Amy and Kate are in the distance, Amy closer. I dive the plane, ask her on radio if she can see me. Trees are in the way. I maneuver to stay visible to Amy. Kate is too far away to see. I'm doing chandelles and lazy eights, dipping below the trees, but still thousands of feet up. (Tall trees!)

8/13/65

I'm flying a light plane on a runway which is also a taxi strip. This creates confusion. Pilots taking off are suddenly confronted with a taxiing plane. If they have enough air speed, they hop over. If not, they screech to a stop. My instructor is in the back, but he's invisible, willful. This seems not to concern me. I let go of the controls and let him fly. He's spastic on the rudder, flitting from one side of the narrow taxiway to the other. He scares me, but I don't take control.

8/18/65
I climb uphill through sewage and return to get a
girl, not sure who. I hope it's Amy, but it may be Kate.
Going up a steep part I slip in the sewage.

But these dreams meant nothing to me. Who, me, a
showoff? Involved in a love triangle? With a ghostly, willful
instructor in my private spiritual airplane? Sewage, slippery
slopes ahead? I paid no heed.

Falling in love, I began writing Amy daily and thinking of
her constantly, and she began answering me. I do not remember what I wrote, or what she wrote back, but I
remember what it felt like. It felt like a transformation. Like
becoming the sun, the wind, the sky, all at once. To me she
felt like the grass, the trees, the flowers, as if, deprived of my
personal sustenance, she would immediately wither and
die. I remember feeling virile and confident, as if launched
toward Manifest Destiny, soaring in my mind's eye high over
the earth, across the heavens like a human comet.

I loved Amy as one who still has not earned a place in this
world, as a young knight on his first quest, with a veiled and
sinister shadow. I loved her as a fool about to be dubbed
perpetually foolish, who longed to be titled wise. I loved her
as one who believes in love, as a child believes in his or her
mother, as one who believes in life, but only one, and too
short. Romantically, hopelessly, deliriously, possessively,
desperately, idiotically, sentimentally, passionately, tragi-
cally, intensely, unrealistically, naively—I loved her in every
way men have always loved women.

Meanwhile, with *The Canadian Air Force Exercise Book,* I
progressed gradually from gentle to strenuous workouts.
Running in place kicked off at dozens of paces per minute
and raced into the hundreds. Sit-ups started with arm
reaches to the knees, but snapped to simultaneous leg lifts
and toe touches. Push-ups began with hips on the floor, and

whipped into flying hand-claps under the chest. Huffing and puffing ten minutes a day soon stretched to an hour, leading me in small increments to heretofore unreachable plateaus. Within two months I was doing a hundred push-ups, three times my previous maximum. And the floor-to-ceiling bedroom mirror began reflecting muscle definition. All in the name of enlightenment.

Insomnia began in September. I'd nod off, but my eyes would pop open after an hour. I'd close them and stay in bed, but awake. My pulse rate continued elevated all night. I didn't miss any work and was astounded that I could function so well. The only deleterious effect seemed to be constantly bleary eyes. A warning? Not to me.

Amy wrote: "Your letters are very special to me, Graham. A friend, watching secretly as I re-read your last for the dozenth time, marveled at my moist-eyed ecstasy. He'd like to write his girl something that would make her melt like that, he said."

I wrote: "Dear Amy, when are you coming to visit?"

She said, "Soon."

I repeated, "When?"

She said, "Don't worry! I'll get there. Be patient!"

"Hurry!" I prodded.

One night, dreaming, I seemed to be in Illinois, agonizing while Amy and another guy made love. She'd told me she had a boyfriend, but was "trying to ditch him." I was jealous and ashamed, as if I'd stepped over a red line into some prohibited and personal area. Yet it felt real. Later, Amy confirmed it had been.

Halloween night, 1965, she arrived, and I drove to Schenectady to meet her train.

AMY

As Amy's train screeched to a halt, my heart was fluttering like a baby bird's, and when I finally spotted her on the platform, I thought it might screech to a halt, too.

"Hello, you."

"Hello, yourself."

We hugged. I drank her in for a long moment, trying to ignore the squadron of butterflies in my stomach. I picked up her suitcases and carried them to my beat-up red Ford coupe, Amy in trail.

"How was the trip?"

"Thought I'd never get here."

I laughed. "I've been thinking that for the last month! You must be exhausted."

"No, scared."

"Why? It's only me."

"That's just it."

"Hell, we've known each other for years."

"Right now I don't feel like I know you at all."

I set her suitcases down beside the Ford and turned to face her.

"You look different," she insisted.

"How?"

"Thinner. Harder."

"Well, you look different, too."

"Disheveled, you mean. Feels like I've been on that damn train for days. I need a bath."

"That's not what I mean."

"What?"

"You're not fifteen anymore. You're a woman."

She smiled.

I shoehorned her bags into the back and we crawled into the front. "I just happen to know where you can get all the baths you want. Would you like a bite to eat first? We can go to a restaurant."

"What would *you* like?"

"Go home, I guess. It's late."

She eased over, put her head on my shoulder, and squeezed my arm. "Then let's go home."

I liked the way she said that.

I headed west on State Street, across the Western Gateway Bridge, through Scotia, then right on Route 147.

"Long way?"

"Mmm, twenty miles. Half an hour this time of night."

"What's The Farm like? I know, you've written me a lot. But tell me again."

"Kitchen is new. Living room has a huge picture window. I've put up two bird feeders, one in front, one in the back. The house sits on a twenty-three-acre woodlot. Lots of room. You'll probably feel lost for awhile."

"Be good to feel lost. Big house?"

"Two bedrooms and a bath upstairs. Another bedroom and a half bath downstairs. The folks have had a lot of work done on it. Three outbuildings, including the garage, which recently burned."

Headed north, we exited Scotia.

"So how long can you stay?"

"As long as you want. Nobody's expecting me."

"Great."

"You have a dog, right?"

"Sergeant. But you won't believe this. I now have a cat!"

"Really! You didn't write me about that!"

"He just started coming around, must've been waiting for you."

A cat lover, Amy clapped her hands. "How neat!"

"He's beautiful, but wild. I've been enticing him inside with evaporated milk."

"No kidding!"

"Just last week, while Cole and I were talking, he ghosted into the kitchen for the first time, as high-strung as a live wire, ready to bolt at the first false move. We just kept talking softly, almost afraid to look. Very special. A visit by a feral cat."

"What's he look like?"

"Solid gray, lean and lanky. I call him 'Simba,' after Rudyard Kipling's lion. 'Sher Khan' would've been better, after the panther, but it's a tongue-twister. You can help me tame him."

"Sounds like a Russian Blue. I can hardly wait to see him."

After a few minutes of silence, I glanced her way.

Amy was staring at me, a slight smile. "Better watch where you're going, mister."

I turned left on Rt. 29, took the next right down Greens Corner Road, left into Dad's driveway and into the still-usable half of the burned garage. We scrambled out. I muscled Amy's bags into the house.

Amy gaped at Sergeant. "He's so big!"

"Robby said he used to dote on his wife. He'll probably dote on you, too."

Sergeant laid his ears back and wagged his tail. Amy knelt and immersed her fingers in his ruff.

"He's gorgeous! Aren't you, boy?"

"Shake hands with your new mistress, Sergeant!"

He raised his paw and took a swipe at her with his juicy tongue.

"He's so furry! And, my God, what teeth!"

"Frightening, isn't it? I shut him in the garage last week when I went to work, just to see how he'd react. Well! He grabbed the double-door by its handle—you know how heavy that is?—lifted it and scrambled out."

Amy laughed.

"The next day I locked the double door. Guess what, he flattened the knob of the other door, turned it with his teeth, and opened it. Absolutely destroyed that doorknob!"

Amy shook her head. "I hope he doesn't bite!"

I shook my head. "He won't. He's a baby around me. Be the same around you in a day or two."

"Where's Simba?"

"Simba only stops in when he gets hungry. The independent sort, you know. I usually spot him from upstairs. Come on up. I'll show you."

The stairway led to a half-size window that opened onto asphalt shingles.

Amy put her arm on my back, bent down, and peered out. Her soft locks brushed my cheek.

"How'd you get him into the kitchen?"

"Moved his milk dish from the windowsill to the top stair, then a few stairs lower, then a few more. He's getting braver by the day. It'll be easier to tame him with you here."

"Oh! I wish he'd come right now. I can hardly wait." Amy glanced behind us. "Is that the bathroom?"

"Yup. You have a clean towel, washcloth, everything."

"How nice! Mind if I disappear for awhile?"

"Not if you appear again."

Later, she returned to the kitchen in her bathrobe, hair tied in back with a red ribbon, eyes bright.

"Feel better?"

"Much." She slid onto the opposite bench.

I'd fixed a plate of fruit, cheese, crackers, and wine. "Tell me about your trip."

"Oh, that's right! You don't know yet! I had to escape from Lucy's house!" Lucy was her sister.

"Escape?"

"We wackos get extra attention, you know. We have this air of unpredictability. In fact, I've been expecting you to go bonkers any second."

She liked to call herself a wacko. Actually she was the baby of the family who liked to act wacko. The rest of them kept an eye on her out of habit.

"Bonkers? Not me, Amy." I grinned.

"You're sweet." She stroked my hand. "My family thinks I might get swallowed by a whale, like Pinocchio. They appointed Lucy my Jiminey Cricket." She touched her nose.

I squeezed her hand. "You don't feel like wood."

"Anyway, Lucy took her lousy job too seriously. If she'd learned I was coming here, she'd have squealed to Mom and Kate and they'd have swooped down on me like a pair of vultures. So I waited until three in the morning and snuck out. Wasn't that neat? Only a nut could've pulled it off!" Amy chuckled, a sweet melodious burbling of mirth.

"What did you do with your luggage?"

"Hid it under a lamppost, walked to a phone booth, called a cab, drove to the lamppost, then to the station."

I chortled. "Does anyone know you're here?"

"No."

"Don't you think you ought to phone?"

"In the morning."

With her dark hair and brown eyes, Amy was very different from her fair sister. Did they actually have the same parents? It was hard to imagine. Kate had been broad-shouldered, busty, and long-legged; Amy was slim, straight, and slender. Kate's eyes had been direct and assertive; Amy's were gentle and compassionate. Kate's beauty was chisled, like a flashbulb going off in a nightclub; Amy's was subdued, like a lone candle in a parlor. Self-assured Kate favored authoritative statements; self-effacing Amy often conceded ambiguity. Where sex and intimacy had embarrassed Kate, Amy seemed unconcerned. She reached for my hand.

"You seem far away."

"I was thinking about your sister."

"Already! I just got here!"

"You two are so different!"

"How?"

"Every way I can think of—facially, physically, temperamentally . . . "

She stuck out her chest. "Mammologically?"

I guffawed, she giggled.

"It must have been hard on you when she left," she mused.

"I'd rather not talk about it. Want more crackers?"

"No."

"Let's go to the living room. I can start a fire."

"Sure."

I took her hand and led the way. She plopped on the couch. I touched a match to the kindling, threw on a few logs, then moved next to her.

"You have a nice name, Graham, did you know that? I've said it to myself every day during the last few months. I'm glad you asked me to stay with you." She rested her head on my shoulder. I put my arm around her and kissed her forehead.

"What was my sister like?"

"Don't ask me. I could never figure her out."

"I mean as a lover? She seems so strait-laced, I have a hard time picturing her like that."

"She was so put out with me during the last year—I almost don't remember. Can't we change the subject?"

"You started it."

"I know. And I want to stop."

The flames crackled. My heart surged with gratitude for the woman who'd returned warmth and laughter to my house.

"I saw Kate last week."

"Oh?"

"The kids, too."

"How're they doing?"

"You've got the neatest kids I ever met. That Scott is a devil. Billy is just adorable. And Laurie is a regular clown. I'm sure they miss you a lot."

The mention, then the memory of my children opened a floodgate of pent-up sorrow. My throat felt like I'd swallowed a doorknob. I bit my lip. My eyes filled. I buried my face against Amy's shoulder and sobbed. She rocked me in her arms like a child.

"I'm sorry. I shouldn't have said that."

The fire became embers as she kissed away my tears.

Finally my hoarse whisper: "I made up the downstairs bed so you'd have a place to sleep."

"Don't you want me to sleep upstairs with you?"

"Yes."

The next two months with Amy were, for me, a crash course in intimacy. Amy assured me I didn't have to worry about getting her pregnant. An old infection had left her uterus scarred. She couldn't get pregnant, ever, she said. At least that's what the doc had said.

We made love everywhere—on the downstairs bed, the sofa, the porch swing, the rug in front of the fireplace, in the bathtub, standing in the shower, in the hallways. We made love wherever and whenever the urge occurred. Touching became our customary disposition. Clothes became an impediment, an encumberance; standard garb a birthday suit. One night as I approached the back door, Amy presented herself stark naked.

"Surprise!" she roared.

Indeed!

Boundaries blurred. Never had I felt so close to another human being. Often I found myself unable to tell where she began and I ended.

Then I had a dream.

BIG DREAMS

The dream:

    A friend and I climb a hill to a cubical stone house—
the place where the old men live. We sneak toward it
and hear the old men murmuring. I stop, but my im-
petuous friend keeps on. He peeks through the trellis,
and an alarm goes off. We bolt.

    A shelty and an old man chase me downhill through
a field. I leap a stone wall, dash to the gully and into
the woods, where I lose the dog and the old man. Veer-
ing right, hoping to find my friend, I come upon a
sewage plant, enter through slats, and stare into three
vats. Twenty feet deep, they are rimmed with three in-
terlocked courses of rectangular slates. If I fall in, I'll
drown. Yet I stride out onto the innermost, precarious
slates.

    The old man, my pursuer, appears and beckons me
to follow. We angle through the woods, meet my friend
and another old man, and climb to a hilltop, where the
old men point to the lights of two cities—one near, one
far. In a foreign language, they tell my friend how to
spot landmarks and avoid dangers on the way to these

cities. My friend understands, I do not. The old men depart, and my friend and I resume our journey.

I awoke excited, yet realized as I brooded on it that this dream was a warning. I, the ego, had approached the cubical stone house where the old men lived. The old men and our male foursome represented my Higher Self. I had blundered into a sewage plant, heedless of my own well-being. The foreign language was the language of dreams. The dark setting called to mind the spiritual darkness I'd brought onto myself since the arrival of Amy. I'd stopped recording my dreams; stopped reading the Bible, Cayce, and Jung; stopped listening to my John 14-17 tape; stopped exercising and worrying about balance. I had embarked on a spiritual journey and, like Lot's wife, looked back. I had put my hand to the plow, then faltered.

Amy, a convent dropout, balked at anything religious. She'd first been intrigued by my John 14-17 tape, then bored. I didn't blame her, but this put me in a dilemma. My old men dream was prompting me to resume my spiritual journey. She had no interest in Cayce. Her curiosity about Jung and dreams seemed superficial. Yet I didn't feel I could proceed without her.

We drove to Bronxville the weekend before Christmas to visit my folks. Concerned for my welfare, they were friendly to Amy and mum about our living together. As the evening progressed, Mom let the good cheer get out of hand, became loquacious, then incoherent. I complained to Dad in private. He blamed it on the sorrow of losing her grandchildren.

We stayed for dinner, then headed home. On the way, I stopped for gas at a cubbyhole station under the Gramatan Hotel. Backing up to gain turning room, I smacked into a green Cadillac that had just pulled in behind me. The middle-aged driver, his glitzy chariot mutilated, was irate, but my rust-bucket was unscathed. We traded addresses and parted.

I ruminated about this all the way home. The threat of a lawsuit intensified my feeling of financial vulnerability. Here I was trying to support Amy while legally responsible for Kate and our three children. That night I had another dream:

Amy and I are necking in a yellow, wheel-less school bus. Orazio Ottaviano, *Gazette* city editor, strolls by and knocks. Irked at being interrupted, I go to answer it. Embarrassed, Amy arises and dresses.

Orazio, clad in shorts, produces a golden-bristled brush and brushes his thighs. Then he hands it to me. I do the same. The brush turns my thighs red. Then he produces two vials and holds them toward me. I sniff. Mint oil! The first makes me blink, the second makes me reel back.

I see that our school bus is parked on a hilltop, which is also a farm, but does not produce macadamia nuts or blanched almonds (which my parents served yesterday). It produces mint-flavored almonds. The almonds are dipped in vats of this oil, as in the vials, then transported down the hill. I see them being loaded onto a ship for world-wide distribution. All around is the ocean.

I awoke excited, but challenged. These two dreams reinforced each other—the old man in the first beckoning me away from the sewage plant, in effect saying climb up and resume your spiritual journey; Orazio, in the second, handing me a golden-bristled thigh brush, in effect bidding me to purify my animal nature, find my way to self-sufficiency and productivity.

What had caused these dreams? Certainly not the ego. Jung's answer was the transcendent function, or the Self,

which I read as God. If this were so, then my animal impulses must yield to a Higher Power.

Amy in my second dream was a symbol for the anima,
the feminine component of a man's psyche. When projected, the anima could entangle a man in exhausting
affairs. Privately, I suspected I'd projected my anima onto
Amy and that, to continue the process of "individuation," I
must withdraw it. But how could I possibly explain this to
her? If I tried, she'd only interpret it as rejection, which in a
way it was.

I began spending more time reading Jung, Cayce, and the
Bible, and deliberately keeping to myself. This made Amy
feel abandoned, but I couldn't help it. I could be remote and
cold if I set my mind to it. Maybe the talent stemmed from
the military, where I'd learned to give and take orders, fly jet
fighters, and live with peril. When threats or challenges
loomed, or decisions needed to be quick, it had its uses.

One bright February afternoon while we were wandering around the nearby cemetery, Amy became fascinated
by the epitaphs. We separated. Noticing an open grave, I was
reminded of the vats in my dreams. But this was only six
feet deep. Feeling clownish, I leaped in.

"Hey, Amy!" I called, ducking.

"Where are you?" she called.

"HERE!" I stayed out of sight.

"Where?"

I kept still.

"WHERE?" she yelled again, closer.

Flat on my back at the bottom of the hole, I grinned to
myself.

She peeked over the edge.

I leered. "Hi!"

She rebuked me: "Graham, you come out of there! You're
not funny! You scare me when you act like that!"

I climbed out.

She was sullen and unappreciative. Did she want me to take death more seriously? If so, I wanted her to take it less. Then I had another dream:

Across the street from The Farm is a huge fire-fighting camp—trucks, tools, sheds, men, much activity. Four large men—one black—wield a huge circular saw next to the road. Dad tells me to go outside and keep them away.

I seek a white marker in my brother's dresser, but find only a yellow crayon. With it I draw a line around The Farm, doubting it will keep the giants out.

Next I am in the snowy backyard beside a narrow, amber stream, holding my bare foot in the water. Two snakes as thick as my wrist slither over my ankle. A third approaches from the opposite direction and, as I jerk my foot away, sinks its fangs into my toe.

I hollered and kicked off the blankets. Amy hollered, too. The next day, reading Jung's *Psychology of the Unconscious,* I came upon this italicized line on page 332:

"*... was bitten in his foot by a poisonous serpent.*"

I nearly dropped the book! To dream about being snakebit one night and read about it the next day was astounding! Who was this doctor of souls, this wizard, whose writing could contain such magic, even after his death? He'd even coined a term for the phenomenon—synchronicity!

And that was not the only surprise. The translator of this book was Dr. Beatrice M. Hinkle, grandmother of Bob Hinkle, my childhood chum, New Rochelle neighbor, and Fuller Brush man.

What did it all mean? Trying to understand, I read and reread this chapter, "The Battle for Deliverance from the Mother."

"The serpent," Jung wrote, "the primitive symbol of fear,

Illustrated the repressed tendency to turn back to the mother . . . "

"The fear springs from . . . the longing to go back to the mother, which is opposed to the adaptation to reality."

"The retrospective longing acts like a paralyzing poison upon the energy and enterprise; so that it may well be compared to a poisonous serpent which lies across our path . . . "

" . . . man does not live very long in the infantile environment or in the bosom of his family without real danger to his mental health. Life calls him forth to independence . . . "

As I pondered the dream, the atmosphere at The Farm grew heavier and thicker. A few weeks later, Amy, also feeling oppressed, took the train home "for awhile." Talking with her on the phone, feeling my snake bite and my separateness, I asked her not to return.

She was devastated.

I was devastated, too. Broken, and shattered. Certain that my loneliness would last the rest of my life. I flopped on the couch and buried my face in a pillow. Then came the images:

> Amy and I are strolling through a beautiful fluorescent garden, admiring the colors and bouquets, touching and brushing the blossoms. Suddenly, she reaches up, picks a glowing-blue fruit, and hands it to me.

I sat up with a start. The Garden of Eden! The glowing blue fruit was from "the tree of the knowledge of good and evil," or, according to Cayce, a step on the path to self-knowledge. I splashed cold water on my face and dragged myself outdoors to cut wood.

Sawing, I pondered my situation. I had no family, no property, and no savings. The bank owned my car; Dad owned my house. My child support obligations stretched interminably into the future. Yet I was still better off than many. I had my job, my health, three squares a day, Sarge, a doodlebug, two days off a week, six free hours a day, the woods, the birds, the streams, good music, *Gunsmoke* on TV, and a room full of the world's best books. I also had my vision and my dreams, but could speak of them to few. Mom, at this point, was drinking heavily, making me feel cut off, frustrated.

A week later, arriving home from the office depressed, I flopped on the bed and slipped immediately into a vivid dream:

> I've been called back into the military and am stationed in Japan. It's dark. The enemy is plotting something for which oil is the counterweapon. A soldier shows me an oil hole in the ground. I dip my middle finger into it, and a voice says, "Diamonds can't stand oil."
>
> A train approaches on a nearby track. The voice tells me to duck, hide, get close to the earth. Staring up at the rumbling train, I see troops hiding among green bales of hay.
>
> Then I am a civilian, standing near the track. A man comes by on a cart and invites me to ride with him. We pump the cart into a city, and I am all eyeballs—weird buildings, lights, crowds, girls in colored silks—a fantastic place!
>
> I look different and am afraid I'll be identified and arrested as an alien. Yet I stop in the street to watch a strip show. Three women peel off their red dresses to display gold ones. They doff these and appear in red, then gold, then red, off and on, until, disappointed, I wander off.
>
> Reaching the dark outskirts of town, I glance back and am startled by a tall man. I think he intends to ar-

rest me, but his countenance is impartial and benign. His eyes glow blue with an unearthly inner fire.

He wears a straw hat like a peasant, but I know who he really is—Death.

He puts both my hands atop my head, in the classic prisoner pose, and surprises me by removing a brandy flask from my jacket. "We'll leave that here," he says, slipping it under a rock. Then he marches ahead and, hands on head, I follow. Our route reminds me of the way home from elementary school.

I turn right, but Death keeps on without looking back. I enter a house. A woman asks, "Well, how was it?" I reply, "I was almost arrested."

This dream astounded me. Something had triggered my immediate awakening just as the dream ended, so that I remembered its vivid details. The feeling of alienation was familiar. I'd often felt that in real life. But bits of this dream confounded me—"Diamonds can't stand oil." I mused about that for weeks. Obviously, they were opposites. Both were valuable and found underground, that is, in the unconscious. But diamonds were the hardest solid; oil was liquid. Diamonds had facets and boundaries; oil flowed. Diamonds were used as an abrasive, oil as a lubricant. Perhaps they represented the alternately abrasive and lubricous face I'd turned toward Amy. Or my desire to be part of a group, yet sparkle on my own.

Again a repeated theme—another man, my shadow, transporting me to a city. Death—a tall, unthreatening Oriental with clear-seeing, glowing-blue eyes, and an intolerance for brandy flasks. What did that mean?

My closing rejoinder—"I was almost arrested"—probably referred to continued development.

Ten days later Mom died.

MOM'S GIFTS

For the next few days I thought about her constantly—who she was, what she believed, the people and things she loved, her gifts to me. True, she'd been drinking too much for the last few years, but in terms of her whole life, that was easy to overlook. During my youth she'd been a beacon, a force.

She loved telling stories. As a tot she had fallen downstairs and bitten her tongue "almost off." Her father had held it in place while they waited for the doctor in his horse-drawn buggy. "By the time he arrived," Mom insisted, "it had knit itself back together, but a little bit longer. And ever since then, I've been able to touch the tip of my tongue to the end of my nose." Her listeners begged her to demonstrate, which invariably evoked howls.

I grew skeptical of Mom's explanation, though, when Don, reaching puberty, exhibited the same ability, thus suggesting a genetic quirk. In the great wisdom of my boyhood, I accused Mom of fibbing. But she never stopped telling her story and never stopped sticking out her tongue, thereby demonstrating that a stuck-out tongue transcends even a son's impudence.

Mom with her tongue out looked anything but beautiful.

Yet she cultivated beauty wherever she lived—vases, paint-
ings, and gardens in her house and yard; and her own
physical beauty—body (solid), skin (smooth and soft), teeth
(no cavities), hands (strong and square), hair (white). And
always books, thousands upon thousands of books! Magazines, book clubs, and newspapers—she read everything
she could lay her hands on. From the Bible to risque novels.
One wall of her living room was devoted entirely to books.

Writing poems and short stories had been Mom's pas-
sion all through my early school years. Don and I had orders
not to interrupt. But, according to "Involvement," a published poem, orders didn't always help:

> My sonnet's form may tear and bleed before
> I finish it, for interruptions fill
> My hours, and mine is not the tranquil store
> Of quiet places where the soul is still.
> My sonnet's twists must curl between my boys
> Who usher me to mend a trouser torn,
> Who call me to witness childish toys,
> Or beckon me to share ideas born,
> Who ask me questions sages never heard—
> And answering which I'd not be writing verse—
> My heart would quiet be—nor sad, nor stirred
> By man's illimitable quest, his aching curse.
> Oh little browsing interrupting sons,
> For you what matter sonnet's halts or runs?

While I was a student at New Rochelle High, I stopped at
her room a few times between classes and sometimes met
her there after school, but never told her what I did during
my first week.

My homeroom, 163, was on the first floor, but Mom's, 207,
was on the second. I excused myself to go to the boy's room,
but sneaked upstairs. She'd cautioned me against needless

interruptions, but I didn't plan to interrupt; I just wondered what she looked like, teaching. As I peeked through the window in her door, she was speaking, gesturing, and pacing back and forth in front of her students. She seemed remote and far away. Afraid I might be caught spying on my own mother, I hurried back to my homeroom.

Mom had been valedictorian of her Perrysburg (Ohio) high school class, setting a grade record that stood for thirty years. She held bachelor's and master's degrees from Oberlin College, where she'd met Dad.

An excellent student, Mom expected me to be one, too, and so was continually disappointed. A week before my regent's finals, she told me that Miss Rebecca Simms, my geometry teacher, had told her I was flunking. Mom said that if I flunked, she'd make me go to summer school, which I abhorred.

"You have one week. I want to see you in your room, cramming, every minute of every day from now until that exam. You understand? If you don't score in the 90s, it's summer school for you. Is that clear?"

I scored 100 on that regent's. Miss Simms gave me a D. Mom was very proud. But that was the first and last time she ever threatened me into excellence. She didn't believe in threats.

All my friends had Mom for senior English, but not me. Mom described it as a no-win situation: "If I give you an A, they'll accuse me of bias. If I have to give you an F, you'll accuse me of bias. Either way, I'll feel hog-tied."

So I took English with Miss Stark next door, received my usual B's and heard my classmates roaring at Mom's jokes. It was certainly a no-win situation for me.

Years later Mom was still remembered as among the school's most loved and respected teachers.

Though living with "my three men," as she called us, she seemed uninhibited by minority status. It wasn't uncom-

mon to glimpse her parading naked through the upstairs
hallway. To her a body was just a body. One day, getting set
to climb into the tub after me, she howled, "Graham! You
come back here and rinse this tub. If I crawled in there, I'd
have grit in my crotch for a week!" Dad never quite got over
that. For years, grinning, he'd prod us: "Better scrub that tub!
We wouldn't want Jeanny to get grit in her crotch!"

Dad often flew to far places in his job as a Wall Street financial analyst. During one absence, she wrote her poem,
"Departure," for him:

> May I be resolute in that near time
> When you will not be with me as you are,
> When days to come will be the less sublime
> With you as distant as some crystal star.
> So let me hold the spell between us now
> And keep the bloom upon the world we share,
> So let me put a kiss upon your brow
> As I might light a candle with a prayer.
> So let me make this day a holy day
> Before you go, that it hold laughter, sweet,
> And golden words which may like tapers stay
> To light the dark in some unknown retreat.
> Oh let me make a heaven of all we know,
> Sustaining me against the day you go.

Despite lifelong commitment, deep respect and love, my
parents had many differences. Mom was solitary, Dad sociable; she liked art and literature, he baseball and politics;
she gardened, he played tennis; she read novels, he history;
she was intuitive, he logical; she was dreamy, he practical;
she saw inside and beyond, he dealt with surfaces; she was
demanding, he tractable; she liked neatness, he seemed to
care less.

Before their marriage, Mom had been horrified by Dad's

mother's remark, "You ought to meet my other son," as if Dad were somehow the lesser. Mom went out of her way never to play favorites between Don and me, even to the date of her death, April 14, halfway between our birthdays.

I arrived downstate for Mom's funeral as many of her friends and relatives were gathering. Like Mom, I believed in the continuity of life, that death was merely a passing to another realm. She was not dead in the commonly accepted sense, I knew. To quote Shakespeare, her favorite bard, she had merely "shuffled off this mortal coil." I sat mute in the corner, feeling her spirit, unable to articulate the vistas she'd helped me glimpse, appalled that my father seemed so unaware of his mate's beliefs. Mom's mourners, every one, seemed oblivious to her personal truth. I scorned their fawning over Dad and their unwarranted attempts to comfort me.

Mom had often expressed the wish that her passing be celebrated, yet I saw nothing but long faces. Personally, I was glad her despair and drinking were over. Feeling gruff, I went outside to get some air, climbed into my car, and, before the memorial service ended, headed home.

Dad, bless his heart, forgave my missing her funeral by blaming it on grief. But I wasn't feeling grief. I'd been mortified by his unabashed sentimentalism and his unquestioned dread of that inevitable other side of everyone's life. I'd also been chagrined, without recognizing it then, by my own inability to express my views without sounding heartless.

On a later trip to visit Dad, I retrieved a prize I'd spotted for Mom in a shop window a few years earlier—a ceramic statuette of an old Chinese man, "straw" hat blue, robe green with a yellow border, beard and hair snow white, face brown, eyes indented, in his right hand a scroll, in his left a water pot. Broken and glued, I'd "stolen" it for $5.

Immediately sensing its meaning, Mom had clasped it to her bosom, explaining that the scroll represented the Intellect, the water pot Intuition, the old man the coming passage from the Piscean to the Aquarian Age.

I also took Mom's art supplies, which Dad said she wanted me to have. Back home, sifting through her canvases, I found in her graceful and flowing script, in oil the color of dried blood, her last message to me—

"Dearest First Born, You Stay, You Be!"

Obviously meant to show what her other two men would not have understood—that she had foreseen and accepted her impending death; it put a lump in my throat.

Soon after she died I awoke one night with a fierce pain in my heart and her voice ringing in my ears: "Graham, I don't want to do this alone. You come with me! I need you as a guide."

Realizing those were not words I had imagined, nor would have attributed to Mom, feeling sure that I had communicated with her spirit, I sat on the edge of the bed and spoke aloud, as if she were physically present: "Mom, I can't go with you! I have work to do here or I wouldn't be alive! You'll have to find another guide."

"It's O.K., Mom," I kept praying. "It's O.K. now. Look for the Light. You'll find your way." That had been her inebriated self speaking, not my Mom, not the Mom I remembered.

Hoping she had heard and understood, I pulled on my levis and strode outside to saw wood.

SNAKEBIT

After Mom's death, the U.S. began massing troops in South Vietnam, and on June 29, 1966, began bombing Hanoi. "Escalation," they called it—nice neutral word. What they meant was full-scale war!

The world seemed an incredibly hostile place. And as a former fighter pilot, I started worrying about being recalled.

As the summer wore on, I decided I did not deserve the poverty, immobility, and loneliness which had been thrust upon me by Kate. This was her idea, not mine. Presumably she had understood Cayce, yet had broken up our family over the pronouncements of a bogus psychic. This was not my fault. The more I thought about it, the more I resented it. At last I fired off an ultimatum—either she come home with the kids, now, or she could forget about any more child support.

Never mind karma or oneness; they were merely concepts. Jung, Cayce, and the Bible required so much effort, and mine had ebbed. Gradually, as if all my big dreams had been little ones and I was just now waking up, I turned my back on myself. I stopped reading, stopped sawing, exercising, and striving for balance. Fate, I decided, had made a mistake.

All of my skills had pointed me outdoors, and now I was trapped in an office. It seemed so unfair! My muscles sagged from constant sitting. I longed for the wild, free expanses of the North, a bracing dash of the Great Unknown.

In a book by Rockwell Kent, noted illustrator, I found a full-page woodcut of a Greenland Eskimo woman. Tracing the lines around her wind-creased eyes, thinking she might have been me, I mooned over her until my own eyes creased.

At the copy desk I spoke only when spoken to, and then tersely. News failed to stimulate. Headlines and photos flitted across my awareness. Nothing seemed worth the effort. The newsroom felt like a cage, my hours in it like a prison sentence.

Letting my personal habits slip, I slept twelve hours a day. Dirty clothes accumulated, dirty dishes piled up. I quit visiting Cole. The lawn went unmowed. I barely managed to feed myself and Sarge, and get to work. Sarge rescued a vestige of my sanity by taking me for walks. Then I had a dream:

> Kate is piloting an XB-50 experimental delta wing jet, buzzing under bridges, racking into steep turns, porpoising close to the ground. Realizing she's not qualified as a pilot, I flee to mid-fuselage, and, as she zooms straight up, bail out. Falling clear, I yank the rip cord, but it's loose, unconnected. The chute does not open. I hit the ground, am killed, but feel no pain, and retain my sight. In the distance the XB-50 crashes. I see smoke. Dad approaches, glances at my corpse, kicks it, says "Humph," and departs.

This dream depicted Kate's taking over "the controls" from me, my feeling of helplessness, my lack of influence with her. Also, my father's remoteness.

When Kate did not respond to my ultimatum, I cleaned

and oiled my '06, gathered my duffel, and, without telling anyone, prepared to flee to Alaska. On the eve of departure, I had another dream:

It's night, pitch dark, and I am escaping from a reform school. I lope over hedges, through yards, across streets. The houses are weird, fairy-tale-ish, like something out of Hansel and Gretel. Facing a wide stream, I turn into a puma and spring across. Magic! Barred by a fence, I become a serpent and wriggle under it. Running again, I notice my hands and feet—they are black and hairy, like a gorilla's. In touch with Nature, I am elated to have escaped, and happy when I arrive at Grandmother's house. I am home!

Grandma is sitting on the porch, her black shawl falling around her, and merging with, becoming the earth. She is the Earth Mother. On a table beside her is a white bowl containing a small head—not bloody or grotesque, but dapper and cute. His eyes glow blue (like Death's in my Japanese dream). His face is clean, and his hair combed. He is her husband, Grandma says, and is clairvoyant. In fact, he had told her I was coming. To see better, I step closer.

Beguiled, bewitched, I peer from this side, then that, until the head, the bowl, and blue light fill my vision. As I stare, the head talks. Finally I step back.

The superintendent of the reform school appears with a strait-jacket. I consider running, but realize I have nowhere to run. I suspect Grandma of conspiracy and feel betrayed. But she merely nods in agreement with the superintendent. Reluctantly, I let myself be buckled into the strait-jacket, noting that my shoulder is chafed and red, where this same jacket has chafed it before.

On awakening, I was stunned. For hours I wandered around in a daze. The dream frightened me, but the message was clear: I must learn to love my work at the *Gazette*, accept the poverty, immobility, and loneliness that had been thrust on me by Kate. Evidently, no matter how dull it seemed to me, my life had a purpose for my Higher Self. I must abandon plans to flee, submit to Kate's demands for money, keep my job, return to the "reform school," bow my head, and get back on the spiritual path.

Through my past reading of Jung, I recognized a "restriction of consciousness" or "abaissement du niveau mental." It was the onset of a neurosis, perhaps even a psychosis, but not all bad, Jung said. Even normal when one is approaching the unconscious.

Thinking I should talk to a psychiatrist, I wrote to a Jungian analyst in New York City named Margit. We corresponded a while, but I could afford neither her fee, nor travel costs.

I didn't call Jack Cooper because I thought he might treat me as "a young, feminine soul." Instead I ordered a book in the Bollingen Series, Jung's life work, and pored over it.

I thought about "my grandma" a lot. Had she really betrayed me to the superintendent of the reform school? Or had I betrayed my best self through doubt and lack of faith? Hansel and Gretel had lied to the old witch by telling her the oven wasn't hot yet. In another fairy tale, the wolf had lied to Grandma by pretending to be Little Red Riding Hood. Perhaps, by wanting to run away to Alaska, I had been lying to the Earth Mother, my real grandma! It reminded me of that TV margarine ad—"You can't fool Mother Nature."

Blue, Cayce said, symbolized the "will." Where had I come across that before? *A Search for God*, Book I. The affirmation for "Cooperation": "Not my will, but Thine, O Lord, be done in me and through me . . . " I started carrying it around with me, repeating it to myself every day.

Two weeks later this dream proved prophetic when I suffered bursitis in my right shoulder, the same one that had
been chafed by the strait-jacket. It incapacitated me for
months.

TURNING AROUND

My shoulder became so sore with bursitis that I couldn't sleep on my right side, often couldn't sleep at all. Sometimes when I did sleep, I'd wake up cradling my wing and moaning. For years I'd burned off excess vitality by chopping and sawing. Now I had to find other outlets.

I didn't go to a doctor because the pain wasn't constant, certainly wasn't life threatening, wasn't even keeping me home from work. Also, I felt sure that somehow I'd caused this myself and that the Cayce readings could tell me what to do for it.

Researching, I found he recommended peanut oil rubs, spinal adjustments, castor oil packs, drinking lots of water, eating more fruits and vegetables, and keeping up the eliminations.

"An attitude of *resentment* will produce inflammation," said reading 1005-7. I'd felt, still felt much resentment toward Kate. Yet what could I do about it now? Forgive, Cayce said. Pray. Learn to meditate.

" . . . don't feel sorry for self if you have chosen the wrong road—*Turn around!*" (462-10)

Alaska, I was convinced, since my grandma dream, was
the wrong road for me. Evidently my journey within also
included healing my bursitis, so I started changing my life
style as Cayce suggested, easiest things first—more water,
more fruits and veggies, and peanut oil rubs. Several times I
went to visit a chiropractor. Also, I started taking walks every day, keeping my dirty clothes picked up, the dishes
done, and the house neat.

My old-men dream had depicted me traveling toward
two cities. Yet in real life I despised cities. The thought of
being cooped up in one made my stomach churn. I wondered where this dread had originated. Another life,
perhaps? Maybe I'd once starved to death and the trauma
had carried over. But never mind another life. What if Dad
sold The Farm, now, in this life? Then I'd be *forced* to live in
the city. Considering that, I held my head in my hands and
spoke aloud, "Lordy, how will I ever get enough to eat?"

At that instant, as if in response, I was startled by a loud
thump on the picture window behind me. Investigating, I
found a gorgeous ring-necked pheasant which had crashed
into the glass. I stared in awe. Was this another example of
synchronicity? A statement that the Creative Forces understood my fear and were promising to nurture me, even in a
city?

Seeing it as manna, I bore it to the kitchen, and though it
wasn't officially Thanksgiving, plucked, stuffed, baked,
prayed, and smacked my lips over it, afterward tacking a
wing feather to my bulletin board, and pressing a tail feather into my wallet—a personal reminder of that inspired
proclamation on our nation's legal tender—"In God We
Trust."

A week later, driving home from the *Gazette* at 2 a.m., I
passed a Great Dane dozing beside the road. Realizing
within a mile that it couldn't have been a dog, I wheeled
around and found a recently car-killed doe. I loaded it into

the back seat, took it home, butchered, wrapped, and froze it.

Gradually I began feeling less depressed. Though I still faced poverty, immobility, and loneliness, and though nothing outwardly had changed, often I became so absorbed in reading Cayce, Jung, or the Bible, enjoying a stump fire, watching the stars, or taking a walk that I forgot my loneliness. A Cayce reading said:

"You only fail if you quit trying. The trying is oft counted for righteousness." (3292-1)

In winter at The Farm, I developed a simple routine which, despite solitude, filled me with cozy feelings of home and hearth. I shut off all but three rooms, and heated only the living room, kitchen, and upstairs bathroom. To prevent fires, I'd turn off the oil burner while I was at work, flip it back on when I returned, torch the logs in the fireplace, trudge upstairs, climb into a steaming shower, amble back down, feed Sarge, cook supper, throw on a few more logs, eat by the fire, wash dishes, and read until sleepy. Then I'd snuggle into my sleeping bag and watch the embers until nodding off.

With my shoulder aching, I couldn't split or saw, but the woodpile was so big it wasn't an immediate problem.

I really missed Scott, Billy, and Laura Beth, but took heart in the Cayce readings:

"Do not *ever* attempt to *force* an issue!" (1982-2)

" . . . know that what is *truly* thine *cannot* be taken away from thee . . . " (2448-2)

" . . . he that is faithful is not given a burden beyond that he is able to bear . . . " (290-1)

Perhaps Kate will change her mind about telling me where she lives, I thought. *Maybe, as our children grow older* ... To ease my loneliness I adopted two more cats, waifs of *Gazette* employees, and now had Simba, who was losing his fear, Tasha, and Tinker Bell, all of whom tolerated a resident chipmunk. With black and gold stripes along a russet back, bright black eyes, and an insatiable curiosity, he'd honk a rowdy "squeak-squeak" while scurrying, tail up, between doorways. Soon he'd explored the whole downstairs, one night even sprinting across my forehead as I snoozed. I named him Squeaky.

Squeaky entertained us all that winter, accepting tidbits from my hand, but jumped up on the toilet bowl one night while I was at work and fell in. Its porcelain sides were too steep and slippery, and Squeaky squeaked no more. I felt terrible, but consoled myself by remembering that all life is a parade, that individuals come and go, that God is good and just and has, no doubt, figured all creatures in His timeless scheme of continuity. So I bowed my head, put my hand over my heart, said a sincere thanks for Squeaky's uppitiness and joy, and, minus taps, conducted a homespun version of a burial at sea.

My shoulder was slow to heal, so I tried another Cayce suggestion—fume baths. I set a pot with boiling water on a hot plate, placed a three-legged milk stool over the pot, stuck my head through a hole in a plastic sheet, sat on the stool, and into the water dumped a dollop of pine, camphor, eucalyptus, balsam, fir needle, turpentine, myrrh, Atomidine, or witch hazel—all had been recommended in the readings. The steam would start my heart pumping and the sweat oozing, the fumes would wash over my skin and waft me into other realms. A perfect place to try meditating.

Soon I started feeling pressure in my head, a flickering in my eyes, a vibration, a stirring, an unquenchable uplift, the kundalini rising—symptoms, Cayce said, of the body centers' opening to the Creative Forces. "Not my will, but Thine, O Lord." It was happening! I could feel it!

Heeding Cayce—"The entity should keep close to all those things that have to do with outdoor activities . . . " (3374-1)—I let Sarge take me for walks in all kinds of weather, any time of day or night.

One April afternoon, sashaying through a nearby field, Sarge, the dog killer, flushed a dachshund, who raced into the woods with Sarge on his heels and me in hot pursuit. The chase ended with the dachshund cowering in his owner's lap, me grasping Sarge's tail in a cloud of dust in the middle of a picnic!

The field owner pointed her boney finger at me and demanded, "Who are *you*? And what are you doing *here*?"

"Nothing, Ma'am." I spat. "Just walking my dog." Grabbing Sarge's collar, I wobbled to my feet and backed away with all the dignity of a craven rout.

The incident had been embarrassing, but I didn't brood on it. In fact, I started laughing. What the field owner had thought or said wasn't important in the larger context of my spiritual search. Only my intentions were important, and I had meant only to save that dachshund.

The Cayce readings offered no instant transformation, but my shoulder was getting better:

> "Little by little, line upon line, here a little, there a little . . . " (262-24)

At the *Gazette* I noticed my attention turning away from myself toward my co-workers, in line with a Cayce aphorism, "To have friends, be friendly."

I began dropping in on Cole again and befriended an old man who lived a mile north of The Farm in the Kennyetto Creek valley.

Rudolph Zimmer kept goats, geese, chickens, and bees,

grew prize vegetables in his organic gardens, and sold homemade cider, goat cheese, honey, and sumptuous brown eggs. Short, wiry and feisty, he wore a goatee and limped. So long had he associated with goats that he'd begun to look (and smell) like one. His beret, I discovered, covered a half-dollar-sized lump on his forehead. He claimed he'd acquired it as a kid when his uncle hit him with a bottle.

"When was this, Rudy?" I probed.

"Ven I vas a boy in Ow-stria."

"Austria?"

"Ja."

"Why did he do that?"

"I dunno." His voice was lyrical. "Long time ago. I forgot now. Meybe I vas a bad boy."

"You, Rudy? A bad boy?"

"Oh, ja." He grinned.

"What did you do?"

"Meybe I zmoked zee corn zilk."

"Your uncle hit you with a bottle for smoking corn silk?"

"Vell, meybe I chase too many dairy maids." He leered.

His father had been killed in World War I, and his mother was forced to let her brother raise her children. Arriving in America as a youth, Rudy worked in steel mills in New Jersey and had bought this farm with twenty years' worth of savings. Now he subscribed to *Organic Gardening* and *Prevention* magazines, and practiced chemical-free soil management before it was in vogue. He despised pesticides.

"Rudy," I once complained, "your apples are wormy!"

"Ja sure! Apples no goot enuf for vorms zurely no goot enuf for you und me!"

At 72, he'd sometimes lament, "Canna do zo much now as I useta." So I appointed myself his volunteer handyman, helped stack his wood (with my good arm), bought a used coffee grinder for making corn meal, and fixed his pickup when he broke its axle. In return he plied me with honey, hard cider, goat cheese, dried goat whey, and other exotic delicacies.

Rudy helped start my first compost pile, advising me how to stack, turn, lime, and aerate it. I learned to prize composting because it transformed rotten stuff into something useful. Also, as with Cayce's home remedies, it fostered a do-it-yourself independence. Composting eventually led to road knacking.

While Rudy farmed all day, I drove a total of forty miles to and from work, often passing dead coons, foxes, possoms, skunks, and woodchucks. Collecting them not only benefited my compost with infusions of wild nutrients, but benefited area motorists with carcass-free roads. I usually deposited them in the VW trunk and left them there till I arrived home.

Since the bug's trunk also provided gas-tank access, I soon fell into disfavor with my favorite gas station attendant. "I ain't pumpin' no gas for you today, pal. Not after what you had in there the last time you stopped in."

On the way home one night, after picking up a smelly raccoon and leaving it in the trunk all afternoon, I also picked up two hitchhikers.

"Where you guys headed?" I piped pleasantly.

"Aaa, errr," one sputtered.

I grinned. "Eh? What was that? I said, 'Where you headed?' "

"RIGHT HERE!" the other wheezed. "LET US OUT RIGHT HERE!"

"In the middle of the bridge?" I kept driving.

They bolted when I stopped for the red light, without even saying thanks. I grinned. Later, Cole and Rudy guffawed.

"Let no day then pass that ye do not speak a *cheery* and an encouraging word to someone!" (1754-1)

My friends and co-workers became my family, and solitude became my friend. Kate still wouldn't tell me where she lived. But I continued writing to Amy, and, holding no grudge, she answered. Praying, meditating, studying the *Search for God* books alone, recalling my dreams, reflecting on the pheasant and the doe, I gradually regained my confidence and mobility.

I began to realize that my once-vaunted self-reliance was an illusion and kept trying to integrate the Cayce readings into my life. I wondered if I could embrace that verse from Matthew: "Take no thought for your life, what ye shall eat, or what ye shall drink... is not the life more than meat...?" (6:25) "Reverence for life," Albert Schweitzer had termed it.

I'd been dispatching garden pests without a qualm, but now began commiserating, "Oh, those poor beasties." Even the rabbits who munched blithely away on my cabbages, the raccoons who crunched unconcernedly on my corn. Surely they had a right to live. Yet I couldn't believe that the Almighty wanted me to sit idly by while my crops were decimated. Sympathetic, Cole built me a live trap from an old oil drum. I set it out and escorted my "pests" over the hill.

One morning a huge buck woodchuck refused to be routed. "SCRAM!" I hollered. "SCAT! GIT!" But he only clicked his teeth and retreated into the weeds. I could have shot him with my .22 or sicked Sarge on him, but instead I rigged up a noose on a long pole, slipped it over his neck, bagged him in burlap, and transported him unhurt to the next county.

Then came the acid test. The farmhouse had become infested with rats. Could I stretch my new-found reverence to include even them? I doubted it. They were too numerous and fecund. I often heard them gnawing the backs of kitchen drawers, tattering Mom's napkins, and leaving droppings amid the silverware. If I banged the living room ceiling, the thunder of their scurrying made me shudder, and neither moth ball spray, nor ether, injected through a drilled orifice, had a noticeable effect.

One evening, with my three cats lolling beside me on the couch, a faint clump occurred at the top of the stairs. It developed at the bottom into an authoritative "CLUMP-THUMP." A foot-long brown rat squeezed under the double doors, ambled into the open, across the rug, and into the woodpile. The cats never batted an eye.

"What the hell is this!" Did they think Squeaky had come home again?

I bounded off the couch, chased that rat into the kitchen, and bashed it over the head with the ash shovel. And yes, I'd killed many rats in the past with poison and traps, but now I felt queasy about it. It didn't fit in with Cayce or reverence for life. I decided on a bold strategy.

"Lord," I prayed, "Source of all blessings and trials, Thou knowest I have killed many rats. And Thou knowest I would like to stop. But I fear it would allow them to proliferate, leave all my drawers in splinters, and my toes gnawed. Lord, I fear. Yet I seek Thy aid."

Praying thus every night, I stepped out on the back porch two weeks later to view the morning snow, and there was an ermine with a rat in his mouth! He had discovered my rats' nest! And he kept coming back until he'd cleaned out the whole house!

HOMEBOUND

.

As the months passed, I began to see myself and my place in the world in a new light.

I took my '06 out of the closet, ran my hand along the stock I'd often linseed-oiled, the sling I'd neatsfooted, the bolt I'd lubed, the barrel I'd scoured. I'd toted this rifle hundreds of miles over some mighty rough terrain. It had fed and protected me well. Wrapping the strap around my arm, pressing the butt against my shoulder, I aimed it out the window, let my cheek rest behind the scope. A photo album of memories came flooding back—

The black bear whose pelt had covered the hole in my wickiup, my first moose with the Junebee brothers off the Taylor Highway, Kate's young moose at Pickerel Slough, the long stalk and kill with Jim Hansen, Robby's Seventy Mile wolf, my first Adirondack whitetail.

Zeke had been alive then.

With Thoreau I wholeheartedly agreed: " . . . that if one advances confidently in the direction of his dreams, and endeavors to live the life he has imagined, he will meet with a success unexpected in common hours . . . "

The cross hairs in their circle of light reminded me of the Cross—horizontal line for matter, vertical one for spirit. I knew where I was headed now. I had a bearing and a glimpse of home.

Breathing deep, closing my eyes, I knew that humankind does not wrest life from the earth, that survival of the body is subordinate to growth of the soul. Turning the other cheek did not come naturally to me. Yet I now knew by experience what I'd tried to say to Kate in Berkeley: that dark and light, cold and hot, rough and smooth, fast and slow, good and bad, true and false, joy and sorrow—any sensory condition—is perceivable only in relationship to its opposite; that above, beyond, and behind them all is God; that true freedom is insight into my own thought processes; and that unconscious resources are best unleashed by the Creative Forces, through fate, having their way with me. Or, as He put it, "Resist not evil." Not by forcing my will upon others. For, as Jung knew, that shields me from my own shadow— the dark side of myself, which longs to make amends with God.

My '06 was a trusty tool, an old friend, a reliable sidekick. Together, we had come a long way. Yet, I knew I'd never fire it again. Cradling its forestock in the crook of my elbow, hooking its butt under my armpit, I carried it to my VW, placed it gingerly on the seat, transported it to Cole's house, and hung it on his wall.

"Whatcha doin'?" He scowled.

"Givin' you my '06."

"Why, for Pete's sake?"

"Don't want it anymore. Outgrew it, you might say."

"Don't you wanna keep it in the closet—just in case you get hungry?"

I shook my head.

This was a symbolic act. By my disarmament I was unfurling my experience of life's continuity over every living thing.

A disgraceful gleam of wetness in my eye was causing

Cole to doubt my sincerity. But I didn't bother to explain. He was only a beneficiary, a witness to my commitment. This was between me and God.

EPILOGUE

An old friend from *The Saratogian*, Bob Mayette, former neighbor and lensman, had photographed me using my VW bug as a garden tractor, plow chained behind it, Kate and our boys waving back at me from the car windows. Mom had called it prophetic.

Kate continued to withhold her address, yet demand child support, a situation I felt stemmed from some responsibility I had spurned in a past life, perhaps as an alcoholic, as Death suggested in my Japanese dream. I believed there must be some soul strength to be gained from my anguish, or Jesus and other teachers would not have stressed loving our enemies. Concentrating on dream and Bible study, staying busy and trying to forgive, I did not press for justice in a material sense.

Billy, our Alaskan cherub, was killed by a truck in Chicago at age eight. I learned about it a month after his funeral through an offhand remark at A.R.E. headquarters in Virginia Beach. Kate had not told me, and I fought another bout with depression.

I lived alone at The Farm for five years, till Dad remarried, sold it, and moved to Arizona.

In 1971 I started seeing an old friend, Sherrill, who was in the process of getting a divorce. I admired her methods—not focusing on the material, not attempting to cast her ex-to-be into outer darkness, not trying to separate him from their three children—David, Chris, and Becky. Sherrill and I soon discovered deep affinities, common ideals, similar woundings, and abiding concern. We were married in 1972 and, through many vicissitudes, still are, recently celebrating our twentieth anniversary, eighteen as members of a Search for God study group.

Through Sherrill I've grown to appreciate the treasure and wonder of womanhood—the art of relating to others while holding fast to one's own ideal. We have become, in Cayce vernacular, "helpmeets" and know the joy of walking hand-in-hand toward shared goals. Based on love and trust, we have built a home and have extended its warmth and laughter into our community.

" ... the highest of man's achievement in the earth—the *home!*" (480-20)

"Do make the home the career, for this is the greater career any soul may make in the earth." (5070-1)

At times I feel as close to David, Chris, and Becky as if they were my own. When your ideal is loving service, I learned through my new family, the Universe will find a way for you to express it.

Son Scott, encouraged by his aunt in St. Louis, called our house in upstate New York on Thanksgiving Day, 1975, and subsequently landed on our doorstep. Laura Beth came to live with us for a year in 1979. I have established friendships with and have been in close touch with both ever since.

What Is A.R.E.?

The Association for Research and Enlightenment, Inc. (A.R.E.®), is the international headquarters for the work of Edgar Cayce (1877-1945), who is considered the best-documented psychic of the twentieth century. Founded in 1931, the A.R.E. consists of a community of people from all walks of life and spiritual traditions, who have found meaningful and life-transformative insights from the readings of Edgar Cayce.

Although A.R.E. headquarters is located in Virginia Beach, Virginia—where visitors are always welcome—the A.R.E. community is a global network of individuals who offer conferences, educational activities, and fellowship around the world. People of every age are invited to participate in programs that focus on such topics as holistic health, dreams, reincarnation, ESP, the power of the mind, meditation, and personal spirituality.

In addition to study groups and various activities, the A.R.E. offers membership benefits and services, a bimonthly magazine, a newsletter, extracts from the Cayce readings, conferences, international tours, a massage school curriculum, an impressive volunteer network, a retreat-type camp for children and adults, and A.R.E. contacts around the world. A.R.E. also maintains an affiliation with Atlantic University, which offers a master's degree program in Transpersonal Studies.

For additional information about A.R.E. activities hosted near you, please contact:

A.R.E.
67th St. and Atlantic Ave.
P.O. Box 595
Virginia Beach, VA 23451-0595
(804) 428-3588

A.R.E. Press

A.R.E. Press is a publisher and distributor of books, audiotapes, and videos that offer guidance for a more fulfilling life. Our products are based on, or are compatible with, the concepts in the psychic readings of Edgar Cayce.

We especially seek to create products which carry forward the inspirational story of individuals who have made practical application of the Cayce legacy.

For a free catalog, please write to A.R.E. Press at the address below or call toll free 1-800-723-1112. For any other information, please call 804-428-3588.

A.R.E. Press
Sixty-Eighth & Atlantic Avenue
P.O. Box 656
Virginia Beach, VA 23451-0656